D0857086

THE NATURE
OF REVOLUTION

Other Books by Carleton Beals

THE BRASS-KNUCKLE CRUSADE

EAGLES OF THE ANDES: SOUTH AMERICAN
STRUGGLES FOR INDEPENDENCE

GREAT GUERILLA WARRIORS

THE GREAT REVOLT AND ITS LEADERS

LAND OF THE MAYAS: YESTERDAY AND TODAY

NOMADS AND EMPIRE BUILDERS: NATIVE PEOPLES AND
CULTURES OF SOUTH AMERICA

STORIES TOLD BY THE AZTECS, BEFORE THE SPANIARDS CAME

WAR WITHIN A WAR: THE CONFEDERACY AGAINST ITSELF

THE NATURE
OF REVOLUTION

CARLETON BEALS

THOMAS Y. CROWELL COMPANY

New York, Established 1834

All the verse, letters, and invocations quoted in Chapter 11 have been re-printed from *Mau Mau from Within* by Donald L. Barnett and Karari Njama, copyright © Donald L. Barnett 1966, by permission of the pub-lisher, Monthly Review Press, 116 West 14 Street, New York, N.Y. 10011.

The statement by the Columbia graduate student quoted in Chapter 13 has been reprinted from the article "Columbia's Senate" by Glenn Col-lins, published in the Fall 1969 issue of *Columbia Forum*, by permission of *Columbia Forum* and Mr. Collins.

2 3 4 5 6 7 8 9 10

CONTENTS

CHAPTER 1

DON QUIXOTE RIDES AGAIN

LIKE BIRTH AND DEATH, revolution is violent change. Mostly an ugly process, it wears the visage of hope for a better, juster world, to achieve which no sacrifice and no enormity are too great. It feeds on martyrdom in the face of suppression.

A revolution seeks to destroy the regime in power in an effort, usually, to correct radically, social wrongs or to establish an allegedly better order. "The [French] Revolution had willed that public burdens be equal, really equal, for all citizens," Count Alexis de Tocqueville told the Assembly of the Second Republic in 1848. "It failed in that. The distribution of public burdens has remained unequal in certain areas. We must see to it that they are equalized. . . . Finally, the French Revolution desired—this desire is what made it not only sacred but holy in the eyes of the world—it desired, I say, to introduce charity into politics. It developed a higher, broader, more general idea than that previously held of the State's obligations toward the poor, toward the suffering citizen."

Lenin wrote, "Marx taught us from the experience of the Paris commune that the proletariat *cannot* simply lay hold of the ready-made state machinery and set it in motion for its own purposes, that the proletariat must *destroy* this machinery and replace it with a new one." Inevitably revolution, whether following the Lenin formula or not, inflicts hardship and suffering on privileged ruling groups, on innocent bystanders, and on many of those it seeks to benefit. Though it endeavors to overthrow tyranny and end injustices by wiping out the power of the privileged elite, it can rarely succeed, once it has entered the palace, unless it imposes—if only temporarily—dictatorial rule, until a new system of law and order can be set up and enforced, sometimes until a new generation comes to adulthood, that accepts the revolutionary criteria and altered social relationships. Thus it abolishes old wrongs at the cost of causing or creating new injustices—at least for considerable sectors of the population. The one notable exception was the American Revolution, but it, rather than trying to destroy a system, was aimed at preserving well-established liberties against shortsighted British impositions.

"It is a revolutionary age we live in," remarked Robert Kennedy, bowing to world consensus. Ever since the American Revolution, which was an incident in British imperialism, the cycle of revolutions has been quickening. The American struggle owed much to French thinking and in turn stimulated the great French Revolution of 1789. Movements of national liberation swept away the great Spanish empire in the span of a generation, broke the Austro-Hungarian empire, and later the British and French empires. Revolutionists seized power in Mexico, Russia, and China, in all of eastern Europe, in Africa, in Asia, in Cuba, and for a time in Guatemala and Bolivia.

A certain inevitability seems involved. Revolutions spring not merely from social injustice but from man's imperfections, biological, psychological, and social, and are fired by his hopes for freedom and his dreams of utopia.

Institutions, as Thomas Jefferson pointed out, tend to grow sluggish. Inevitably governments grow away from the people, become insulated in massive police power and bureaucratic cynicism, and grow hopelessly corrupt. Wealth increases, becomes concentrated; misery piles up. The social arteries harden, and presently the brain stroke becomes inevitable. Jefferson knew this and spelled it out in the Declaration of Independence. A double movement, which no man can stop, is at work in modern civilized societies, said De Tocqueville in 1848. While the standard of living rises, the number of those needing the support of their fellow men to obtain a small part of those benefits increases. The Second Republic, after the overthrow of Louis Philippe, tried to eliminate the discrepancy, but was soon betrayed by Napoleon III. Revolutions appear to be as unavoidable as the cycles of change and catastrophe in nature itself, as certain to occur as the march of generations, for youth is born into a world he did not make, which often bores him, hurts him, stifles him. Today he strikes back in almost every university in the world.

Robert Kennedy summarized the problem in his *To Seek a Newer World:* "Our answer is the world's hope; it is to rely on youth—not a time of life but a state of mind, a temper of the will, a quality of the imagination, a predominance of courage over timidity, of the appetite for adventure over the love of ease." He added that the cruelties and obstacles of our swiftly changing planet would not yield to obsolete dogmas and outworn slogans. The planet could not be moved by those who cling to a present "already dying," who prefer the illusion of security to excitement and change.

Simón Bolívar, the great Latin American liberator, once said that a revolution could not be "made." It could be neither hastened nor held back. When the time was ripe, it would occur, and once started, no power could stop it. Since he led one of the most far-reaching revolutions in all history, he likely knew whereof he spoke.

Wendell Phillips, the abolitionist, said the same thing more explicitly: "Revolutions are not made; they come. A revolution is as natural a growth as an oak. It comes out of the past. Its foundations are far back."

Lenin had a less Calvinistic and fatalistic view, though he recognized that a revolution had to mature. He saw it as the culmination of a historical process that had to run its course. Yet he did not precisely see himself as a helpless instrument but rather as a dynamic maker of history. He also believed in the possibilities of timing. A revolutionary movement could be bungled, causing a setback of years. Thus he wrote the Bolshevik Central Committee on November 6, 1917, the eve of the take-over, that the hour had struck, that any delay would mean they might lose everything. "We must at any price, this evening, tonight, arrest ministers and disarm the military cadets." The political task was unimportant. It would be clarified "after the seizure. To delay action is the same as death."

Nevertheless, revolution is not a narrow conspiracy or the product of conspiracy, though conspirators are inevitably involved. Friedrich Engels, author of *Socialism: Utopian & Scientific*, a close friend of Karl Marx and one of the fathers of modern revolution, remarked: "The times of the superstition which attributed revolution to the ill-will of a few agitators have long passed away. Everyone

[?] knows nowadays that wherever there is a revolutionary convulsion, there must be some social want in the background which is prevented by outworn institutions from satisfying itself."

Of course, the phrase "International Communist Conspiracy" is the stock bogeyman of the attorneys of so-called witch-hunting committees in Congress. General George Grivas, leader of the revolt for Cypriot independence, remarked that the British lost the struggle because they could never get it through their heads that the uprising was not a conspiracy; it was a movement of the people that could not be permanently suppressed by force.

Government everywhere is loathe to listen to grievances, but rather aggravates irritations by indifference, tokenism, or repression. Police power grows more brutal and desperate, and by clubbings, tear gas, and tanks, accelerates the violence temporarily suppressed. Resentments flow together to create alienation and resistance, much as the peace movement and Negro demands have made common cause in recent demonstrations in the United States. Even nonrevolutionists who have the temerity to criticize the government in power are apt to be harassed, persecuted, jailed, or killed in both totalitarian and democratic lands. The aim of all governments is to protect the established order. The emotions of patriotism are easily aroused against dissenters, even when they are the real patriots. There are always plenty of laws to get such people behind bars whenever their opinions threaten to arouse followers to action. Often they are involved in years of prolonged, costly court appearances, which sap their energies and their resources, viz., Benjamin Spock and codefendants, as also the leaders of the Women's League for Peace and Freedom, and the Women Strike for Peace, David Dellinger, William Worthy, Rap Brown, Eldridge Cleaver, Adam Clayton Powell, Robert Hutton, and Huey Newton, founder of the Black Panthers, some of whom, of course, consider themselves revolutionists. Carry Nation destroyed property, but as she herself pointed out the property was being used illegally. And her arrest by the Post Office Department because her magazine discussed masturbation was certainly overt persecution that caused her considerable financial loss. Need we mention Thomas Paine, William Lloyd Garrison, Stephen F. Austin, the father of Texas, and Henry Thoreau? Francisco Madero was jailed in San Luis Potosí, escaped, abandoned conventional politics, and led a successful revolution to become president of Mexico. Fidel Castro resorted to the

Cuban courts, had his candidacy for the Cuban Chamber of Deputies thrown aside by Fulgencio Batista's coup, was sentenced to fourteen years in prison, and came to lead a successful revolution. He was merely following in the footsteps of José Martí, the father of the first Cuban independence movement. Numbers of Irish patriots were jailed but came to hold high and respected posts in the Irish government. Jomo Kenyatta, like other black leaders, spent many years in jail before he became the head of the free state of Kenya. The list of victims in the Soviet Union, Yugoslavia, Hungary, Greece, Czechoslovakia, South Africa, Spain, the Dominican Republic, Mexico, and the rest of Latin America is tragically long. From time immemorial, governments have been more apt to use police power than to redress grievances. Such force is invariably applauded for a time by the unthinking majority. Police power can bloody many heads, but few are bowed. As Eldridge Cleaver has said, police clubs can crack skulls but not ideas. The blaze is not extinguished by such violence. A new leader, usually more militant, invariably replaces those rendered *hors de combat* or killed. The fire creeps along underneath the surface and bursts out afresh in another spot. "If the Gods had a little more pity," wrote former President Juan José Arévalo of Guatemala, "they would have enlightened the Police Rulers . . . that the social agitators are the best assistants imaginable in pointing out and solving problems of government."

But reform, not to mention revolutionary change, inevitably runs foul of much existing privilege and all ingrained custom. Even the most miserable citizen has some status quo to defend. He is more apt to growl over his gnawed bone than to risk leaping the barriers for pie in the sky. But driven desperate or inspired by more militant souls, he will grab for the pie.

Ralph Roeder, author of the monumental biography of Benito Juárez of Mexico, declared: "No revolution is ever lost, however abortive, no reform ever fails completely. Its results may be abolished but . . . the movement returns pendulum-wise by the very momentum of the reaction."

It is a point-counterpoint process. A people has to become mad, i.e., possessed of an *idée fixe*, before it can move into revolution. Such a semipathological state takes hold of the mass mind, usually because the government, the rulers, have grown mad first. Destruction is always one of the products of madness, and is a cumulative disease on both sides. Thereafter it takes time to understand or reconcile the divergent words and ideas. If they cannot be, revolution is inevitable.

Governments are usually unable, however well intentioned, to rectify abuse with sufficient celerity. Governments themselves are the prey of conflicting interests among the elite themselves. It is thus difficult to channel unrest within the bed of existing law or to provide the new laws required. Law always lags far behind social realities; it rarely catches up with even the status quo. The mildest reform requires long periods to come into effect. The idea is in the minds of many men even before it gets into print. From then on, however desirable the change, it is an uphill road. In this country, readier for change than most, it often requires seventy-five years for a new idea to take legal form—and by that time it often has no particular meaning, is already belated.

After twenty-five years of exposition in Populist newspapers, the subtreasury plan for government storage of surplus farm products, price supports, and loans to farmers, was put forth by C. W. Macune, head of the Farmers' Alliance. It was urgently needed, but the Populist movement rose and fell. Small farmers lost their homesteads; their sons were driven into the cities. Not until the Great Depression did Henry Wallace put into effect a modified subtreasury plan, but by then more subsistence farmers had been crushed, so that those who benefited from the Wallace program were mostly larger landholding companies or such great plantation owners as Senator James O. Eastland of Mississippi, who receives a subsidy of more than a hundred thousand dollars from the federal government, while his Negro sharecroppers nearly starve.

True, the new large-scale farm system is often more efficient, more scientific, even though millions have had to adjust themselves to an uprooted way of life. The point made here does not concern the pros and cons of this colossal technical agrarian revolution, but rather the long period involved in providing legal channels for measures of economic reform. Delay breeds revolution.

All dictators harp a great deal about law and order; so do most presidents, especially when the going gets tough. An executive, if he heads a government in which outmoded laws can be changed by the representatives of the governed, has some right to use the stale phrase, though to do so may not bespeak great intelligence. Even in the United States the law-making process has become special privilege. Most progressive laws are bottled up and smothered in tightly controlled congressional committees; laws that do emerge are likely to be the bastard children of wheeling and dealing in smoky rooms. Laws made by the majority often are ill considered or favor privileged elements and work hardship on many minorities. If the minority is a considerable segment of the population and a rising force that cannot be denied, "law and order" talk becomes downright foolish. More and more men and women are willing to go to jail rather than submit. Robert Kennedy sensed this when law-and-order phraseology was batted around at the time of the Watts disorders. It is not *their* law and order," he commented mildly. Simón Bolívar said bluntly, "The expression 'law and order' is used by those in power, not by us, as a false slogan to justify their abuses. We are not interested in their law or their order, but only with justice."

Revolution always follows its own law, its own order. This to the Establishment is always disorder and lawlessness—as indeed it is—at least till the revolution succeeds. The revolutionist invents his own language and converts men to its use. Most humans are loyal to phrases, not to the meaning behind them, but the tooth and the truth crumble in their mouths. For years all talk out of Moscow sounded insane. Gradually many of the phrases used have been accepted or at least adopted everywhere in the world, and have eaten into our more complacent language, subtly undermining some of our long-cherished conceptions. Even our beautiful words *democracy, freedom, the right of self-determination* have been turned topsy-turvy, and have lost their original potency, especially as our politicians dote on watered-down double-talk and sanctimony.

Thus the advocates of established law and order, the upholders of the status quo, and revolutionists are unable even to talk to each other. Nothing, for instance, is more reasonable and thoughtful than Columbia University President Grayson Kirk's résumé of the violent student upheaval. The statements of the British Board of Trade and the blundering Tory Parliament before the American Revolution were likewise reasonable—and also self-righteous. By then the language and the idea gap had grown too wide to be bridged. For the British Tories there was no other solution, despite some minor concessions, than to punish the colonists. The error was fatal. And it is one that is always being repeated.

And so every testing of old law by rebellious spirits brings about

ever harsher enforcement. Injustice is compounded. Victims or martyrs display bloody heads and fill the jails. This merely promotes
the revolutionary cause, provides greater momentum and justification. "When government becomes the law-breaker," remarked Rap
Brown, the Black Power advocate, "we cannot allow the government to be an outlaw, especially when the crime is against the people."

To interviewer Robert L. Allen, Brown remarked (shortly after
his "white" conviction in New Orleans), "Revolution is an
evolutionary sort of thing." This was not double-talk. He was referring to the prerevolutionary stage. "Rebellions are a legitimate step
toward revolutionary struggle, but they are not revolution." Riots
are just "the toys by which the people prod the powers that be to
make them jump." His language reached a vulgarity which *The
New York Times* would not print. It became a harsh verbal thrust
at conventional gentility—brazen, uninhibited, powerful, and soul-
shaking.

The notable Mexican Reformation leader, Valentín Gómez
Farías, said, "There is no lock strong enough to prevent the progress of the world." The word *progress* can be debated. That revolution is necessarily beneficial or that all change is desirable cannot
be sustained by any ideal criteria, except those of the instigators.
But here we are concerned with the realities. Every revolution that
succeeds in due time becomes accepted—all its truths, distortions,
and lies—though perhaps not by the first several generations of diehards or superidealists who find the new credibility gap unsur-
mountable. Irrational emotions, since the elite long remain blind to
the existing gap, take over. But once an idea—and that is what revolution is before all else—gets hold of a people and shakes them
loose from the arms of existing authority, there is nothing, not even
governments or armies, more powerful. Once Humpty Dumpty has
been broken, he's broken, and can't be put together again.

We have chosen to describe briefly eleven modern revolutions,
how they came about, the elements in society that provided their
struggle, their aims, methods, and accomplishments. We have
started with the American Revolution for independence, the grand-
daddy of them all. It succeeded the religious upheavals of Europe,
which in past centuries had seen the overthrow of feudalism and
the emergence of modern capitalism.

The American Revolution was a revolt of colonies against the mother country, a type of revolt that still agitates much of the world. In the case of the American Revolution it was in good part an effort to preserve the system of liberty that had evolved out of earlier ecclesiastical totalitarianism and had finally entrenched itself in the local methods of government, the town meeting, and free communications. It was an effort to preserve these liberties rather than an effort to establish a new system, though the setting up of an independent republic was indeed revolutionary in the days of the divine right of kings, and was so considered by the ruling elite of Europe until the overthrow of Klemens von Metternich of Austria by the 1848 revolutions. Maximilian was sent to Mexico in 1866 in good part in an effort to block the spread of republican doctrines in the New World. Naturally the initial establishment of the American republic brought many political and economic changes, not even fully foreseen by the participants.

The French Revolution owed part of its success to the American example. Lafayette was one of the chief participants, though soon swept aside by more radical leaders. It was propelled by much longer philosophical preparations, went far beyond mere political change, was rooted deep in the economic and cultural life of France. It cut deeper and broader, had more of an egalitarian and humanistic character, than did the American Revolution. The class aspects of society were far more emphasized.

The monarchs of Europe combined against the Revolution by war caused it to be changed into chiefly a nationalist revolution, and monarchy was reestablished in France for a half century. Nevertheless the Napoleonic wars destroyed the structure of feudalism, on which their dynasties rested, and they, too, were mostly destroyed.

Both revolutions were largely a product of the industrial revolution and made possible the rise of capitalism, already advanced in England, soon to take hold in the United States and France, and presently in Germany and other parts of Europe.

The independence struggle in Latin America was continent-wide. It was inspired by both the American and French revolutions. That fifteen- to twenty-year upheaval saw the overthrow of the great Spanish empire. This struggle has significance for the present conflicts in the United States, for into it was injected the battle of the races and their cultures. Unlike the French Revolution, it did not succeed in destroying feudalism. Hence it failed to provide the basis for either capitalism or democracy, and the rule of the great landholders, the church, and the military was perpetuated under national flags, the traditional system imposed four centuries earlier by the Spanish conquistadores. After about 1820 the Spanish rulers moved out; the white Creoles (men of European descent) took over, but they were soon overshadowed by the mestizos, the men of mixed blood. The Indians became citizens but remained in the shadows, as they do in most of these countries to this day, still fodder for eventual revolution.

Our camera-eye swings back to Europe. The Paris Commune of 1871 is more significant as a symbol than as a revolution. It was hailed by Marx and later by Lenin as the first bona fide proletarian revolution. Actually it was far from being purely proletarian— though it was socialistic. It was also the product of national survival, or nationalist pride, a result of the defeat and overthrow of Napoleon III and the humiliation of France by Prussian arms. It was the child of disaster, but it never gained control of France. It was bottled up in Paris and overwhelmed shortly by the forces representing the old landed aristocracy and the new bourgeoisie. Capitalism resumed its ascendancy. Napoleon III, though an anachronism in the world, had done much to strengthen the power of the new industrial and financial elite, and the Paris Commune was merely a brief interlude, a portent of future troubles, and it would likely never have occurred except for the imperialistic lunacies of Napoleon, a series of blunders and stupidities that brought France to the brink of disaster. He lost his shirt in Mexico, with the Maximilian-Carlota enterprise. It was an early Vietnam adventure, and France paid dearly for the folly at home and abroad, even though, when the warning bells rang, he pulled out swiftly and completely, not worrying about French honor and pride or saving face. Capitalism reigned triumphant in Europe and the United States. It messed up the rest of the world with bloody colonial wars, appropriating needed new materials obtained with coolie labor from subjugated colonies or puppet governments. Wealth and power, if not social justice, were the prizes, but the standards of living improved for large sectors of the populations. The Great Power alliances became a precarious balance of ill-concealed military and economic rivalry.

A significant check to the imperialist grabs, a great warning light against future aggression, came with the Mexican Revolution and the first Chinese Revolution of Sun Yat-sen. In 1910 the Mexican Revolution began as a tame enough political overthrow, but soon deepened to a thoroughgoing social upheaval, a semiproletarian and Indian revolt. It is especially significant as the first revolution against the capitalist colonial system, the alliance of foreign capitalism with the native aggression overlords, an alliance symbolized by the rule of Porfirio Díaz and his *rurales*.

The Mexican Revolution became the prototype of the nationalistic revolutions, which have since broken up the Austrian, French, German and British empires in Europe, Asia, and Africa.

The differences between the Soviet and Chinese revolutions in the two greatest land empires and the largest blocks of peoples on earth are essential to the understanding of the revolutionary principle and the present politics of the world. Their threat to America, its conversion to a militaristic power, and the impact on the minds of America, both revolutionary and counterrevolutionary, will affect the course of events in the United States for perhaps a century or more. The techniques of revolution in both countries need to be known.

Africa is a continent shaken with revolutions—nationalistic, pro-Western, anti-Western, pro-Soviet, pro-Chinese. The role of democracy in such upheavals, the role of Western interventions and meddlings, should be known. And the struggle there has special importance for understanding the black revolt in America. The presentation is here limited to the long bitter struggle of Kenya for liberation, a tragic and beautiful record.

Two examples of counterrevolution, that of Mussolini's Italy and of the rise of Fascist Spain, are included: the causes and methods, and the significance for war and peace of the shilly-shallying of England and the United States, and the interventions of Nazi Germany, Fascist Italy, and the Soviet Union. The formula of counterrevolution is evidently an oversimplification. Both revolution and counterrevolution hurtle down the same historical road, one facing forward, one backward.

The surging current of revolution takes us to Castro's Cuba. No revolution has been more inadequately told about in the United States, or told about with more venom and more foolish adulation, than that of Cuba. Such reporting is of little value in understanding the revolutionary process that is bound to overtake most of Latin America in the years to come. A survey of that area and its present sad political state is presented.

Finally there is an analysis of the student, black, and peace movements in the United States. These are yet far from constituting a bona fide revolution, though they are typical preludes to revolution. The examples chosen for inclusion in the book should provide a better comprehension of the forces involved and the possible outcome, whether we are at the crossroads or not, and which road we tread upon.

By the phrase *The Nature of Revolution* we refer to the causes, the prerevolutionary climate, the fissions in the social fabric, the methods and the mechanism (if it may be called that), the conditions for success, and the results of social upheavals. A tentative definition seems called for. The word *revolution* is often used loosely for any abrupt or violent change. But violence per se—even though an increasing crime rate betokens the sickness of the social order— does not constitute revolution; it is rather a symptom of social dislocation and corruption. "A hungry man," said Lenin, "can't distinguish between a republic and a monarchy." As Juan Perón said cynically when he cracked down on recalcitrant Argentine university professors, "The people are interested in shoes, not higher education."

Certainly most palace-guard revolts or Praetorian Caesarism, whether in Rome or Latin America, do not represent real revolution; however much blood is shed, they are usually instigated by puppets of the elite, who at the same time further their personal ambitions by taking advantage of social misery and social unrest. Without such evils, coups of this sort could scarcely occur. The *cuartelazos*, or barracks revolts that take over governments in South America, and today in Africa and for some years in Saigon, resort to revolutionary slogans and extravagant promises to the people, but do not constitute valid revolution. They are bastard expressions of illiteracy, economic oppression, race hatreds, social dissolution, militarism, and vicious ambitions. The War of the Roses in England had far-reaching ramifications, but scarcely represented basic change in the social structure.

The overthrow of the state by force is as old as recorded history,

[*12*]

if rarely such a generalized sport as today. We like to ascribe all this to Communism, but we may be deluding ourselves. Revolutions occurred long before Marx and Lenin. Our own revolution for independence can scarcely be laid at the doorsteps of those two gentlemen, nor can the French Revolution, those of Mexico and China, nor the independence movement in Latin America. Whatever overriding dogma of Communism, nationalism, freedom, or democracy is involved, the pattern, aims, and methods of each overturn are different. No two are identical; each is as unique as the individual fingerprint. Each springs out of the particular soil, climate, traditions, and social institutions of the people involved. If similar economic, religious, political, or nationalistic doctrines provide a motif, often these merely mask the real reasons for revolt. Nor do such dogmas, even if reiterated ad nauseam, long determine the actual course that a revolution, once in power, will follow.

Similarly the situations that have gestated such upheavals are varied indeed: They have occurred after war-defeat and after war-victory. Paraguay was largely victorious in the long bloody Chaco War against Bolivia (1929–1938), but both Paraguay and Bolivia had revolutionary overturns, and both are now ruled by reactionary dictatorships. Revolutions have occurred in ruined lands and in highly prosperous lands, in primitive communities and in complex modern societies. They have been staged *for* the people and *against* the people—"counterrevolution" is the stock phrase. More revolutions seem to be inevitable. The latest reported in October 1969 in Chile and in December in Panamá were merely puffs of smoke, but those countries as do others, stand at the brink. The United States may well ruin itself by trying to stem them everywhere, as the 1969 Nelson Rockefeller report proposes that we do—in a well-disguised manner.

Revolutions around the world have been made or led by all kinds of leaders from all ranks. They have been made by slaves, plebs, peasants, cowboys, feudal lords, Catholic friars, Protestant preachers, lovers of Allah, Buddhists, students, doctors, lawyers, merchants, thieves, manufacturers, capitalists, sea captains and traders, soldiers, veterans, sergeants, generals, sailors and admirals, aviators, poets, artists and writers—and politicians. President Rómulo Gallegos, one of Latin America's greatest novelists, was coauthor with Rómulo Betancourt of the Venezuelan pseudorevolution. Even the

[13]

proletariat is usually led by the elite. Karl Marx was a professor; Lenin and Trotsky were intellectuals, never workers. Castro was a lawyer, son of a rich landholding family.

One thing all revolutions have in common: Invariably they are started by militant minorities; they represent the ousting of a governing "elite," sometimes the elite of a different class or race or group; by the proletariat, middle class, bourgeois, feudalists, upper class—by Indians, Negroes, mestizos, Creoles, brown men, yellow men, white men.

Marx and Lenin believed that "revolution" must constitute a far-reaching change in the economic and class structure of society. Of course, for those two thinkers there could be only two basic revolutions in all history: the overthrow of feudalism (which still awaits being overthrown in most of the world) by the bourgeois or capitalist class (which the two theorists considered a step forward); and the overthrow of capitalism by the workers and peasants, i.e., the establishment, according to them, of the ultimate ideal classless society, ergo, the *last* revolution. For instance, Marx blasted the French 1862–1867 occupation of Mexico, but felt that a similar seizure by the United States would be helpful to Mexico, or at least preferable. With the workers' revolution, all injustice would be eradicated, the state would wither away—that is the title of one of Lenin's longer essays. People thereafter would live in the everlasting utopia of happiness, unexploited by any privileged class. (In time, likely, the chief enemy would become boredom.) Actually the Russian "proletarian" state has swelled beyond all previous dimensions, rivaled only by the "capitalist" bureaucracy in the United States. Big statism—Hobbes's Leviathan—so feared by the American Founding Fathers, seems to have overtaken both Communism and capitalism—with no end in sight, except tragic ruin. Nor is Russia—despite advances in literacy, education, technological miracles, and some economic betterment—free of privileged rulers, for saying which a leading Yugoslavian writer was long jailed. As a big state, Russia acts much the same in Czechoslovakia as the United States acts in the Dominican Republic—except for the catchwords, and even some of those are identical.

Years ago, Secretary of the Treasury Henry Morgenthau told me at a dinner party in his home: "They say that Russia jumped from feudalism right over capitalism into communism. You know what? The United States is going to jump right over communism into

[*14*]

chaos." His facetiousness has become almost flowery prophecy.

There is, however, another step forward (?), one taken by the Fascists in Italy, the Nazis in Germany, and the Falangists in Spain, viz the military and police state. Fascist revolutions have a weakness for shirts: the blouse-wearers of Napoleon III, Black Shirts (Italy), Brown Shirts (Germany and Chile), Blue Shirts (Italy), Green Shirts (Brazil), Gold Shirts (Mexico), Silver Shirts (United States), or the shirtless armed thugs of Dictator Juan Perón of Argentina. Not all such shirted marchers are wholly opportunists, but there looms ahead the horror of 1984, with its plethora of electronic snooping devices, the perverted regimentation of thought and conduct, and heels-over-head phraseology—permanent war is called peace; slavery is called freedom; aggression is called liberty. I once asked Huey P. Long of Louisiana if the United States would become Fascist. He responded, "Of course, but we'll call it 'Democracy.'" Fascism represents, among numerous other things, the last desperate effort of monopoly capitalism to survive, a counterrevolution of the diehards. Mussolini and Hitler were both closely allied with the big industrialists. Ironically, Hitler's associates, just prior to their downchute into war and catastrophe, began taking over the property of the industrialists. Foreign occupation has since restored in half of Germany the former monopoly capitalism, commonly known as "free enterprise." Communism rules the other half, so the story is far from ended during this bizarre era of armed "peace." Today's effort—in both West and East Germany —to maintain the status quo by police power is likely to make the resultant violence and revolution, or war, more terrible.

What is the nature of revolution? When Rap Brown was asked about revolutionary ideology, he snorted. A program weakens militancy; it tends to divert rebellion into reformist channels and make it part of the Establishment once more. *A revolution can have no program,* he reiterated firmly. It must develop its own program as it develops. Asked about socialism, he snorted again. Socialism run by white racists? The Negro, he believed, would receive the same despicable treatment as before.

Revolution is born of an abnormal state of mind, sensitized by an accumulated body of experience. Revolutions are psychological explosions resulting from irritations commonly economic in origin, and they are conditioned in their programs by the stock of knowledge and aspiration peculiar to their time and place.

[15]

Many Americans are fond of saying, with a prodigious sigh, that the United States is a sick society. Certainly the decline in our public services is approaching tragic proportions. We call on more electronic devices and get poorer mail service than a generation ago. Some of our railroad trains are as bad as those of the banana railroads of Central America. We spend more than ever on medical care, but have slipped way down in public health standards—eighteenth in infant mortality, a death rate higher than in Cuba. Our air is polluted; our lakes and rivers and beaches have become putrid. We no longer have enough decent homes to house our population. Our vitaminless cardboard bread is not fit to eat. We have finer school buildings and much barren education. Teachers, coerced by empty-headed flag-wavers or by militant fanatics, often can hardly call their souls their own. Need the list be stretched out?

A sick society, unless it has the health reserves to cure itself, is a sitting duck for disorders, the establishment of a police state, or revolution. For the nonce we have to listen to the sickening hot-air spray of self-seeking politicians.

It is a long dark tunnel, but before we plunge down the red road of revolution or into the disasters and grief of the police state (some say we already have), we should at least take stock of the revolutions that have shaken this earth and altered society: how and why they came about, what were their tools, what results, good and bad. Since our own "Great Society" was born of revolution, we must admit that revolution is not entirely evil. Of course, there are those who claim today that the American Revolution was never a revolution, a claim made by both Tories and leftists.

Still, the Daughters of the American Revolution have announced no changes of name. Charles Beard saw in it no basic change. Vernon Louis Parrington in his great *Main Currents of American Thought* called it "a puzzle." It is a puzzle that we need to understand.

John Adams wrote in 1818 that the true history of the American Revolution could not be recovered, for it was effected before the struggle began. Half the Revolution, he said, was in the minds of the people. How did it get there?

CHAPTER 2

THE REVOLUTION OF 1776

THE SONS OF LIBERTY from Norwich, Connecticut, the town of rattlesnakes—which infested every crevice—rode into Windham, the town of frogs—where the bullfrogs were so numerous and so vocal, people said they couldn't sleep. The Sons of Liberty rode four abreast, white staves lifted. Three trumpeters sent echoes across the rolling hills. At their head went two men in red with laced hats. Each man in the column wore a red band catercornered across his chest. In their saddlebags they carried eight days' rations. They were riding to the Connecticut River to intercept the crown's stamp-tax agent, Jared Ingersoll, and force him to resign. The year was 1765. The British-imposed stamp tax had stirred up all the colonies, and people were determined that it should not be collected.

They had started out after a mass gathering around the Norwich Liberty Pole, with its blue, gold-starred liberty cap, where Ingersoll was burned in effigy. Similar ceremonies had been held in nearly all the nearby towns. Additional recruits for the Sons of Liberty expedition were gathered in Windham, Lebanon, and villages en route. They rode on to the Connecticut River, one thousand strong.

Another contingent, led by Zebulon Butler, rode out of Old Lyme for New Haven in an effort to intercept Ingersoll before he left that city.

The main body to the river was led by John Durkee, "the bold man of Bean Hill"—Indian fighter, farmer, tavern-keeper, and West Indian trader and smuggler. The story of Durkee is an epitome of the Revolution getting underway. He had been born in frog-infested Windham, December 11, 1728. He came of a good family, the second child of Deacon William Durkee and Susan Sabin. She was a relative of daring Captain John Sabin, who had founded nearby Pomfret in 1698. The great John Eliot of Massachusetts, who had preached to the Indians there half a century earlier, had called it an Eden, New Canaan, and Arcadia—the fairest bit of earth he knew. Durkee's youth was colored by a murderous "Wild West" feud over land titles—a violence promising little future or safety—and at twenty-two he went off to the new settlement of Norwich, where he started a tavern on Bean Hill. Three years later he married Martha Woods, a daughter of a well-to-do farmer.

Norwich was perched on a rocky eminence above the Yantic River at its junction with the Shetucket, not far from where New London, a busy port of entry, stood on the wide Thames River. The steep streets of Norwich, even after being cobbled, could hardly be traversed on icy days. It had been settled late because of its rocky soil, good only for goats, and its swarming rattlesnakes. A local legend tells of a fiddler, a Pied Piper, who lured the snakes from the rocks into the river. Even before that, the Indians had cultivated beans on the more fertile hilltops, and no soil grew better beans. The first settlers learned how to cultivate them—"Bean Town," it was long called. It was beans that Durkee raised on the acres about his tavern.

By the time he moved there, the community had a plain meetinghouse and a small courthouse, facing a high, small, irregularly shaped green. There were two taverns, a general store, an apothecary shop, whose owner had waxed rich, importing and concocting drugs. The best house in town had been built by John Bradford, son of a governor, to encourage settlement, but came to be owned by the Huntingtons, rich folk, whose name later made railroad history in the West. Durkee got his property for a song, because discouraged residents were moving out. Many went to Danbury, which, like Norwich, soon also became known as Bean Town. But most went to Nova Scotia, where the British had defeated the French and English settlers were in demand.

It was an exchange, for hundreds of Acadians, driven out of their homes, settled in Norwich. A few prospered, and Durkee's daughter eventually married one of them, but the majority were soon run out by lynch law.

In March 1756 Colonel George Washington passed through New London on military business, for colonial troops had to be recruited to fight in the expected war with France, which came that May. He was already famous for his exploits in fighting the Indians, when accompanying General Edward Braddock's redcoats in the fiasco of the expedition against Fort Duquesne. In February 1757 Durkee was appointed a second lieutenant in the Fourth Company of the Connecticut Regiment, to serve under the bungling earl of Loudon for the invasion of Canada. Durkee's captain was a good friend, Joshua Abell, owner of a successful iron foundry in nearby Fitchville. The following year Durkee was made a captain of the Ninth Company of the Third Regiment, under Colonel Eliphalet Dyer of Windham. Zebulon Butler was regimental quartermaster. Later, Dyer and Butler became associates in the Sons of Liberty. Durkee's company was stationed near Lake George, and there he met another friend, Captain Israel Putnam of Pomfret, head of the Seventh Company and later a Revolutionary general. Durkee's company was given the task of rounding up stragglers from Loudon's disastrous Wood Hill battle and preventing their being killed by hostile pro-French Indians. It was a Fenimore Cooper story: single-filing through dense forests, ambuscades, body-to-body knife-fighting, scalping.

On returning to Bean Hill, Durkee joined with his fellow officers Abell and Elisha Lord (son of the owner of the other tavern) to engage in West Indian trading. They purchased a sixty-ton sloop, one of the first ever built in Norwich, and christened it the *Three Friends*. Durkee already had considerable experience in river trading and handling smuggled goods. He had organized a small gang to beat up nosy crown officials and trounce informers with stout oak staves. The new venture prospered.

In the spring of 1762 Durkee went as major in the Third Connecticut Regiment of 2,300 men to join the earl of Albermarle's expedition against Cuba. Around Havana Harbor he found 44 British warships, 150 transports, and 14,000 landing troops. The British had already seized the fortress, La Cabaña, alongside Morro Castle at the entrance to the harbor, but yellow fever had stricken half the force. With the arrival of colonial troops, the wall between Morro Castle and La Cabaña was blown down, and Durkee's men were among those who streamed in. The assault cost two thousand lives. The troops then fought step by step through the suburbs to encircle the city, which was pounded with six thousand shells and grenades daily. It capitulated, and fifteen million dollars in gold and silver were captured. Three and a half million were distributed to the troops. Durkee did not feel the colonials were treated equitably in the sharing of this loot, and for all their sacrifices, Cuba was handed back to Spain in the subsequent peace treaty, about which the colonial governments were not consulted. On the way home to Connecticut yellow fever raged aboard the vessel. John Durkee was among the handful of survivors.

By then he had had his stomach full of being lorded over by British officers. His tavern became a center for malcontents against British rule and the manufacturing and trading restrictions. It was to become the pivot of the Sons of Liberty movement in Connecticut.

Britain even closed the western frontier, to prevent the exodus of settlers and to preserve the western lands and forests as a royal monopoly. Emigration was forbidden. Ohio settlers were ordered out, to the anger of Virginia and New England land companies. George Washington and Benjamin Franklin—and Durkee—had invested in several. A new edict made all forests crown property and prohibited the unlicensed cutting of timber and the extracting of natural products. This spelled ruin to the shipbuilding industry, which already surpassed that of the mother country. British companies were going bankrupt too; men were being thrown out of work, so after the war the financial pinch was even tighter in England than in the colonies. The result on both sides of the Atlantic was depression and unemployment. Heavy war debts had to be met in both areas.

Early in 1764 the burdens in America became heavier, for England was determined to get larger revenues out of the colonies. The new revenue bill—the Sugar Act—directly affected Durkee. It placed duties on non-British textiles, coffee, and indigo, on molasses and Canary and Madeira wines, and banned foreign rum and French wines completely. The duty on non-British refined sugar was increased, and to the dutiable list were added iron, hides, whale fins, potash, and pearl ash. Duties on all foreign goods, which first had to go through England, were doubled. Smuggling became more profitable than ever.

Measures were taken to tighten controls. Warships were stationed along the coast and in ports. Customs inspectors and collectors—previously local men—were now appointed in London. Worst of all were the new heavy registration fees and bonding for all New World vessels and their cargoes. The act also established a vice-admiralty court in Halifax, where informers could bring colonials to trial rather than in local courts. The accused had to prove innocence, post bond for all costs, and journey to far-off Canada.

All local currencies were forbidden and outlawed. These issues had helped finance the wars fought in England's behalf. Dismissal, plus heavy penalties, was prescribed for all local officials and even governors who violated the provisions.

James Otis of Boston raised the cry of no taxation without representation. Samuel Adams, defying the royal governor, had the assembly set up Committees of Correspondence to keep other communities and colonies informed of events and to arrange for concerted action. The idea spread to every town, city, and province. Merchants and workmen began boycotting British goods.

The last straw was the above-mentioned Stamp Act of March 22, 1765, to go into effect November 1. It was the first attempt to impose an internal revenue system dictated by London. It hit just about everybody. All business and nearly all goods were affected: legal documents, beverages, dice, playing cards—every merchant; every banker; every lawyer, land speculator, and printer; every farmer; every worker. It taxed newspapers, books, pamphlets, insurance policies, ships' papers, licenses. The fact that the money raised was for the specific purpose of financing British defense forces to "protect" the colonies failed to make it more palatable. Rather, it seemed, the colonists, who already had their own war debts and their own militia, were being taxed for their own subjugation.

Incredulity and rage were spontaneous. Samuel Adams sent word to the Committees of Correspondence to organize the Sons of Liberty to take any and all necessary militant action to prevent enforcement of the act. This was the beginning of overt civil disobedience, willingness to use violence and to go to jail, a process that provokes counterviolence, repression, a never-ending cycle of discord. The clandestine reunions on Bean Hill began.

James Otis got the Massachusetts Assembly to call for a meeting of colonial delegates in New York to discuss the steps to be taken against the Stamp Act. Five assemblies promptly responded to this appeal, and when the congress opened, all but four of the colonies —and these had expressed their approbation—had delegates present. The congress put together fourteen resolutions denying the right of England to tax the colonies without representation. It condemned giving jurisdiction to admiralty courts. Petitions were sent to the king, the House of Commons, and the House of Lords.

An economic boycott by the colonists was already underway. The leading merchants of New York, Philadelphia, and Boston agreed to ban all British imports until the Stamp Act was repealed and trade regulations were modified. All over the land women got out their spinning wheels to make homespun. Seventy wheels were customarily present in the house of Sons of Liberty member Ezra Stiles in Newport. By November, when the act took effect, practically all business had halted; courts had ceased to function.

The colonies were bursting at the seams—more people, growing towns, new enterprise, new energy. The early settlers had been afraid of "the howling wilderness." They had come from tight little villages and from the tight little isle of England, and the great spaces of the New World appalled them. Like children pulling the curtains to shut out the dark, they placed restrictions on departure from the towns, tried to hem their people behind walls, and, in their fear of the unknown, the Indians, and the wilderness, they set up ecclesiastical autocracies. The pastors railed about the evils of the frontier, where men lost their religion, became wastrels and sinners. But bit by bit people slipped away or rebelled against church dictatorship that imitated the cruelties they had fled from in England. There, beyond the pale of church authority, the old values were broken down. Soil-rooted Americans were born.

In 1630 the Reverend Roger Williams, one of the great minds and free spirits of his time, had left England rather than take a compulsory oath to the Church. He soon was ordered to take an oath to obey the secular authority of Massachusetts. He escaped to the smoky Indian wigwams rather than be arrested and perhaps tortured or shipped back to England. He went on through the deep forests to found Providence, Rhode Island, where gradually his congregation joined him, and a new utopia was set up, the ideal commonwealth of the brotherhood of man.

The Reverend Thomas Hooker, a more discreet man, finally obtained permission to settle the Connecticut Valley, and led a large band with their oxcarts and belongings through the wilderness and under the Dutch guns near Hartford. There they threw off allegiance to Massachusetts and to England. The Fundamental Orders adopted were the first truly democratic constitution on the continent.

Though few new immigrants came to New England, the early settlers had big families—eight, ten, twelve, children—and the primogeniture laws, favoring the oldest son, set the other offspring into motion to find places where they could make a living. Acreages were too small to be divided up anyway. In the South, land monopoly and slavery drove freeholders to more western homesteads, where they were joined by new immigrants from Europe. Well before the Revolution, the population was pressing against the Alleghenies and the Appalachians. In spite of crown restrictions, they drifted on beyond to West Virginia, the Ohio and Kentucky areas. It had taken more than a century for the necessary population and necessary worldly goods to be accumulated for the westward trek. The tight walls were breached.

By then crown restrictions were more of a barrier than either physical hardships or danger. People had grown more self-reliant. They had learned to fight Indians, and four major wars had seen the creation of colonial militia units, which went forth to the north and west to fight the French and their Indian allies. They had moved against Spain in Florida and in the West Indies. But when a mother country finds it necessary to arm and utilize native troops, the end of colonial rule is in sight—viz. Africa, South America, Asia. Sooner or later the new weapons and skills are used against the imperial ruler.

If New England had received little fresh immigration, in the middle colonies and the South new breeds rapidly filled up the interior: the Scotch-Irish and Germans by hundreds of thousands. French Huguenots, a large Dutch population in Connecticut and New York. The Swedes took over Delaware. None of these peoples had loyalty to England, and the great grandsons of earlier New England settlers had become Americanized. They lived in log cabins; ate corn and turkey, wild game and honey; wore coonskin and homespun. The old ties were breaking down. Everywhere the local people were incensed by the rents on absentee-owned property— formed by early crown grants. Often the aristocratic British families had never seen their properties—not for a hundred years.

There were broad geographical divisions. There was a great cultural gap between the large tobacco and indigo plantations of the South and the New England homesteaders, and both differed from the manorial system in New York and Pennsylvania. The inland frontier was another area with different customs and peoples. A pluralistic society was being born.

Differences were appearing everywhere, between town and

homestead and plantation, between the coast and the interior. Sometimes these differences turned into armed revolts: the early Bacon rebellion in Virginia; the Regulators in North Carolina; the Paxtong boys in Pennsylvania, the battle of Connecticut settlers, led by John Durkee from Norwich, in the Wyoming Valley, claimed according to ill-defined crown grants by Connecticut but parceled out by Pennsylvania to a few large land-grabbers. These various disputes and open warfare were projected on into the Revolution against the British.

Within the new cities the contest between the ruling elite, the bankers, traders, and lawyers, and the disenfranchised artisans and laborers, growing in self-consciousness, was often acute. The indenture system of semislavery was breaking down. Dire penalties and punishments did not deter the indented from sneaking off to the cities or the frontier. Naturally they were scornful of authority, both colonial and British.

Economic interests constantly clashed with those of the mother country. From the first, fishing had been a major source of livelihood. Within a few years after settlement, Plymouth waxed prosperous on fishing. Nothing riled the New Englanders more than the British restrictions and duties on maritime products and activities. American whaling stations were set up in Antarctica two centuries before Admiral Richard Evelyn Byrd's publicized exploits.

New industry was arising. Little shops, often using water power, sprang up all along the rivers. England forbade the manufacture of iron and steel, sailcloth, and textiles for export. Massachusetts defied the orders. In Virginia and Maryland the British in 1706–1708 forbade the founding of new towns so as to prevent the starting of new industries. Trying to salvage her home industries, Parliament lengthened the list of prohibited manufactures. A spirit of flagrant disobedience grew up even among the well-to-do. All the time, the colonial market was expanding as the demand for goods increased in the towns and on the frontier and abroad. Diverse fresh energies were called into being everywhere.

The new industries changed the attitudes of whole communities. The journal of that great scholar Ezra Stiles abounds with accounts of his trips to new mines and factories. He is exuberant over the many new inventions. He himself started the raising of silkworms in Rhode Island in 1771—three thousand of those worms were "cocooing," and he distributed millions of mulberry seeds to every corner of Connecticut, even to Long Island and Vermont. New textile mills, paper mills, and powder mills were to be found in many places. The great newspaper brothers Samuel, Thomas, and Timothy Green started a paper mill, and Thomas planned to make paper out of seaweed. Abel Buell, the great engraver, had discovered a new amalgam for type, which he designed, and with a subsidy from the assembly he set up a shop in New Haven. Another New Havener, Isaac Doolittle, built and sold the first commercial printing press. Others were built in Newport. New printing methods were developed.

Parvenu wealthy groups had arisen, plantation owners, shipbuilders, traders, slave runners, rum makers, and rum peddlers. The new traders, who often made a fantastic fortune from a single voyage, flouted the navigation acts, ignored the barriers of the Spanish and French empires, and became semipirates, defying the might of the great powers, whose local officials often enriched themselves by conniving with the Yankee intruders. Two thousand American ships and more plied the seas. Customs houses in the colonies were bypassed, and even before the Sons of Liberty, dark-of-the-moon corporal punishment was meted out to informers and nosy officials. Open violations soon became the order of the day. In 1768 the Sons of Liberty and others carried a boatload of foreign wines openly through the Boston streets, and the revenuers and other officials dared not interfere. One of the wealthiest smugglers was John Hancock of Boston, known to later generations only as the first signer of the Declaration of Independence but recognized in his own time as "the Prince of Smugglers." When customs officials tried to seize his freebooter ship *Liberty*, they barely escaped with their lives at the hands of Hancock's gang of smugglers and the Sons of Liberty. One result was the Boston Massacre, when British troops fired on demonstrators, killing five, the first a Negro.

From 1750 on, more and more newspapers were started. An editor was put on trial in New York (1752) for criticizing the governor. His acquittal was notable. When the New Haven *Gazette*, edited by a nephew of Benjamin Franklin, appeared in 1754, its front page was a ringing editorial, set in italics, in behalf of freedom of the press and against tyrants. Just before the Revolution new newspapers were appearing on all sides, along with books, pamphlets, and handbills. The colonial mind had reached its lowest uncouth level by about midcentury, but the reawakening could not be held back. The old Calvinist and Puritan doctrines began to crack; a measure of religious tolerance made headway. It all represented a new continental force, which had started from a few little springs, had bounced along as little brooks, and had grown to wide streams. The rains came, the cloudbursts came, bringing the flood toward the sea of full independence and freedom.

The first open resistance to British encroachment on old and new liberties and enterprise came chiefly in the elected colonial assemblies and legislatures. True, the vast majority of the people, thanks to property and religious restrictions, had no vote—one in fifty in Philadelphia, one in seven in Rhode Island. Even so the assemblies were as colonial in their roots as tobacco or corn. Gradually they had freed themselves from imperialist interference and had limited the powers of royal governors, whose salaries they paid. (Only Connecticut and Rhode Island named their own governors.) The assemblies came to promote public works and new enterprises, to expand education and primitive public health. A few had issued paper money (which England in turn prohibited) to help finance war costs. They regulated wages, prices, and many intimate personal matters, such as dress, church attendance, and morals. At the start their concepts were often medieval, but gradually the expansion of industry and trade, the new jostling in the towns and cities, forced a more modern outlook.

The first protests against British impositions were mild and accomplished little beyond awakening the people. As resentments deepened and festered, anger was directed alternately against the king and Parliament. A powerful London Board of Trade to keep check on the colonies had been set up. It met daily, considering complaints, examining every bit of colonial legislation, and discarded everything that threatened the interests of the British landholding class, manufacturers, and traders. The needs or rights of the colonists were ignored. British colonial policy was never directed so much at raising revenues in America—though this provided the immediate *casus belli*—as at preserving or expanding the rights and profits of the British manufacturing and trading class: control of shipping commerce, the stopping of industrial competition, the monopoly of the fur trade, and—this was important—the provision of bureaucratic posts for the younger sons of wealthy families. The idea, which gathered effectiveness under the Protestant Cromwell dictatorship, was to acquire cheap raw materials from the colonies and to sell them high-priced, exportable, fabricated goods —the same pattern as that followed by the empires of today, against which so much of the world is now rebelling. The colonies had to buy solely from England, and British goods cost from 25 to 40 percent more than those of competitors. This slowly reduced the southern plantation owners to staggering insolvency and bondage to British speculators and loan merchants.

As Thomas Jefferson put it, the British buyers gave the tobacco grower good prices and credit till they got him immersed in debt. They then reduced the prices to such a degree he could never clear off his debt, which was hereditary. The planters saw no alternative but revolt. At the same time in England itself taxes rose, and the wars to seize Canada, India, and other outposts piled up a fantastic debt, not lessened by the huge standing army and large fleet. Empire was not a sweet story for most of the people.

If most colonial leaders merely wanted redress, a few of them, while not at first advocating independence, saw this as an inevitable and desirable outcome—such figures as Samuel Adams, James Otis, Patrick Henry, and John Randolph. James Otis called together the Continental Stamp Act Congress. Samuel Adams' Committees of Correspondence, even before the Stamp Act, were setting up Liberty Poles on village greens, where men rallied to listen to news and to protest against the British laws. The real break with England came with the Stamp Act and the formation of the Sons of Liberty, who forced every crown stamp agent to resign, even before the act was to go into effect.

In Boston they burned the admiralty court records, ransacked the home of the comptroller of currency and the mansion and library of Chief Justice Thomas Hutchinson, the biggest landholder in the colony, and by open violence forced his brother-in-law Andrew Oliver to resign as stamp agent (August 15, 1765). They hung him in effigy and burned the figure before his house.

The Connecticut people were particularly outraged by the appointment of Jared Ingersoll as stamp agent for the colony. He had been sent to London to lobby against it, but had accepted a post to administer the act—"a barefaced betrayal of trust."

Town meetings in New Haven and elsewhere called on him to resign. He received threats of death. His initials, he was reminded, stood for Judas Iscariot, and he would go down like "chopped hay" along with all others who enforced or obeyed the hated law. Not daring to bring in stamps from New York, Ingersoll rode off for Hartford, to try to get the Connecticut General Assembly, which was opening in September and where he had great influence, to back him.

Zebulon Butler's New London contingent of the Sons of Liberty arrived too late to intercept him, and rode hell-bent-for-leather north on his trail. He had left the previous night, in the company of Governor Thomas Fitch and an assemblyman, and had slept in Middletown at the Stonehouse Tavern. But when Durkee's men reached there, he had already ridden on. They caught up with him near Wethersfield and escorted him into town in formation, white staves lifted, trumpets shrilling.

Durkee told him he had to resign then and there. He refused to resign to an unauthorized gang of men—only to the authorities who had appointed him.

Durkee ordered him into the tavern. He refused to dismount, saying he would go on to Hartford or return to New Haven.

According to the account later written by Ingersoll, the conversation, reduced to quotes, went like this:

"You shall not go two rods from this spot until you have resigned."

"What will you do to me?" Ingersoll demanded.

"It will be difficult to pacify my men," Durkee warned him, "unless you resign."

"I can die now just as well as any other time," Ingersoll answered.

"We can take you prisoner to Windham until you change your mind."

Ingersoll answered pleasantly that he was very fond of Windham and would be delighted to visit there for awhile.

The angry shouts grew louder, and Durkee forced him into the tavern. There the Stamp Act agent stood at the window where he waved at assemblymen he knew who were riding to Hartford. The growing crowd outside grew more turbulent, and Durkee ordered him away from the window. "Quit enraging the people."

Groups rushed inside to demand that Ingersoll be delivered to them.

"What good will it do you if I resign? The government will appoint someone else. Is it fair for two counties to dictate to all Connecticut?"

"It does not signify to parley," retorted Durkee, losing patience. "A great many people are waiting for you to resign. You have no other choice."

Only after three hours, when tempers were completely frayed, did Ingersoll finally write out his resignation. A proviso that Ingersoll would never again act in his present official capacity was added.

Ingersoll had to stand up before the infuriated crowd and swear to his resignation loudly and reiterate the promise never to serve again. He was told to give three cheers for "Liberty and Property" —the slogan of the Sons of Liberty—which he did, throwing his hat into the air.

He was then taken on to Hartford in formal procession. "Death on a white horse," he said bitterly, "and Hell following."

Another vast crowd was gathered before Government House, where the assembly had just convened. Ingersoll was made to mount a table in front of the tavern and repeat his promise never again to serve. Resolutions were adopted to be put before the assembly. Governor Fitch promised to have the Stamp Act declared invalid. Satisfied, the Sons of Liberty circled the Government House three times, white staves lifted, trumpets blaring, then dispersed across the hills to their homes.

Fitch reneged on his promise, and Ingersoll announced that his resignation had been obtained under duress. But nobody bought his stamps, and Governor Fitch was thrown out, along with all assemblymen who had backed him. Durkee was elected to the new assembly, which had a distinct Sons of Liberty tinge.

Well before this trouble Durkee had had his own tribulations. The various trade and tariff acts had disrupted the fabric of trade. Joshua Abell pulled out of the shipping venture. It was continued as Durkee and Lord, which took over all "appurtenances," including the *Three Friends*, which was at the moment at sea on a voyage to Antigua. In 1767 Lord died "greatly insolvent." Durkee had to mortgage his home, tavern, land, and other properties, and as trade ground to a halt, he could not weather the difficulties.

To recoup, in cooperation with his former commander and friend Eliphalet Dyer, he led a big land-settlement expedition to the Wyoming Valley, a rich area claimed by both Connecticut and Pennsylvania.

The battle for the valley—during which the Bean Hill man built

Fort Durkee and laid out Wilkes-Barre—is one of the most thrilling, and bloody, episodes of frontier life in American history. The Connecticut people were aided by the Paxtong brothers, already in revolt against the Quaker regime. Twice Durkee was taken in chains to Pennsylvania. The last time he lay in filth for two years and came out broken in health, but soon plunged into the Revolutionary War.

No city in America bears a nobler name than Wilkes-Barre, Pennsylvania, founded by John Durkee. Colonel John Wilkes and Isaac Barré were members of Parliament who spoke out against coercing the colonies, and for their pains were thrust as prisoners into the Tower of London. Barré, in his speech against the Stamp Act, alleged that "sons of liberty" could not be oppressed by laws or arms, words that provided the name for the Sons of Liberty, which came to spearhead American resistance and civil disobedience, the basic instrument in the overthrow of British rule and the winning of independence.

The Sons of Liberty were the violent arm of the Committees of Correspondence. The methods, philosophy, and direct action were typical of revolutionary undertakings from that day to the present Black Power movement. Their punitive methods quickly divided the fish from the fowl. Respectable law-abiding citizens decried their actions, but step by step were forced to align themselves openly for or against independence. Civil disobedience forced the issue and wrote out principles in letters of fire for all men to see. Indifference could no longer stand erect in the winds of doctrine.

The Sons of Liberty provided a cover for many desperate individuals, but on the whole they were led by responsible men, in some places by wealthy citizens. In Rhode Island "a mob" was led by John Brown, one of the wealthiest men in the colony, to burn a tea ship in Providence Harbor. The leaders in New York City were wealthy men in high position.

The Sons of Liberty formed secret military alliances in all the colonies. At one reunion attended by John Adams, who was to become the second President of the United States, he found present among others two distillers, two braziers, a painter, a printer, two jewelers, and a ship's captain. As secret enforcers they looked into the opinions of all citizens, trounced merchants who violated the nonimportation agreements; they burned down the barns of Tory farmers;

became night riders, and before long day riders. They strung offenders up, sometimes on the Liberty Pole itself.

After the Sons of Liberty terrorized all stamp agents into resignation, no stamps could be sold. Durkee ordered everybody, under threat of violent reprisals, not to buy stamps. Town after town, even colonial assemblies, fell into line. Deeds could not be filed. Courts were closed for all civil suits. Business ground to a halt. Fasts and prolonged sit-ins in churches were staged under black drapes.

The boycott of English goods forced British companies into bankruptcy. By January 17, 1766, London merchants were up in arms. Thirty towns in England petitioned for immediate repeal. Benjamin Franklin, acting as agent for Pennsylvania, Georgia, and Massachusetts, kept telling Parliament and the British public that because of the French and Indian Wars, the colonies had no money to bear the burden, and that attempts to collect it by armed force, as crown minister Sir Richard Grenville demanded, would result in open rebellion. With the aid of William Pitt, the hated measure was repealed March 1, though Parliament insisted, even so, that it had full authority to make any and all laws it chose binding upon America. For each concession given to the colonies, the other hand always took something away. The trade laws were also modified, ironing out the unfair duties on non-English sugar and other products, but henceforth all products destined for England from the European Continent had to clear British ports and pay even heavier preliminary duties.

The Sons of Liberty next concentrated on the hated Quartering Act, by which the colonies had to provide free quarters and provisions for British troops. Tension mounted all spring and early summer. The New York Assembly refused to vote money for quartering General Thomas Gage's troops. British troops destroyed the Liberty Pole in Bowling Green. A pitched battle occurred between British troops, using bayonets, and the Sons of Liberty. Isaac Sears, their active leader, was wounded. The following year Parliament and the Boards of Trade suspended the assembly's legislative powers.

By June 29 Parliament was back at the whipping post and passed the Townshend Acts, new import duties on glass, lead, paints, paper, and tea, all vital for colonial economy. Pewterers (a major industry), builders and glaziers, printers and newspapers, were hit, and every colonist, until then, drank tea. Even more irksome were the enforcement measures. Hated writs of assistance or John Doe search warrants could be issued by court justices. New admiralty courts were imposed. A Board of Customs Commissioners, directly responsible to the British treasury, was set up in Boston.

The answer? Colonial merchants met together to enforce new restrictions on British imports. A Boston town meeting drew up a long list of goods to be boycotted. Providence and Newport imposed an overall nonimportation agreement. New York followed suit and set up a committee to promote domestic industry and employment and saw to it that all these measures were enforced. Soon the boycott was legalized. By 1769 every colony except New Hampshire had adopted nonimportation agreements, and in most places no payments of debts to Englishmen were permitted.

The colonial attitude was set forth by wealthy Pennsylvania farmer John Dickinson, who had the showiest mansion in the colony, just outside Philadelphia. His *Letters from a Farmer in Pennsylvania to the Inhabitants of the British Colonies*, published in the *Pennsylvania Chronicle*, were reprinted as a pamphlet, distributed, and widely read. "Behold the ruin hanging over your heads." Behold the "tragedy of American Liberty." He denied the right of England to tax the colonies, declared the Townshend Acts unconstitutional, and denounced the suspensions of the New York Assembly as a blow to the liberties of all the colonies.

"We have been prohibited from procuring manufacturies . . . anywhere but from Great Britain." The colonists were prohibited from manufacturing anything themselves. "We are exactly in the situation of a city besieged. If England made the colonists get their necessities from her and could order them to pay whatever taxes she pleased they were as abject slaves as those in wooden shoes and with uncombed hair."

Arrogant abusive bureaucrats were being foisted on the colonies. George III, with his doctrines of absolutism, was leagued with the corrupt trade monopoly of the East India Company. He was "trying to destroy a hundred and forty years of self-government in the New World."

Samuel Adams had the Massachusetts House of Representatives send out a general letter to all colonial assemblies. The acts violated the principle of no taxation without representation; the colonists were not represented in the British Parliament. He attacked recent ministerial maneuvers to make royal governors and judges wholly independent of the people and the assemblies, which paid the salaries, and called for united action.

Governor Francis Bernard ordered the seditious letter withdrawn, and when this was refused, dissolved the General Court, March 4, 1768. Wills Hill, the earl of Hillsborough, prime minister of the British cabinet, ordered all governors if necessary to dissolve the assemblies. But the Massachusetts Letter was endorsed by the legislatures of New Hampshire, New Jersey, and Connecticut. Virginia sent out its own circular letter, endorsing the Massachusetts stand.

Bernard called the assembly back into session and ordered it to expunge the circular letter from its records. After long debate the house refused 92 to 17 to obey and was at once dissolved again. The 17 "rescinders" were threatened, harassed by the Sons of Liberty, and all were defeated in the next election.

In New Haven—where typefounder Abel Buell and wealthy merchant-smuggler Benedict Arnold were leaders—by threats and beatings they drove the Glassites, or Sandemanians, a Scottish Tory sect, out of their meetinghouse on Gregson Street, which Buell took over for his foundry. When suit was brought against him by Tory printer James Rivington in New York, a big Sons of Liberty contingent rode out of New Haven to New York, smashed his plant and made off with the type and metal. Rivington had to flee to London. Buell helped the New York Sons of Liberty pull down the lead statue of George III on Bowling Green. The metal was sent north to Connecticut to be made into bullets for patriots. Buell tried to make off with it for his foundry and had hard work talking himself out of jail.

Tension mounted everywhere. Militia units were set up by town meetings and colonial assemblies and by Committees of Correspondence. Training bands were maintained in nearly every community. The more militant members then were the Sons of Liberty, who became the minutemen, pledged to instant action. Those in New Cambridge had blue uniforms, which they hid, when not in use, under woodpiles or in secret closets.

Presently the Sons of Liberty, dressed as Indians, dumped tea into Boston Harbor and elsewhere. Ships were burned, as in Rhode Island.

The uproar among London Tories was fury unleashed. Earlier Lord North, who had taken over as prime minister in 1770, had said he would grant no redress until the colonies were prostrate. A member of Parliament shouted that "all their woods should be burnt down." Another inquired why the Americans, "a strange sort of people," could not make their claims by argument but always had to decide things "by tarring and feathering."

The British proceeded to close the port of Boston to all commerce. Town meetings could not be held anywhere without the governor's consent and only for purposes he might designate. The ban was not obeyed anywhere, not even in Boston.

A wave of protest swept through the colonies, which began collecting food, supplies, and ammunition to be sent to aid the port. In Farmington, the third largest community in Connecticut, a thousand people gathered about the Liberty Pole, bearing streamers with such mottoes as PEACE, LIBERTY AND SAFETY or NO TAXATION WITHOUT REPRESENTATION, and surmounted by the blue liberty cap decked with gold stars. An officer of the training band read Parliament's "infamous" Boston bill closing the port and imposing penalties.

Jeers greeted the reading. "Is this law a crime?" sang out the officer. A roar of "yeahs" came back. "Shall it be hung to the Liberty Pole and put to death as a common criminal?" Another roar, "Shall the law be burned?" A still louder roar. "Let your will be carried out." The bill was cast into the fire. A little puff and curl of flame, it was gone.

The Sons of Liberty were present. Their chief local leader, sixty-year-old John Wilson of nearby Harwinton, where he had carved his homestead out of the wilderness, was a prominent pillar of the church and his community, a selectman and member of the Connecticut Assembly. As somber as the Harwinton forests, a man of inflexible self-righteousness and faith, a passionate patriot, he stood at the Farmington burning, lean, hard-bitten, his arms akimbo. He was the first to step forward as a volunteer to collect supplies for beleaguered Boston. The crowd burst into song.

And so the fires before the Liberty Poles ran faster than ever through the hearts and minds of a hundred villages in every commonwealth. Sparks of freedom ignited the whole Atlantic seaboard. Already the call had gone out for the first Continental Congress.

When the Boston Port Bill went into effect, the towns stopped all work and the patriots dedicated themselves to fasting and prayer in churches draped in black. The villages were silent except for the steady beat of drums, which made the rounds all day, all night. In Boston, too, there was silence, the wharves idle, the fishing boats swinging unused with the tide in the harbor. At times the ominous tread of redcoats was heard. In New Cambridge First Church, the Reverend Samuel Newell preached a sermon on the "Misery and Duty of an Oppressed and Enslaved People." The Church of England, the "Tory Church" was empty. For some time its members, mostly well-to-do Chippin Hill farmers, had not dared meet. Their minister, an active Tory, had hidden out.

In New Cambridge, Hezekiah Gridley of the Sons of Liberty turned his home into a warehouse for goods to be sent to Boston. Amos Barnes, a leading merchant, was put in charge of the collections. A great store of wheat and rye and Indian maize, pork and beef was accumulated and rushed on to the Boston selectmen for distribution to those "incapacitated, to provide a necessary subsistence in consequence of the late oppressive measures." Before June was over, Sam Adams wrote a special letter of gratitude. Such supplies, some sent a thousand miles from as far away as Georgia, had to be shipped by wagons and oxcarts over primitive roads. Great cavalcades of such vehicles converged on the New England port day after day. All the colonies, aroused to militant resistance, prepared for the struggle ahead.

Everywhere now, despite British troops, flags hung at half mast, and new streamers were flown from Liberty Poles as fast as the redcoats cut them down.

On September first, General Gage seized the powder of Charleston. It was reported that six Americans had been killed. All the towns about flew to arms, and about four thousand armed volunteers swarmed into Cambridge. In some towns every able-bodied man rushed out. The women prepared food and made bullets.

The news flew across Connecticut and New Hampshire, and by Sunday at least thirty thousand men were on the march toward Boston. Thousands more had gathered in readiness in Pennsylvania and Maryland, and George Washington was preparing to lead at least ten thousand Virginians to the scene, before the fact that the report of deaths was an error became known. Most volunteers turned back to their homes upon hearing that the news had been false. But the half-stoked fires remained ready to burst forth.

Not until Sunday, February 25, 1775, did General Gage send out another raiding party—from Castle William, the island fort in Boston Harbor—this time to try to seize some ordnance in Salem. The party landed at Marblehead, five miles from Salem. The Salem people rushed from the churches and hurriedly pulled their guns across a drawbridge, which was then raised. The British officer Colonel Alexander Leslie, later made general, threatened to fire on the thirty or forty armed militiamen, and the crowd assembled on the other bank. Nobody budged.

The Reverend Thomas Brainard stepped forward, advising Leslie that if he fired he would certainly be cut off before he could get back to his vessels. Leslie said that if the drawbridge were lowered, he would march across it for thirty rods, then retire. This was finally agreed to. A line was drawn; when his men got that far they would turn back or be fired upon. Before all his men had even put foot on the bridge, Leslie ordered them to pull back. He went at once to Marblehead and reembarked. Had he not done so there would have been deaths, and the war would have begun quite some months before it did.

It came on April 18, 1775, with the Lexington-Concord fight. As the news of that encounter flew in all directions, every colony sprang to arms. Money, ammunition, supplies, were sent out. Men left their work instantly; they dropped their plows in the fields, as did Colonel (soon to be General) Israel Putnam, Durkee's friend of Pomfret, Connecticut. Preachers led men out of their churches and women set to work making bullets, weaving blankets, making clothes. They went into the fields to finish planting the crops. They milked the cows and did all the other necessary chores. Any laggards were stirred to life when the news of Bunker (Breed's) Hill brought thousands more to the front. In the rear the Sons of Liberty stood guard and punished or drove out Tories. A hundred thousand pro-British colonists, most of them the well-to-do members of the communities, fled to Canada, to England, or to the Bahamas.

For its own defense the town of New Cambridge, west of Hartford, authorized the purchase of thirty hundredweights of lead, ten thousand French flints, thirty barrels of powder. The minutemen drilled. A Committee of Safety, headed by Joseph Byington, was set up to investigate violators of orders of the Continental Congress. Tea drinkers and black marketeers of British goods were pulled before them. Horse-racing, gaming, cockfighting, and shows, all were banned by Congress and the local authorities.

The town committee looked into the activities of all persons suspected of being unsound in their political sentiments. Presently Nehemiah Royce and others "were excommunicated by Town Vote as enemies of the country"—it was so advertised—and their children were denied admittance to the schools. Nehemiah and several others disavowed being Tories and had their rights restored. Others refused to retract.

As the dispute moved on to a wider war, bitterness against American Tories intensified. The people of New Cambridge, who even before actual hostilities, stripped themselves of animals and grain and got together military supplies and homespun, gazed sourly on the Chippin Hill Tories, where fat cattle grazed and the fields were fair. Presently the Sons of Liberty raided their herds and butchered the animals for meat for the fighting men. John Wilson said the Tories harbored enemies of the cause, that they gave shelter to the king's messengers and guided them on their way, which could bring death to thousands.

The Tory farmers rarely slept in their houses, and in the daytime the women sounded conch shells for the men to flee from the fields to a refuge known as the Tory Den, a secret cave in the hill ledges. The patriots did catch Chauncey Jerome, strung him up to an apple tree by his thumbs, and prepared to apply a hickory cane to his bare back. He escaped and ran deer-swift over the line into Plymouth to the home of his brother-in-law, who stood the raiders off, gun in hand. Stephen Graves escaped to the Tory Den time and again, but was finally strung up and beaten. Joel Tuttle was hung by the neck on Quarry Hill Green. A tanner cut him down, and Tuttle crawled off to the Tory Den.

The Reverend James Nichols, of the Church of England, and Moses Dunbar, a Chippen Hill recruiter for the British army, were captured and sent to Hartford. The minister was released, but Dunbar, the father of sixteen children, was tried and condemned "to be hanged up by the neck between the heavens and the earth until he shall be dead."

He escaped. The *Hartford Courant* described him as about five feet eight, with short curly hair and a beard of "sandy color . . . a down-look round face, hollow eyes," and wearing a red greatcoat. He was apprehended and hung on schedule, after the Reverend Nathan Strong told a "prodigious" concourse of people of the lessons that should be drawn from the unhappy event.

The Chippin Hill residents guided Tory marauders and gave asylum to them in April 1777 after they and several thousand British raided and burned Danbury, the main supply center for the new Continental army. Four persons were burned alive in Captain Ezra Starr's house, and when the meat houses were set on fire, fat ran ankle-deep in the streets. American General David Wooster was killed in the bloody fight that ensued.

The people of New Cambridge rounded up seventeen Chippin Hill residents and lodged them in the Hartford jail. They denied all knowledge of the Danbury raid, claiming they had been misled by the Reverend Mr. Nichols. All took the oath of fidelity to the Continental Congress, paid jail costs, and were released. Similar stories could be told of most communities in the colonies, particularly in New England. The abandoned mine pits near Hartford, which served as a prison, were packed with Tory prisoners.

On returning to Norwich from prison in Pennsylvania, John Durkee was put in charge of the local militia. They marched north, May 23, 1775, in time for the battle of Bunker Hill. He was made a colonel in charge of the Twentieth Regiment. When Washington finally had to evacuate New York City, Durkee helped guard the rear during the retreat across New Jersey. Once he had to abandon supplies and leave dinner simmering in the mess kettles. He covered the retreat at the Delaware River. His unit guarded the crossing in a night of driving rain and sleet. He was steadfast during the darkest hours of the Revolution—at Trenton, Princeton, Morristown —then rushed off to Norwich to get more recruits. He was back in time for the Germantown battle, and presently was at White Plains, helping to hem the British in New York.

Meanwhile in Wyoming Valley, where Durkee had founded Wilkes-Barre and fought for so long, six hundred Connecticut settlers were scalped by British-allied warriors of the Six Nations, and three thousand were driven from their burning homes. Durkee rushed there. After a successful campaign he was brought back and stationed on the bank of the Hudson opposite West Point, but he soon had to return home to Norwich on sick leave. The war was won when he died.

What did the long battle for "Liberty and Property" bring to the Thirteen Colonies? Before it was over, the Continental Congress and Samuel Adams' Committees of Correspondence became the real governing powers in the colonies; they punished offenders, confiscated Loyalist properties, fixed prices, collected army supplies, fitted out privateers, recruited men. "What an engine!" his friend John Adams exclaimed retrospectively.

The crown governor in New York advocated burning every committeeman's house and was himself willing to give twenty silver dollars for every one turned in to the king's troops.

Independence was the first reward of peace—thirteen states under the Articles of Confederation, drawn up while the battles were still going on. All colonial royal and proprietary governments were replaced by republican state governments, and all but the two that had already elected their own governments drew up new radical constitutions, which liberalized the political system, established free speech, a democratic judiciary, religious liberty, and the secret ballot. Nearly everywhere entailed estates and primogeniture were abolished. These had been pillars of land monopoly and the rule of the elite. The frontier was opened. The states were granted a vast western empire from the Atlantic to the Mississippi. The elimination of all British, royalist, and company officials and representatives broadened the bases of government and property ownership, and provided new jobs. This change was reinforced by wholesale confiscations of royal lands, proprietary estates, Tory properties, and big landholdings. Many such properties were seized during the Revolution and broken up into small homesteads. The De Lancey and John Morris estates in New York were sold to 275 and nearly 250 persons respectively. All rents to the crown and private British owners were abolished. The Anglican Church was disestablished and ceased to be supported by taxes. Religious tolerance was accepted. The rigid doctrines of Calvinism, already breached by Ezra Stiles, pastor of the Second Congregational Church of Newport and president of Yale, gave way to the more amiable doctrines of Unitarianism. Slavery was abolished in all New England and Pennsylvania, and the slave trade was prohibited or heavily taxed in eleven states. The indenture system withered away. Penal codes were reformed. Voting restrictions were eased or abolished. A number of state capitals were moved into the hinterland (viz Harrisburg, Pennsylvania, and Albany, New York) for security reasons and in answer to the rising influence of the frontier population.

A new land act opened up the Northwest Territory to land settlement. The lands beyond the mountains were available to homesteaders for insignificant prices. Much of it was sold to land companies that agreed to bring out settlers. Foreign trade was carried on with any part of the world. New ventures were made into the Pacific; exploration of the coast, as far as Alaska, expanded trade with the Orient. Robert Gray, a Martha's Vineyard man sailing out of Boston, made the first trip around the world under the new American flag. Above all it was an eager era of new enterprise: new factories, improvement of roads, turnpikes, and canals. Science took great leaps forward. New books poured from the presses. Art was advanced. Nearly everybody got a leg up by the Revolution or had access to new opportunities at home or in the West.

For a while, however, there were dreadfully hard times. The veterans came back to ruined, mortgaged farms. The merchants and financiers came into full control in Boston and elsewhere. There was real suffering as farms were foreclosed. A secondary revolution against the Boston speculators occurred. Daniel Shays's Rebellion came within an ace of taking over Massachusetts. George Washington was very upset. But Jefferson considered it a healthy symptom. Rhode Island tried to alleviate suffering by paper currency issues and by repudiating debts, which won it the nickname "Rogue's Island."

However, the ruling elite pretty much kept control of wealth and government, even staged a sort of counterrevolution, with the new Constitution drawn up in 1787. But despite all the checks and balances a broader basis for democracy was established. This was further emphasized by the Bill of Rights, the first ten amendments, which guaranteed popular freedom from abuses recently perpetrated by the British.

But not until after the anti-rent strike, the "Tin Horn and Calico" revolt, which began in 1839 in New York State was any real headway made against serfdom on the great patroonships of the Van Rensselaers, the Stuyvesants, et al. Men were killed; men went to jail. The rebelling tenants, exploited and abused, held from father to son in debt-slavery, denied even the right to have visitors in their shacks without permission, revolted, often disguised as Indians, blowing their tin dinner horns from the crags. They fought off sheriff's deputies and armed posses, burned court summonses, roughhoused rent collectors and land agents; their revolt was broken time and again, but little by little changes were edged into the state laws, and in the end the great empires were dismembered. But the ugly system was not wholly destroyed until after the Civil War.

The American Revolution had enjoyed little intellectual preparation, and it was chiefly growing resistance to the escalation of impositions and suppression. Whenever the British made one step back in the form of concessions, they took two steps forward in the form of new duties, new taxes, new regulations. Violence met violence; raids, riots, armed conflict, stormed out of the differences. England was interested in her own welfare and commercial advantages, with little concern for colonial needs and little knowledge of the system that had grown into being and was flourishing in America.

If theoretical guidelines were lacking, the struggle represented a conflict of cultures, economic interests, and political systems. Though the mother country had made some concessions to her own homegrown Liberals and Whigs, she was unable to grant the same rights to the colonies. Imperialism scarcely ever does. Even most Whigs were for repression. Overseas, England knew only how to apply absolutism and autocracy whereas the Americans by that time had had a century and a half of evolving democracy, predating that in England itself, and were not inclined to abandon their system and way of life for the inferior pattern of England or submit to police and military attempts to crush it. Autonomy was an issue. The colonists had believed at first that an accommodation could be made, that they could obtain due recognition of their own institutions. They alternately blamed their grievances on the king and on Parliament. Parliament was, of course, a closed gentleman's club, made up of feudal landholders and the new bourgeois manufacturers, bankers, and rich traders. They were intent on stamping out New World rivalry and colonial free enterprise. Adam Smith might believe competition to be the life of trade, but the merchants and manufacturers in Parliament much preferred the safety of monopoly. On their side the colonies, developing rapidly, were less and less inclined to accept curbs on their initiative and energy. The crown's claim to all frontier lands struck a blow not only at the rise of a free homesteading class but set up a British monopoly on fur trading. When the British navy patrolled the coast, the smugglers and merchants were badly mauled. Trade dropped, bankruptcies shook the colonies, and the activities of the new western land companies were smashed. The arbitrary 1763 Greater Proclamation Line along the crest of the Alleghenies shut off the entire West.

The first protests came from the top colonial leaders, the elite colonial assemblies, whose rights had been expanding for a hundred years. Such protests did not get far, until resistance spread down to the people. Only then was it possible to get some redress. By then the situation had become ugly.

In New England, town meetings were quick to take up challenges. These in themselves were incomprehensible to an aristocrat —like Governor Thomas Hutchinson who called them "mobs." Unlike the colonial assemblies, in town meeting there were few limitations on voting rights, except freeman status and (not everywhere) church membership. Personal wealth was not often a requisite. Hutchinson, the wealthiest landholder in Massachusetts, complained that things had reached the point where a gentleman could no longer enjoy "ordinary courtesy." Respect for their betters was draining out of the minds of the colonials.

The intellectual father of the Revolution, the source of most of its theory—more than either Jefferson or Franklin—was Samuel Adams of Boston. He drew his ideas from many sources, such as Plato, Cicero, Milton, Sir Algernon Sidney, and David Hume. For Adams, Montesquieu was a source of intellectual strength, as he became presently for the French Revolutionists. Adams relied greatly on such classical philosophical jurists as Grotius, Pufendorf, and Vattel, who were widely read in America. Adams also cited Coke and Blackstone a great deal, though he was aware they were reactionary. His great mainstay, as for so many of the revolutionary leaders, was John Locke, the British philosopher, author of *An Essay Concerning Human Understanding*. Locke, too, went to France, where he consorted with physicians and naturalists. Locke was no revolutionist, but a temporizing liberal, who would have had little sympathy with American freedom, though he wrote a bold essay on toleration, and his *Two Treatises on Civil Government* was a defense of individual liberty, in terms of property. But if any one man was responsible for the ideas and theories of the American Revolution, it was John Locke.

His thinking loomed gigantic in his day. He cleared away much ecclesiastical and feudal thinking by setting forth a sensible view of human cognition and the mental processes of forming generalizations. However, he flouted his own findings by blindly accepting a medieval concept of God, which must have aroused derision from the French thinkers of his day. Equally *non sequitur*, he set forth an ironclad concept of government as being established almost entirely for the purpose of guaranteeing property rights. The ideal status quo had been established after forty-seven years of disorder when in 1689 the bourgeoisie, growing in influence, ended personal monarchy and established the priority of Parliament. Locke averred the parliamentary system could not be changed, though any encroachment on England's Magna Charta or property rights by the crown or by Parliament became something to be resisted. Here he wove some bright phrases, useful to the colonists, about individual liberties and the defense of personal property. Locke's slogan "No taxation without representation" swept the colonists toward overt rebellion. "Liberty and Property," the slogan of the Sons of Liberty, was right out of Locke. Like Adam Smith he was the philosopher of modern capitalism—except that he had little conception of how revolutionary the new capitalism and property rights really were.

It was this mechanistic and institutionalized philosophy that Samuel Adams seized upon. He scarcely knew the more humanistic philosophy of the French Physiocrats and Encyclopedists, with their vastly wider range over the fields of man and knowledge. Only Thomas Jefferson was well grounded in the French Enlightenment. Adams supplied part of what was lacking in Locke by his own fervent belief in democracy. Adams believed in democracy more profoundly than any American before him—for that matter, more than most Americans since. He had no fear of majority rule, for he knew tyranny was always the work of minorities. He did not grasp that majorities, too, could act as the horrible instruments of oppressions, as under Hitler in Germany and others, of late, in the United States. From early manhood, though for a considerable time he concealed this, Adams dreamed of full independence, i.e., republican and democratic government. He undertook a tremendous task and carried it through. His steadfastness of purpose, his iron will, his courage, his grasp of all aspects of the problem, his ceaseless energy, make him rank with the outstanding revolutionary leaders of all time.

He was a newspaper man, a tremendous polemicist, an organizer. As a member of the Massachusetts General Court, he both enjoyed immunity and had a platform. He was the man most hated by aristocrat Hutchinson and by every Tory.

His first aim was to win English liberals to his side. His studies at Harvard and his extensive erudition served him well. He based his propaganda, first, on the theory of natural rights; second, on the rights of the colonists as British subjects under the crown and Parliament, ergo constitutionalism. *Constitution* is a charming word, he remarked to a friend.

As it became evident that Parliament was the persecutor, the instrument of imperialist coercion, Adams stressed more emphatically a third thesis, to which English Whigs were even less willing to subscribe, viz. that by charters granted the colonists prior to parliamentary rule colonial rights predated British constitutionalism. These early compacts represented the "only medium" that connected the colonies with the mother state, hence were superior to Parliament. Then, as the charm of constitutionalism and legal sophistry faded and became less meaningful, as the lack of colonial representatives in Parliament became more significant, he bore down more heavily on natural rights. Men, he reiterated, certainly had a natural right to change an existing constitution for a better constitution. The Magna Charta, he pointed out, had been wrested at sword's point from King John. Ergo, any act of Parliament against the Magna Charta was evil (John Locke again, plus citations from Coke and Vattel), and "peradventure" it might be "rescued and preserved from total destruction," only with sword in hand. In any event the charters had given the colonies the right to make their own laws for their government. Such shifting arguments today seem quibbles, but they were athletic stances in Adams' day and provided telling arguments for legalistic minds disenchanted with British impositions.

Above all, Adams was a publicist: the first American since Roger Williams to appreciate the power of public opinion and to wield it —and organize it. He used all the instruments at hand to promote his crusade. He was an indefatigable letter writer, article writer, and speaker. "Every dig of his pen stings like a horned snake," complained Governor Francis Bernard. He mingled with merchants, statesmen, fishermen, mechanics, and farmers.

One of his chief bases of operations was the Cactus Club, an early discussion group set up by his father, which admitted not merely the elite but merchants and mechanics. The younger Adams utilized it as a training school for leaders and to lay out such programs of attack on British rule as the nonimportation agreements, which wrought havoc with British trade and disturbed England and the colonies so profoundly. It was at the Cactus Club that he planned his Committees of Correspondence, which set up a continentwide grass-roots network of action and information.

These gave him a leverage in every community. Hutchinson sputtered so badly over the Committees of Correspondence that he lost all control over his gentlemanly language. Adams was not only propagating ideas; he was building up popular instruments for the Revolution.

He also took discussions to town meetings and in Boston to Faneuil Hall, where he swayed men like trees in the wind. Infuriated, Hutchinson characterized them as "indecent." Adams thundered back, defending "the Reasoning of the People" outside the closed aristocratic clubs. Every "transient person," he declared, had a right to "animadvert" publicly on anything under the sun. He intended to exercise that right whenever he chose "without asking any man's leave." "In these times of Light and Liberty, every man chooses to see and judge for himself"—the bulk of the people were democratic. Hutchinson called him a "Master of Puppets." Adams laughed scornfully. He did not conceive of his following as puppets but as free men. He sent out word to the Committees of Correspondence to take people's attention off "picking up pins" by directing them "to great great Objects."

Adams maintained that he was not a Leveler, referring to the faction in Parliament about 1647 that wished to abolish all rank, but he insisted, nevertheless, that extensive equality was the design of government at its best. He scoffed at fears that the people might abuse liberty. Was this a valid argument for denying liberty to them? Denial was a worse abuse of liberty. Was anything less desirable for mankind than slavery?

From the start he realized the necessity of breaking down subservience to English officialdom and the ruling class in England and the colonies, and he laid bare the selfishness and corruption of the existing autocracy. He aroused fury in privileged quarters, and was highly pleased when Hutchinson accused him of "robbing men of their characters." He intended, he flung back, to show them up for what they really were underneath their robes of authority. In the end Hutchinson had to take refuge in England to escape the wrath of New Englanders.

Adams' most persistent and telling attacks were against servile judges and the system of justice. He brought judicial decisions under public scrutiny, showed how the jurists prostituted their profession. He sought to demoralize New England law and denounced Blackstone for reinforcing unjust English law. The only proper test of law was whether it was "consonant to natural reason." Law had to meet the needs of the people. He well knew that to shake faith in law and the courts and to promote defiance of the law were basic prerequisites of revolution. Every harsh sentence or twisted decision, which tended to mount up in hours of stress, reinforced his arguments. He clipped the claws of judges and courts, exposed their graft, and kicked them out of dual jobs in the court and the legislature. Little by little, popular respect for the judiciary turned to derision.

Judges and leaders were forced to choose between accepting royal money or answering to the people—and sometimes the mob. They were forced to serve revolutionary purposes or get out. The sovereign people had a right to withstand the abusive exercise of legal and institutionalized crown prerogatives, and Adams told both the governor and the judiciary that the people had a right to change the fundamental law and not merely the administration and interpretation of it. Anything injurious to the people could not be considered binding. And the people were not the wealthy cultured minority, but all the workmen, yeomen, and merchants, "all the homespun people hitherto treated as pawns."

He prepared the way for the Sons of Liberty to strike out against royal authority, against the recalcitrant legislatures, to close down the courts. Overt civil disobedience, willingness to defy police power, to utilize violence, was the beginning of the end—though it would require ten years of such violence to awaken the people to a realization that the only solution was independence. Other leaders were equally courageous: Isaac Sears in New York, Charles Thompson of Philadelphia, Patrick Henry of Virginia.

By the time Thomas Paine published his *Common Sense* in January 1776, the Revolution was well underway—Lexington, Bunker Hill, and George Washington in command. But the pamphlet, read by everybody in the colonies, swept away the last doubts about the need for full independence, which in turn meant republicanism and government by the people. The words were clear, simple, hard-hitting—for every man. Paine's epigrammatic arguments appealed particularly to the free men of the frontier, to artisans and yeomanry, and particularly merchants and shippers.

Society is produced by our wants, and government by our wickedness. . . . Society in every state is a blessing, but government even in the best state, is but a necessary evil; in its worst state an intolerable one. When we suffer, or are exposed to the same miseries *by a government,* which we might expect *without government,* our calamity is heightened by reflecting that we furnish the means by which we suffer . . . the palaces of kings are built upon the ruins of the bowers of paradise.

Paine went on to examine the contradictory nature of royal authority and English constitutionalism. The latter was merely the base residue of two ancient tyrannies plus new republican dressings.

First—The remains of monarchical tyranny in the person of the king.

Secondly—The remains of aristocratical tyranny in the persons of the peers.

Thirdly—The new republican materials: in the persons of the [House of] Commons on whose virtue depends the freedom of England.

The first two were independent of the people and contributed nothing toward freedom. A thirst for absolute power was the disease of monarchy. Though the Commons could check the king by control of finances, the king could veto all the legislation it passed. This was an absurdity. "As a man attached to a prostitute is unfitted to choose or judge of a wife, so any prepossession in favour of a rotten constitution of government will disable us from discerning a good one."

The British king based his right to govern on the Norman Conquest. No man in his senses, Paine continued, accepted this. "A French bastard landing with an armed banditti, and establishing himself as King of England against the consent of the natives, is in plain terms a very paltry rascally original. It certainly hath no divinity in it." The plain truth was "the antiquity of the English monarch would not bear looking into." He set forth all the evils of hereditary monarchy. "Of more worth is the one honest man in society and in the sight of God than all the crowned ruffians that ever lived."

He listed in detail the advantages of independence as compared to colonialism: the benefits to commerce, business, international prestige, and freedom from entangling alliances and war, periodically inevitable in a Europe divided into rival states. Nor could the colonies be repeatedly drained and their commerce ruined by subservience to British policies. Even if Parliament conceded anything to the colonies, which were always secondary, there was no assurance that it would be generous the day after tomorrow. It had repealed the Stamp Act, but in a year or so new oppressive measures undeceived Americans. It was not in the power of Britain to do this continent justice. It was too distant and too ignorant of American needs. The colonies could not carry on business by running to them with three or four thousand petitions and waiting four or five months for an answer, then spending five or six months explaining them—absurd, anyway, for a continent to be governed by an island. They belonged to different systems.

Did Bunker Hill make sense if the battle were merely for the repeal of a law? Freedom had been expelled from the whole world, including England. America must quickly prepare "an asylum for mankind."

After *Common Sense*, and its impact, the Declaration of Independence was almost inevitable. It came that July. It was Jefferson, with his humanitarian ideas and his intimacy with French thinking, who altered the Sons of Liberty slogan "Liberty and Property" to "Life, Liberty, and the Pursuit of Happiness." As one writer put it, "He watered the tree of liberty with the blood of tyrants" and emphasized the right of a people to alter or abolish a government they did not desire. The theory of government in the Declaration went far beyond Locke by asserting that governments are instituted among men, deriving just powers from the consent of the governed.

Is this the kind of government we have today? We like to think so, but actually our government has grown so powerful, so wealthy, so complex, with so many wheels within wheels, so many echelons of power, that the pristine formula is certainly tarnished. What yesterday was complacency and comfort and chromium, the belief that the American system was perfect, has been swept away. Obviously the Great Society is remote indeed from perfection, and a new revolution, a twentieth-century brand of the Sons of Liberty rides the streets and the ghettos, torch in hand.

CHAPTER 3

THE FRENCH REVOLUTION

As IN THE AMERICAN COLONIES, the modern French enlightenment began to emerge in the middle of the eighteenth century. Little by little, the new way of thinking, based in good part on the rise of the sciences, seeped down to the people, ate away the monarchical regime and the foundations of the feudal, aristocratic, and ecclesiastical system grown so corrupt. The fools were not the thinkers, as many believed, but those in power who threw them into the Bastille. The police grew frantic at the mounting violent civil disobedience. The regime could not comprehend that the laws were no longer adequate or just, or enforceable by police power. Even if goodwill had come into being, it would have come too late to change the laws or to promote justice. Privilege had become too entrenched either to permit or to carry out the required changes.

If any one event signaled the inception of the new Enlightenment—despite such prior philosophers as Bacon, Locke, Descartes, Leibnitz—it was the publication in 1748 of Baron de Montesquieu's two-volume *L'Esprit des Lois,* his last literary opus, colossal in its wide historical and economic erudition and its felicity of style. Previously he had published an important study on the reasons for the grandeur and decadence of Rome, ending with the Turkish capture of Constantinople. Within a few years *The Spirit of Laws* had been translated and widely distributed. It influenced the thinking of the American revolutionaries, particularly that of Thomas Jefferson and Samuel Adams, and became part of the literary baggage of the intellectuals of the French Revolution. (An American correspondent first came upon Fidel Castro lying under a tree in the mountain forest, his telescopic rifle by his side, reading Montesquieu's *The Spirit of Laws.*)

Montesquieu himself was no revolutionist, nor was he greatly concerned with republican government. He believed in a limited monarchy, which became the initial issue on which the French Revolution pivoted, and he hated despotism. His main concern was for a state that governed with moderation and toleration for all beliefs and religions. Thomas Paine, of course, was to consider toleration merely a negative sort of state concession; the true desideratum was freedom of conscience for everybody.

The virtues of a republic, according to Montesquieu, consisted of equality, frugality, and the universal loyalty of the people to their government and their country. Equality, while including, ipso facto, political participation and democracy, was chiefly economic. The failure of Greek democracy was due to its inability to create representative government when individual participation became impractical.

One of his best anecdotes is about Charles II of England. Seeing a prisoner in the pillory, he asked him why he was being punished. "For libeling the minister." "You fool!" exclaimed the king. "Why didn't you libel me, and nothing would have happened to you."

Montesquieu's work yielded many quotable passages that appealed to the American mind, as they also did to the French. Above all, it had a humanitarian breadth that was lacking in the more mechanistic British philosophers. Its premises were justice, liberty, tolerance:

The might of a people is more terrible than a tyrant. The impetuosity of a people knows no limits of danger.

History is replete with examples under a monarchy of civil war without revolution; under despotism, of revolution without civil war.

The benefit of despotism is peace, law and order. This is false; it is merely the peace of slaves.

In monarchies men enrich themselves by the law; in Republics, by evading the law.

Crime does not undermine Republics; only indifference.

In Rome, those who were free were very free; those enslaved, very enslaved.

In a free state, it does not matter whether people think rightly or wrongly; it is enough that liberty results. In a despotism it is poisonous if one reasons either rightly or wrongly.

Spain abandoned natural wealth for symbols of wealth [gold and silver]. In place of great treasure, it should have made a great people.

Bastard children are more hated in Republics than in monarchies.

Montesquieu stimulated all the great prerevolutionary thinkers. Among the greatest was Denis Diderot, editor of the *Encyclopédie*. Friedrich Engels wrote, "If anybody ever dedicated his whole life to enthusiasm for truth and justice—using the phrase in its good sense—it was Diderot." The French thinker had a tremendous thirst for knowledge in every field, particularly in science. He wrote with verve, humor, satire, and was never happier than when demolishing the false idols of politics, society, religion, or sexual taboos. On the positive side he set forth what was later to be the Darwinian concept of evolution, the origin of species by unusual mutations, a century before the English scientist. He had a clear conception of chromosomes and genes—though not naming them as such—long before the facts about biological transmission were known. Leibnitz had developed his idea of the "windowless monad"; but Diderot had a workable concept of atoms and molecules in physics and biology. An atheist, he was among the first to challenge medieval proofs of God and the hereafter.

Commissioned in 1746 to translate and adapt *Chambers's Encyclopaedia,* he built a new shining edifice of universal knowledge. Among his contributors were the intellectual giants of the day: such writers and philosophers as Jean Jacques Rousseau, François Marie Arouet de Voltaire, Bernard le Bovier de Fontenelle, and Claude Adrien Helvétius; metaphysicians Marie Jean de Caritat, marquis de Condorcet, and Etienne Bonnot de Condillac; mathematician Jean le Rond d'Alembert (for a time, coeditor); historian Abbé Guillaume Thomas François Raynal; Italian economist Fernando Galiani; naturalists Georges Louis Leclerc, comte de Buffon, and Louis Jean Marie Daubenton. The first two volumes of this great work were suppressed, though later allowed to appear. The last volume, published twenty years later, had to be printed and distributed clandestinely. Diderot made the *Encyclopédie* into "a philosophical engine of war," said one contemporary. The reason for his initial difficulties, aside from the material itself, was his publication in 1746 of *Philosophic Thoughts,* which, thanks chiefly to the Jesuits, was denounced and burned. An unsuccessful effort was made to suppress his *Promenade of a Skeptic* the following year. He had to hide out while he wrote *Letter on the Blind for the Use of Those Who See* (1749). He spent three months in jail, luckier than many other writers who were thrown into the Bastille for years without trial. The ferocious taxation to pay for the Seven Years' War, the corruption at court, the flagrant ostentation of Madame de Pompadour, created unrest and satire, a spirit of resistance that could be held back only temporarily by police terrorism.

A Swedish professor named Björnstahl, according to John Morley in the second volume of his *Diderot*, saw him at the Hague in 1779 and was enthralled by his charm, vivacity, and original observations on any and every topic:

Who could fail to praise him . . . He often told me he never found the hours pass slowly in the company of a peasant, or a cobbler, or any handicraft worker, but often had found the hours passed slowly in the society of a courtier. For, of the one, he said, one can always ask about useful or necessary things, but the other, so far as anything useful is concerned, is mostly empty and void.

The French writer was a critic of literature, drama, and music, a novelist, and a playwright. He entered into savage polemics in favor of the new popular music of the "Buffoons." In his novel *The Indiscreet Toys*, which he wrote to get money for his mistress—his marriage had proved disastrous—he utilized an Oriental setting to expose the sexual and immoral aspects of court life, and lashed out at the corruption of the priesthood. He indulged in a delightful satire about the location of the soul in the body, which he averred was not in the head but in the feet at birth, gradually rising to the legs and loins. Carlyle angrily described the novel as "the beastliest of all present, past and future dull novels"; one needed a bath and clean raiment after its filth. Actually, though it is scarcely a novel, it is delightful, witty, lucid, scintillating with imagination, most of it better, clearer, more spritely, than much that sexually impotent Carlyle ever wrote.

Diderot's *Discourse of a Philosopher to the King* was a daring proposal to help the exchequer at the expense of corrupt priests, who were very rich and dangerous. "Sire, if you want priests, you don't need philosophers, and if you want philosophers, you do not need priests; for the ones, by their calling are friends of reason and promoters of sciences; the others, the enemies of reason, are the favorers of ignorance. If the first do good, the others do evil." Philosophers cost little, but the priests were very costly, and by ridding himself of them, he could also rid the country of all their lies. It could be done by a progressive appropriation of church revenues. The sums involved were immense: "150,000 men to whom you and your subjects pay about 150,000 crowns a day to brawl in a building and deafen us with their bells" and tell 18,000,000 people that "a king is nothing, nothing at all. They open shop when others close, i.e., about a third of the year. Since you have the secret of making philosophers hold their tongues, why not employ it to silence the priests?"

"What is the world?" he asked in his *Promenade of a Skeptic*. "A complex, subject to revolutions, which ever indicates a continual tendency to destruction . . . a transient symmetry, a momentary order."

The questions he asked of the crown, the church, the aristocracy, came to be asked by more and more people until the whole corrupt superstructure finally crumbled. Diderot, along with Paul Henri Dietrich d'Holbach and Helvétius, made up the great triumvirate of pre-revolutionary thinkers. Voltaire and Rousseau were luminaries, shining in their own bright heavens.

The roots of revolution went far back and deep into national misery and autocracy. The notable Cardinal Richelieu, Armand Jean du Plessis, had made war the fixed system of government. Famine resulted. In 1670, peasant revolts in four provinces were savagely suppressed by scorched-earth methods which laid waste a large part of France. The saying became that everybody in France was a soldier, a beggar, or a smuggler. The feudal aristocrats ruled the ant heap, and absolutism became absolute; taxes multiplied and skyrocketed. Madame Françoise Athénaïs de Montespan, leading mistress of Louis XIV, flaunted her luxury, power, and bigotry. She was controlled by the Jesuits.

Cardinal André Hercule de Fleury took over in 1720 at the age of nearly seventy, ushering in the vice-ridden court of Louis XV. He ruled for eighteen years in a fog of old age, cruelty, and intolerance. The splendiferous Madame Jeanne Antoinette Poisson de Normant de Pompadour became a petticoat prime minister. She ran the navy, raised armies, flung out ministers in disgrace. She severed old alliances, and in concert with Maria Theresa of Austria and Elizabeth of Russia, converted Europe into a "petticoat continent," but lost Canada and India. A century of war with England ensued.

There was some showy "progress," like the magnificence of the colonnade of the Louvre, rising out of tyranny and superstition. Madame Josèphe Jeanne Marie Antoinette imposed her cruel destructive policies on her husband, Louis XVI. As corruption, monopoly, frustration, and cronyism expanded, the freedom of French writers shrank. The intellectual heroes became villains and lawbreakers, and most spent some time in jail. Rousseau's *Emile* was condemned in 1762. Voltaire spent four years in jail and twenty-eight years in exile.

In one of Diderot's most difficult financial moments, Catherine II of Russia bought his library, which he could keep in his possession until his death. In 1773 he journeyed to the Russian court. He died in 1784, five years before the Revolution of which he was one of the chief intellectual progenitors.

Weak and vacillating, Louis XVI was a gross glutton, who rarely rose sober from the table. He was interested only in hunting, tinkering with door locks, and drawing maps. Marie Antoinette, sister of Emperor Leopold—"the hated Austrian," she was called—asked her mother, shortly after her marriage, whether a husband was not supposed to enter his wife's bedroom. One of her children, the dauphin, or crown prince, was rumored to be the son of one of her most faithful paramours, Count Fersen. Her extravagances, her luxury, her gambling, helped bring on bankruptcy. But she was the only man the king had around him, remarked one of Mirabeau's collaborators.

By the end of 1788 things had reached such a sorry pass that the king, hoping to allay discontent and to cool off the food riots, but chiefly because he needed more money for the bankrupt court, was persuaded to call elections for the three-tiered States-General, which had never been allowed to meet for more than half a century. It was to convene at Versailles on May 4, 1789.

The elections let loose floods of oratory, amid the riots of the hungry and mounting popular fury. The peasants were worse off than the lowest savages. They went barefoot, wore rags, slept in hovels on the dirt floor, and a good part of the year subsisted on roots and bark. The greatest orator of all was Honoré de Mirabeau, known chiefly for his profligacy, his duels, and for having spent much time in prison. His father once called him a "chatterbox and a noodle." Mostly he had been jailed on *lettres de cachet,* secured by his father, which meant being held without charges and without trial. One Englishman was thus held in the Bastille for thirty-six years without knowing why he was there. At one time or another Mirabeau's father similarly jailed his wife and other children and everybody else against whom he had a grievance. Once Mirabeau escaped and eloped to the Netherlands with the young wife of a wealthy aged friend of his father. He and Sophie as he called her, Marie Thérèse de Monnier, lived there, half starving in a garret, until he was hunted down and arrested. Mirabeau then spent forty-one months in a small, dark cell, which ruined his health and his eyes, for he was an omnivorous reader. From his cell he wrote his Sophie many passionate love letters, which rivaled in their own way the celebrated letters sent to Héloïse by Abelard; they were later praised by Victor Hugo. Sophie herself was sent to a prison for prostitutes, and finally, after their relationship had been broken off, she committed suicide in 1789.

Mirabeau was said to be "the ugliest man in France." His face was gouged by smallpox, which he had contracted at the age of three. To a female admirer who wrote asking what he looked like, he replied, "Imagine a tiger with a face scarred with smallpox." He had married Marie Emilie de Covet, daughter of the wealthy marquis de Marignane, a "hideous," dumpy girl, hoping to receive a handsome dowry, which did not materialize. She was a terrible gambler, and he soon left her. He repaired his fortunes on the eve of the elections by an affair with dreamy-eyed Madame de Nehra, who was both beautiful and wealthy. At first sight he was so repulsive she backed away in disgust, but was soon seduced by his wonderful smile and charm. He swore eternal fidelity and abandoned her for the voluptuous tricky Madame Le Jay.

A Paris newspaper during the campaign called him "a mad dog." "A good reason to elect me," he retorted, "for despotism and privilege will die from my bite."

He was the choice of the voters of Marseilles and Aix. He accepted the call of the latter, where he had a far greater majority. In general the candidates of the Royalists were decisively defeated, and those candidates who promised to bring "woe to the privileged orders," the so-called friends of the people, though badly maligned by the press and by other media, were chosen. The people had suffered too long. They were clamoring for a change, and they voiced their discontent and desire clearly in the first election held in two generations. The campaigners opened the door to a new era.

Mass, celebrated in the cathedral of St. Louis, and attended by the king and queen, was held for the members of the States-General on May 4. The following morning, the first session was held in the vast Salle des Menus Plaisirs, which seated five thousand people. The assembled body was divided into three chambers: the clergy; the nobles; the Commons, or Third Estate. The first two represented less than three hundred thousand people; the Commons, the rest of France's inhabitants—now estimated at twenty-five million—of whom only taxpayers had the right to vote, cast five million ballots. Thus the delegates of the Third Estate equaled in number those of both the two upper bodies.

The clergy and nobles were allowed to enter by the main doors; the commoners by a small side entrance—after everybody else was seated. The king and queen, clad in regal robes, sat on a high dais under a purple velvet canopy, spangled with golden fleurs de lis, surrounded by members of the royal household attired in superb gowns and jewels. Below them stood the resplendent royal guard.

At a lower level sat the head of the cabinet, Jacques Necker, and the other ministers; on the right, the clergy in surplices and robes; on the left, the nobility, wearing black, with red and gold capes and plumed hats. On the floor were seated the members of Commons in plain black coats and knee breeches. Looking up at the king, Mirabeau remarked audibly, "Behold the victim, already adorned." The Commons refused to remove their hats—a studied discourtesy and in itself an ominous warning to the regime.

From the first, Mirabeau, one of the few nobles among the six hundred commoners, seemed to dominate his fellow delegates, indeed the whole assemblage. He came in with a determined step, a bitter smile on his mouth. His spirit was proud and lofty. All eyes turned to look at him. He was ugly, but his heavy shock of black hair was like the mane of a lion. His eyes flashed. Madame de Staël, the handsome, richly attired daughter of Minister Necker—she had seen Mirabeau at Mass and was now in the balcony with other elegantly gowned women, ambassadors from all over the world, and the nobility of the realm—described him vividly and added, "His whole person gave you the idea of power, an irregular power, but a power such as would figure in a Tribune of the people. He knew everything and foresaw everything."

The king gave a short address; then Necker droned on for three solid hours. Mirabeau called him "a clock that is always slow" or, at other times, "the bookkeeper." Necker talked of finances, new taxes, the raising of more money—nothing about the social ills of the country.

The following day the Commons met alone in the big auditorium. They demanded that the other two bodies join them and that the voting be by poll of all members. The clergy and nobles insisted that the vote be by chambers, which automatically meant the continued domination of privilege and would nullify anything done by the larger body. A deadlock resulted. That same day the king's council suppressed Mirabeau's newspaper, *Etats Generaux*. Mirabeau told the Commons, it would appear the next day as *Lettres à mes commettants*. "Instead of enfranchising the nation, they seek only to deepen its chasms."

Etienne Dumont, in his *Recollections of Mirabeau,* to whom he was a "ghost writer" blowing into "the mighty trumpet," provides the most intimate source for the utterances and events of the leader's life.

The king ordered voting by separate chambers, whereupon the Third Estate (*Tiers Etat*) declared itself the National Assembly. The nobles refused to submit. The archbishop of Aix, speaking to the Commons for the clergy, flourished a loaf of black bread, "the food of the poor," and said that instead of quibbling they should all get to work bettering their condition.

A loud voice, said to have been Robespierre's, rang out, "Go tell your colleagues that if they are so impatient to assist the poor, they had better come down and join the friends of the people."

"That man will go far," said Mirabeau. "He believes what he says."

The day would come, not far distant, when Maximilien Robespierre would weep over the death of his favorite canary and send thousands to the guillotine.

On June 20 the deputies of the Commons found the hall closed on the pretext that it was being prepared for a visit of the king three days later. It was surrounded by soldiers. The deputies angrily demanded admittance. Their president, Jean Bailly, an astronomer, calmed them down, and they went to the Tennis Court, a miserable building without seats. There, after considering a protest march on Paris, they swore with raised hands not to adjourn until they had provided France with a constitution.

The Tennis Court was closed by the soldiery the next day on the grounds that the queen was using the place for a game of tennis. The door of the Recollet monastery was slammed in their faces, so they gathered in the church of St. Louis. The rising fury of popular wrath and the determined stand of the Third Estate brought considerable dissension in the other two orders. It was soon obvious that more extensive changes were required. Both bodies were split; the lower nobility and the lower clergy could no longer be controlled by the great seigneurs or by the church hierarchy, and it became evident that the privileged orders were impotent to take command of the situation.

There at the church of St. Louis, the Commons was joined by nearly all the clergy, led in by the archbishop of Vienne, and a few of the nobles. The solid antipopular front was really broken.

On June 23 in a royal summons, the king promised the Third Estate that he would present a new political policy. The Commons therefore repaired again to the Salle des Menus Plaisirs. As before, they had to enter by the side door. It was still closed, and the rain was pouring down. They finally took their places, soaked to the skin and angry. No cheers greeted the king, no "Vive le Roi." "Silence of the people is the lesson of kings," declaimed Mirabeau.

The king revoked all the laws passed by the Assembly, which had abolished noble titles and privileges. The feudal rights, he declared, were property and hence inviolable. He ordered the three chambers to meet and vote separately. The nobles applauded loudly. "Silence there," roared Mirabeau. The king ordered all to adjourn and withdrew.

The Commons held their ground; Mirabeau harangued them. "What is this military dictatorship. . . . Twenty-five million people are looking to us for certain happiness. . . . A military force surrounds this Assembly."

Marquis de Druer came from the king to remind them of his orders to adjourn. Bailly advised him he had no place, no voice, no right, to speak in the National Assembly. "Go tell your master that we are here by the will of the people and only the power of the bayonet can eject us."

"Let us proceed to deliberate," Abbé Sieyès, one of the great polemicists of the popular cause, said quietly.

The king, informed of their defiance, exclaimed petulantly, "Oh, let them alone."

That morning he had dismissed Necker, who refused to endorse his policy. Now he begged him to stand by, but on July 11 he was ordered out of the country. At this juncture, forty-seven of the nobles definitely joined the National Assembly. "We have come to aid in the regeneration of France." Enthusiastic cheers.

The king plotted a *coup de main*. His younger brother, the Comte d'Artois, arranged the details. Comte de Broglie, "a high-flying aristocrat, capable of any mischief," now head of the army, quietly brought in thirty thousand troops, mostly foreign mercenaries from the frontiers, and surrounded the Assembly. On July 9 that body asked the king to retire the troops. He replied haughtily that he alone had command of the armed forces. The Assembly began to hold day-and-night sessions under its president, the aged archbishop of Vienne. Marquis de Lafayette, who had fought in the American Revolution, was made president of the night gatherings. On July 11 he had the deputies adopt a tentative bill of rights so that some record of principles would survive the threatened dissolution.

German cavalry under Prince Lambesc rode into the city to protect the Tuileries. Near the bridge he struck an old man with a sword. The crowd seized the stones piled there for repairs and attacked the troops. Lambesc had to retire.

In the courtyard of the Palais Royal—which Louis Philippe, duc d'Orléans, cousin of the king, had thrown open for public meetings —the young, poverty-stricken lawyer Camille Desmoulins leaped onto a table and shouted, "The King's dismissal of Necker is the signal for a massacre. This very night they intend to butcher us."

Desmoulins snatched a twig from a courtyard tree. "Let us hoist a green cockade . . . . I call you my brothers to liberty. To arms! To arms!" The cry swept all Paris: "To arms! To arms!" Crowds poured into the narrow streets and boulevards. During the night men and women provided themselves with every weapon they could: guns, swords, knives, blacksmiths' hammers, carpenters' axes, iron crowbars, pikes, halberds, roasting spits, clubs. Jails were broken into; debtors released. The door of St. Lazare monastery was smashed; the food and wine consumed; and fifty wagonloads of grain carted off. Food stores were looted. It was a wild spectacle. Cavalry galloped through the throngs at full tilt, headed for points they were to protect. Artillery rattled through the alleys. Frightened well-to-do citizens frantically buried their money, papers, and valuables in the courtyards. A National Guard was hastily organized in every district. Lafayette was put in command.

The church bells began ringing at dawn on July 14. Breaking into the Hôtel des Invalides, the crowd seized twenty-eight thousand guns, artillery, swords, sabers, and halberds. In the afternoon an endless black sea of people swarmed toward the massive fortified Bastille. The prison rose grim and forbidding in the worst quarter of Paris, where cutthroats, beggars, the poorest workmen, lived in stinking hovels. It had the resources to stand off an army. It was considered impregnable. But the warden, a general, could not bring himself to fire on the people, and after several hours a white flag was run up. By mistake a Swiss contingent opened fire. It enraged the mob, and all the defenders were killed, all prisoners released. In due time the place was torn stone from stone.

At Versailles the king went early to bed. The queen visited the royal troops in the Orangerie. With her own hands she filled their goblets with wine, conducted the officers to her apartments, where they drank more wine and toasted her, pledging to give their lives for her honor.

It was late when the Duc de Liancourt rushed into the royal bedchamber and aroused the king. "Sire, the Bastille has been seized."

"A revolt?"

"No, a revolution."

The king went back to sleep. The officers of the royal guard, also unaware of what was going on, were getting drunk in the queen's apartment.

In the morning the king, accompanied only by his brothers, appeared without warning before the National Assembly. He told them that he had ordered the withdrawal of troops, that he was recalling Necker, and that on the morrow he would visit Paris. He won applause. Many believed he could be separated from the nobility and the clergy. By then he was being abandoned by the army.

Already his ministers were flying to the frontier. One hated official who had said, "Let the people eat hay, I feed it to my horses," was captured, killed, and his head carried on a pike with a wisp of hay in his mouth.

De Broglie's forces were easily routed, and the general, too, fled north for safety, as did the Comte d'Artois and the queen's own most devoted friend, Madame de Polignac. Bishop Charles Maurice de Talleyrand-Périgord abandoned the king in his own fashion; he went over to the revolutionists, saying, "Everyone must look after himself." Napoleon later called him "a silk stocking filled with excrement."

On July 17 the king was escorted by a hundred deputies to Paris. He was met by Bailly, who had been made mayor and who presented him with the keys of the city. "These are the same keys that were given Henry IV," said the mayor. "Henry IV reconquered his people; today the people have reconquered their king."

He was taken to the Hôtel de Ville, and there he permitted himself to be decorated with the tricolor cockade of the Revolution. He won the applause of the crowd, but when he got back to Versailles, Marie Antoinette furiously obliged him to take off the revolutionary emblem.

The bastilles, the local barracks, the feudal castles, were stormed all over France and taken over by the people. In numerous centers the army joined the revolutionists, as it soon did in Paris.

The months following the Bastille's fall saw the mushrooming of revolutionary clubs, representing all shades of popular opinion. A woman's club took a prominent part in the events that shook France. Workmen's clubs were numerous. The Jacobin club saw the emergence to power of the triumvirate: Danton, Marat, and Robespierre. Shortly the Girondists, the constitutional monarchists, were forced out of the Jacobins and started their own club, headed by Madame Jeanne Manon Roland; Lafayette and his moderate followers, also forced to leave the Jacobins, founded the Feuillants. As radical as the Jacobins were the Cordeliers, from the district of that name, headed by Danton, in which Marat was also active.

The Assembly, meanwhile, assumed governing powers. Besides abolishing all titles and feudal privileges, church property was confiscated. *Lettres de cachet* were done away with. New paper money, *assignats*, based on church lands, at the moment almost unsalable, were issued. These were presently put out in such quantity that they depreciated and eventually became almost valueless. Speculators in land, goods, and money flourished.

The king and queen with her son, the dauphin, in her arms, attended a glittering banquet in the Royal Theatre in honor of the mercenary Flanders Regiment. Enthusiasm mounted with each toast, swords were drawn and oaths of allegiance given. The tricolor cockade was torn off and trampled underfoot, and the women replaced it with the white ribbon of the Bourbons.

The event was denounced in fiery speeches in the National Assembly and by angry orators in the Palais Royal. "An orgy while the people cry for bread!"

On October 5 a young woman, beating a drum, gathered a crowd of women. They marched on the city hall and took it over. In the belfry they found a priest hiding and hanged him. The shout went up, "There is bread at Versailles!" The crowd became a marching army. Cannon were dragged along. Riding astride one of them was Théroigne de Méricourt, madame of the most aristocratic *maison de joie* and a leader in one of the women's clubs.

They found the king was out hunting. When he returned, a deputation, headed by the president of the Assembly, demanded grain and food for the city. He put a promise in writing. But the crowd did not disperse, though rain began falling in torrents and a bitter cold wind was blowing. Some of them forced their way into the National Assembly, where they interrupted the debate and called for Mirabeau. Others started bivouac fires and huddled near them during the dismal night. Some began scuffling with the palace guard. About midnight the drums of the National Guard, led by Lafayette, were heard. By 2 A.M. order was restored at the palace. Mirabeau arrived at the Assembly at 4 A.M., rebuked the noisy women, and lifted the session.

Early in the morning the crowd found a gate of the royal château open and surged in. A palace guard fired on them. An infuriated mob of thousands overwhelmed the guard and battered in the doors.

The queen, hearing the shouts, rushed half dressed to the king's apartments. The crowd surged through the corridors, overcoming every guard, and battered down door after door, shouting, "Death to the Austrian! Her head on a pike! Her entrails in our aprons!" They burst into her quarters, found her bed warm but empty.

The National Guard arrived and drove the demonstrators out at bayonet point. Lafayette rushed to the king's quarters to promise him protection. The crowd continued to roar outside, and the king went to the balcony. They shouted for the queen. She presented herself with the dauphin. "Put the child aside," they yelled. She obeyed. Lafayette knelt and kissed her hand. The mob demanded that the monarchs go to Paris. On Lafayette's advice they entered the royal carriage. The National Guard streamed along in disorder with loaves of bread on their bayonets. The crowd pressed after them, singing ribald songs and carrying the heads of two royal guards on pikes. Women, wearing heavy grenadier hats, danced and shouted insults.

The king and queen were held in the Tuileries, the old palace put up two centuries before by Catherine de Médicis and later burned in 1871 by the Paris Commune. They were now hostages of the people. There Louis complacently gorged himself, slept soundly, and devoted his daylight hours to his hobby of making clumsy locks. The Assembly also moved to Paris, meeting in a riding academy nearby. It voted the king and queen twenty-nine million francs to maintain the court.

Some order was established in Paris, but Mirabeau, who wished to become prime minister, in place of Necker, sent warning to the court that within three months the city would probably be a "hospital and certainly a theater of horrors." He believed that he was the one man in France to save them from the yawning abyss, that without him they would perish. But to a suggestion that he be made a minister of state, the queen exclaimed, "If he wants money, gorge him with it. But Mirabeau as minister, never!"

Forbidden by the National Assembly to take any public office, he nevertheless made a secret deal to advise the court, to which he swore loyalty, and was put on the payroll for six thousand francs a month, payment of all his debts, and credit for a million francs. He had one and only one interview with the queen on July 3, 1790. Taking precautions against being assassinated—his nephew stood guard at his carriage—he saw her in a remote kiosk in the gardens of St.-Cloud. She said that the interview inspired her with horror and made her sick. But she had flattered him, and he had declared his loyalty to her. They had been bitter enemies, and there was no trust between them. He kissed her hand at parting, saying, "Madame, the monarchy is saved."

After being put on the royal payroll, he began entertaining lavishly in the Chaussée d'Autin, purchasing costly plate, jewelry, rare engravings, and books. On his death his library was sold for 140,000 livres. He rode about in a handsome blue carriage and negotiated for the magnificent Le Marais estate. He was now serving two masters—an impossible position—but he paid no attention to warnings by his friends. Camille Desmoulins admitted that he personally had been corrupted by Mirabeau's hospitality: "His Bordeaux and maraschino . . . [made it] very difficult to resume . . . republican austerity." Long before this, a pamphlet had circulated, "The Great Treason of Count Mirabeau." But seemingly Mirabeau had not been corrupted. "He would take money from anybody," said one enemy, "but he could not be bought." He continued to thunder his demands for reform in the Assembly, but none of his advice was heeded by Louis.

When Benjamin Franklin, a beloved figure in France, died, Mirabeau gave him a fulsome eulogy as a true friend of France and had the deputies wear mourning for three days. Lawyer Maximilien Robespierre, usually a fastidious dresser, had to borrow a coat. It was so long it dragged on the floor.

Elaborate plans were made to celebrate the fall of the Bastille at the Champs Elysées. The equestrian statue of Louis XIV trampling on the provinces was torn down. An amphitheater for a million people was prepared. Delegates from every village and district were invited, and every road in France was crowded with pilgrims, who were greeted with food, shelter, flags, flowers, and music. Bands played. Cannon boomed. It reflected the ecstasy of newborn liberty.

The morning of the fourteenth was dark and gloomy, and soon heavy rain drenched the vast assemblage. The king and the queen and their suite sat under the usual golden fleurs-de-lis canopy. Mirabeau had sought to preside over the affair, but was passed over in favor of Lafayette, who had become an enemy. Talleyrand officiated at the altar, with three hundred priests and a hundred censer-swinging choristers. One hundred thousand guardsmen stood by, and Lafayette paraded back and forth on a prancing white charger.

As revolutionary fervor mounted, Mirabeau came under bitter attack from the radical Jacobins and the newspapers, but he overwhelmed his enemies by sheer majesty and oratory, and in February 1791 he was made president of the National Assembly. By then he was a sick man, but never more eloquent. He often appeared in the Assembly, with his head bound in bandages and blood trickling down his cheeks from leech bites, and turned his frightful visage on the gathering. He was going blind.

He died, after a few days' illness, on April 2 at the age of forty-two. The country held its breath in shocked disbelief. One hundred thousand marchers conducted him to his grave in the Panthéon of France's notable men, where he was buried alongside Descartes. Cannon were fired; the bells of all Paris tolled; muffled drums set the pace for the four-mile march to his grave. There twenty thousand muskets shook the walls of the city.

"Do not rejoice," King Louis told his wife. "We have lost more than you know."

Jean Paul Marat rejoiced more than the queen, and in his paper he called on the people to thank the gods for the downfall of their most redoubtable enemy. Robespierre joined in the exultation.

The revolution seemed to have achieved Mirabeau's goal of a constitutional monarchy when the king, queen, and their children appeared in the National Assembly on August 14, and Louis swore allegiance to the new constitution. It began with a bill of rights, guaranteeing freedom, property, and security. However, voting rights were restricted; elections were to be indirect; and only property owners could hold office. It was far less advanced than the American Constitution, which had provided much of its inspiration. It was scarcely to be expected that it would satisfy the proletariat or the radical clubs. As for Louis and Marie Antoinette, they returned to the palace and wept. The king sent an urgent message by a special messenger to his brother-in-law, Leopold of Austria, to help him throttle the revolution, destroy the constitution, and guarantee his own divine rights. He was moving the country, not to a new stability, but to war—civil and international.

As a result the new September Assembly—no reelection had been permitted—was controlled by the Girondists (named after one of the provinces), which had become the most powerful Paris political club, largely ruled by the strong, determined, but handsome Madame Roland, described as "dazzlingly beautiful as a Greek statue." She was then thirty-seven, wife of an elderly cabinet minister, the mistress of the radical Georges Buzot. She was well versed in English philosophy and the great rebel literature of France, and was a facile linguist.

The king treated the new Assembly with vast contempt. He had left only the support of Lafayette, whose abilities did not match his virtues, and the rich nobles, many of whom were now émigrés gathering with armed forces on the frontiers of France. At the same time Lafayette was loyal to the constitution, and the queen said bitterly she would rather perish than be saved by him. She felt no gratitude that he had rescued her at Versailles.

Lafayette withdrew from the radical Jacobins—with whom he was falling out of favor, and who were now dominated by Marat, Danton and Robespierre—and tried to form a constitutional party with the more moderate Feuillants and such men as Bailly and Sieyès. Danton was the leader, also, of the far more radical Cordilliers. A great orator, able to arouse the masses, he was almost as ugly as Mirabeau, but he was a successful lawyer with great audacity and still greater vanity. He was determined to overthrow the monarchy, though as yet most men were not republicans. Clearly he was the coming man, who would sway the destinies of France.

As the émigrés and foreign troops massed on the frontiers, Danton called for the raising of an army and a declaration of war. Many Jacobins, however, including Robespierre, opposed war, fearing that it would strengthen the more moderate Girondists in their control of the Assembly. For the same reason, among others, the Girondists advocated war.

Danton saw clearly that it could not be avoided and that prompt, strenuous preparation was necessary. Hostile armies were marching toward France, and on February 7, 1792, Austria and Prussia signed an agreement to intervene to quell the revolution.

The king did nothing, and the Girondists assailed him and his ministers. He was forced to dismiss them and bring in Madame Roland and Charles François Dumouriez, also a Girondist. The latter had the full confidence of Danton, though later he would turn traitor to France. Madame Roland was destined to commit suicide. Unable to withstand the pressures of the rising tides of patriotic passion, the king on April 21, 1792, sent a declaration of war to be passed by the Assembly. It was adopted under the whiplash of Danton's burning tongue, and war made him the undisputed master of the Assembly. He seemed to be the only man who could save France at this perilous hour.

The Girondists doubted the reliability of troops led by royalist officers and, for patriotic and narrower political reasons, voted to gather twenty thousand provincial volunteers to be encamped near Paris. The king vetoed the proposal. His veto, construed as antipatriotic, inflamed all France.

A great public demonstration was planned for June 20 to celebrate the Oath of the Tennis Court. Fifty thousand people were expected to converge on Paris for the affair. On that day Antoine Joseph Santerre, a wealthy brewer, who had been the first man across the drawbridge at the storming of the Bastille, and Marquis Saint Huruge led eight thousand men from the poorer *faubourgs* to the Assembly. Many wore the *bonnet rouge* of "Liberty." Nearly all were armed with clubs, hatchets, scythes, and battle-axes. One man carried a calf's head on a pike labeled, "Head of an Aristocrat." Another carried a pair of black breeches on a long pole with the slogan, "Long Live the Sans-Culottes." It was estimated that by the time they reached the Assembly they numbered thirty thousand.

The National Guard merely opened their ranks and let them surge into the hall, where their spokesman demanded a bill of rights and a dismissal of the king's ministers. The president of the Assembly prudently told them all the proposals would be considered. The crowd chanted *"Ça ira"* and shouted "Down with the Veto."

They then rushed on to the Tuileries, where they swept aside the terrified guards and broke down the doors, shouting, "Where is the king? Where is the Big Veto?" They dragged a cannon up the main staircase to the second floor. An observer on the fringe was Napoleon Bonaparte. When the king, in a red liberty cap, emerged on the balcony, he exclaimed, "What madness! How could they allow those scoundrels to enter? They should have blown four or five hundred of them into the air with their cannon; the rest would have taken to their heels."

Inside, the attackers broke down the doors with hatchets. When they hammered on the door of the king's apartments, he ordered it opened at once and faced the angry mob and their pikes and hatchets. Only a few servants, several members of the National Guard, and aged Marshal de Mouchy d'Acloque remained by his side. The marshal, seated on a chair, addressed the menacing intruders: "Citizens, this is your king; respect him. We stand at his side ready to die rather than let you injure him."

The monarch was baited by screaming men and women for two hours. No veto! No priests! No aristocrats! A drunk offered him a glass of wine. He gulped it down. He was forced to put on the *bonnet rouge*, and in it he spoke to the crowds outside, crowded below the balcony.

Marie Antoinette, "the hated Austrian," whom they really wished to kill, had fled to the council chamber, where two hundred members of the National Guard gave her protection. Santerre, the brewer, stood by her side asking the rioters to respect her. When a man put a *bonnet rouge* on the head of the dauphin, the brewer tossed it aside. "The boy is stifling. It is too hot for him."

Various deputies, after much urging, got the rioters to leave and disband. The palace was cleared by about seven that evening.

Lafayette rushed from the front and demanded that the insurrectionists be punished. But the queen angrily scorned his offers of assistance, and he returned to the front, abused by the Royalists, scorned by Desmoulins, intrigued against by Danton, who feared his popularity.

The armies of Prussia and Austria continued to advance, and on July 11 the Assembly called for eighty-five thousand volunteers and ordered cannon fired at regular intervals to alert all citizens to the danger to the fatherland. July 14 was celebrated in the Champs de Mars. A huge tree set up in the center was bedecked with the symbols of royalty, feudalism, and the church hierarchy: crowns, blue ribbons, tiaras, cassocks, cardinals' hats, St. Peter's keys, aristocratic escutcheons, legal papers, and records. The king, obliged to attend, was asked to take the oath to the constitution and set fire to the tree. He took the oath but said feudalism was already dead and refused to set fire to the tree. His refusal was considered hostility to the revolution. It was the last time he ever appeared in public.

Prussia finally declared war on July 20. On July 25 the head of the Prussian army, Karl Wilhelm Ferdinand, duke of Brunswick-Lüneburg, issued a proclamation to the French people, denouncing abuses and property seizures in Alsace-Lorraine and the Netherlands, the domestic anarchy in France, the attack against the church and the crown. The Prussian army, he said, was pledged to restore the king and his authority. The National Guard, if they resisted were to be punished as rebels and disturbers of the peace. The regular army and its officers were to submit to the legitimate sovereign, the king. Present civil officials were to continue in their positions, pending the decision of the monarch. All inhabitants resisting the invasion would have their houses pulled down or burned and be punished by all the rigors of the laws of war. Those in Paris who did not support the king, including all members of the National Assembly, of the National Guard, and all other officials would be subject to military execution.

After such a proclamation the king's fate was pretty much sealed.

Following his veto, which had created such an uproar, volunteers began marching from Marseilles. They reached Paris on July 30, 1792, and were given a feast at the Champs Elysées by brewer Santerre. A quarrel developed with the royal troops nearby, the Sons of St. Thomas. The Sons were sent flying and sought refuge, many of them streaming blood, at the Tuileries, where they were protected by the National Guard and had their wounds attended to by the fluttering ladies of the court.

The explosion was at hand. The Assembly was threatened daily by armed rioters in the gallery demanding the deposition of the king. Soon this included a demand for the arrest of Lafayette. His effigy was burned in the garden of the Tuileries. Danton organized his followers to strike the last definite blow against the throne. He rallied the men of Marseilles at the Cordelier club. Desmoulins was by his side. They thundered against the "Crimes of the Court": "Citizens, your King has betrayed you. Rise in your might and strike down the usurper . . . this very night. To arms! To arms!"

At midnight a cannon was fired in the Course du Commerce; drums were beaten throughout the city; and Desmoulins and others raced about arousing the people. The bells in all the steeples were rung. "The alarm bells are the voice of the people," shouted Danton. "They sound the last hour of kings: 'Ça ira.'" The streets were soon jammed. In the morning all the shops were closed, and the call went out. The attackers assembled. Santerre and others were raising a mob in the Faubourg St. Antoine. Robespierre, having no faith in the enterprise, went into hiding. Marat hid in a cellar. The Tuileries, they knew, was well guarded by six thousand men.

On the morning of August 10, the royal commander was ordered to present himself before the Paris Commune and did so on instructions from the king, but with great misgivings. He listened to diatribes against the king, himself, and the guards, but was allowed to depart, then was seized en route and shot by a friend of Danton's. His head was stuck on a pike. The men of Marseilles, followed by a horde of armed civilians gathered by Santerre and Danton, headed for the palace.

The king reviewed his forces to prepare for the expected attack. But he was so irresolute that the shouts of "Vive le Roi" died away. "All is lost," murmured Marie Antoinette, watching from a window. "The King has shown no energy."

[69]

The king decided to flee. With the queen and their children, he presented himself at the Assembly, asking for protection. This was given, and he was ordered to occupy a box in back of the president's rostrum, where he and his family remained for seventeen hours listening to the excited debates regarding his person. From time to time he pointed out the more distinguished deputies to the dauphin. He ate an apple and sucked an orange. When food was brought, he ate it and drank wine with his usual gusto. As the tidings came from the assaulted palace, the deputies, particularly the Girondists, grew more and more bitter against him.

A body of Royalists, disguised as National Guards, it seemed, had tried to slip inside the palace to defend the king. They were discovered and shut in a building near the National Assembly. A crowd gathered, shouting for their blood. A National Guard officer cooled them off, but Théroigne de Méricourt, wearing a black hat with a black plume, a pair of pistols and a dagger in her riding habit, leaped upon a cannon and stirred the crowd by her eloquence, urging them to drag the Royalists out. The doors were forced; the prisoners killed; their bodies flung from the windows. Their heads were severed from their bodies and borne aloft on pikes. A few heads were tossed about by street gamins, who caught them on sticks.

At the Tuileries the attacking soldiers and the crowd surged into the gardens. While a parley was going on with the officers of the Swiss Guard, soldiers inside began firing, and the attackers were driven out of the courtyard. A second attack was launched. The king sent word from the Assembly to halt the defense, and the Swiss Guards fled, except for a few who refused to abandon the doors of the king's apartment. These were all killed. The palace was smashed from end to end and looted from top to bottom.

The Assembly debates drew to a close, a vote was taken; and the king was formally deposed. The verdict by motion of Pierre Victurnien Vergniaud was made unanimous. At two in the morning he was escorted to the Feuillants' convent as a prisoner. The following day Danton was made minister of justice by a vote of 222 to 62, and became the virtual dictator of France. He had marched to power over the looted ruins of the Tuileries.

Meanwhile the Prussian army continued to advance and on August 24 seized Longwy in France, and Verdun was endangered. If it fell, the road to Paris would be open.

Danton strode before the Assembly on August 28 and called for unlimited national defense. Rather than let the Prussians take Paris, it would be reduced to ashes. "There is no time to be lost. We shall go forth and join the army of the Fatherland."

But the citizens could not march forth with an enemy of the republic at their backs. The Royalists must be terrorized and destroyed. "When a vessel is in a storm, threatened with shipwreck, the crew throws overboard all that endangers its safety." Close the gates of Paris and seize all conspirators against the republic. Every minute counts. "We must make house-to-house searches . . . tomorrow."

The following night from twelve to fifteen thousand people were dragged to the jails. On September 2 sixteen priests, who had been interrogated at the Hôtel de Ville, were being taken to be detained as suspects when they were quickly surrounded by a crowd. A priest angrily struck a soldier with his cane. At once the soldier ran the priest through with his sword; the crowd closed in; and all but three of the sixteen were killed.

The mob marched through the streets calling for the death of all prisoners. Prisoners were brought from their cells, hurriedly tried by twelve citizen judges. Many were liberated, but those handed over to executioners at the door were bludgeoned, run through with swords and pikes, or shot. The same went on in every *arrondissement*. The judges were men of the working class, clad in woolen hats, hobnailed shoes, and coarse aprons. They sat around tables littered with papers, bottles, wine glasses, dirty dishes, pipes. For three days the bloody work went on.

The extraordinarily beautiful Princesse de Lamballe, Marie Thérèse Louise de Savoie Carignon, a close friend of Marie Antoinette's, was struck down; she was torn to pieces, and her head and heart carried through the streets by drunken celebrants. Her head was then placed on a window of the queen's bedchamber, and later was taken to a bar, where toasts were drunk to the health of "Madame Veto's" friend.

The carnage was the result of centuries of cruel oppression and an accumulated spirit of vengeance, which to the end France's rulers were unable to measure. The immediate fury, compounded by fear, was caused by the invasion of formidable armies threatening not only the revolution but France itself. The slaughter was perhaps no worse than that carried on by the state against the Huguenots. During the century, a million Frenchmen had died in the useless wars of Louis XIV and Louis XV. Uprisings had been put down with wholesale butchery. Millions had died like sheep from hunger and disease. Already people had been slaughtered en masse in three provinces by an attempted White Guard counterrevolution, about which the world heard little—only about the deaths or flights of aristocrats and the burning of their châteaus.

Actually, as in all revolutions, most people tried to carry on their normal tasks and way of life. During "the Terror," which lasted until June 1794 (followed by the terror of the counterrevolution), twenty-three theaters, a larger number than usual, continued to perform to full houses. Sixty dance salons were open every night. Businesses stayed open, except in moments of extreme excitement when mobs roved the streets. When the September executions were over, Danton, who had done most to bring the republic into being, said, with an air of satisfaction, "We have rolled a river of blood between the Revolution and its enemies."

It was Danton who pushed the sending of three hundred thousand men to the front. Lafayette was ousted, and General Dumouriez put in charge. Among his favorite subordinates was General Francisco Miranda, a Venezuelan. The Prussians were defeated at Valmy on September 17, and the French revolutionary soldiers moved on to victory after victory, entering Brussels in triumph November 16, 1792, singing the "Marseillaise." Dumouriez visited Paris as a hero and shared a box at the opera with Danton. Robespierre and others feared he was scheming to march on Paris and declare himself dictator: "He menaces Paris, more than he does Belgium and Holland." They had reason for their suspicions.

A secret iron chest belonging to Louis XVI was found. It contained correspondence with enemies of the republic. He was brought before the convention and charged with innumerable crimes against the republic and against public order. His trial began on December 26. The voting on his fate started on January 15 and lasted for three days. The wives of the delegates showed up in ballroom gowns. Waiters served ices, beverages, and sweetmeats. Special quarters were provided for the mistress of the Duc d'Orléans. Bets were placed on the outcome. Workmen filled the amphitheater. The Jacobins in the lobby and mobs outside shouted for "death!" A message came from the king of Spain in behalf of clemency. "Insolence!" shouted Danton. This was "enough for a declaration of war" against a country that had refused to recognize the republic. "No dealings with tyranny!" The king was ordered executed within twenty-four hours.

January 21 was bleak and cold. Louis was taken to a carriage with his confessor and two gendarmes. The trip, to the public square where the guillotine had been set up, took two hours, with death drums beating, through silent streets where all windows were closed. One hundred thousand troops with cannon surrounded the open space for the dense crowd. The king attempted to speak to the spectators, but his words were drowned out by drums, and he was seized and thrown on the plank. His body was taken to the Madeleine cemetery and pitched into a ditch. His head was placed between his knees, and he was covered with quicklime.

The mobs now turned against the Roman Catholic Church. The foreign invaders had announced their intentions of restoring church property and privileges. Some members of the hierarchy conspired with the émigrés, but others favored the revolution. The archbishop of Paris publicly renounced his faith and took off his vestments. Priests, monks, and nuns followed his example, and since church marriages had been abolished, many married by civil law. Bells and pewter were melted down for cannon and bullets. Silver vessels were made into coins. All over France the churches were looted, and the vestments worn by the demonstrators. Crosses were borne aloft in derision, and holy water sprinkled on the heads of the crowd. In Paris the protestors, singing a mock "Te Deum," entered the hall of the National Convention and with some of the deputies danced "the Carmagnole" and sang the wild "Ça ira."

Dumouriez won more important victories in Holland, then prepared to march on Paris, destroy the convention, and seat the Duc d'Orléans on the throne. But in March his forces were suddenly defeated by the Austrian army, and he was driven out of Belgium in ignominy. The revolutionists turned against him. The ensuing uprising of the people of La Vendée, chiefly because of the new decrees against the church, was serious and was not easily put down. With eight hundred men he surrendered to the Austrians and thereafter fought against France. He soon retired and made his way to England, where he died in 1823.

Danton had been a friend and supporter of Dumouriez, and he came under severe attack by both the Girondists and Jacobins. A diversion was created by Marat, the ex-physician, who led mobs to pillage the meat shops. The new revolutionary tribunal (the Committee of Public Safety) brought Marat to trial on April 22, 1793. Danton tried to get the charges dismissed. He feared the precedent of arresting and trying a deputy. The Girondists hotly accused Danton of being a defender of anarchy and anarchists. The Paris Commune then decreed that twelve Girondist deputies be turned over to the revolutionary tribunal for trial. Maximin Isnard, a leader of the Girondists, warned that if a hostile hand were raised against them, Paris itself would be destroyed. But the Girondists had little influence in the Commune, and no control over the conspirators.

Danton, consumed with rage, turned on Isnard savagely for his tumultuous and insurrectionary words. A mob gathered outside the Assembly hall to attempt to arrest twenty-two Girondist deputies, charged with being enemies of the Revolution. Finally on June 2, all twenty-two were excluded from the Convention or Assembly. It was a dangerous move. They had strong backing in the provinces if not in Paris, and two thirds of the departments threatened to revolt. The situation was serious.

Under the latest constitution, that of 1793, the executive committee of the Convention was converted into the Committee of Public Safety, which took over all power, a revolutionary tribunal. Danton won control over it on April 6. Twelve committees were created, and six ministries established. Omnipotent emissaries took over the army and the provinces, installing all-powerful revolutionary committees everywhere. From this time on, the Convention became a debating society, torn by impotent factions.

Danton faced the situation with complete calm and boundless energy. "Let us make war like lions, let us establish a revolutionary government that can utilize the entire national energy." He asked for fifty million francs at once, mass conscription of all unmarried men from eighteen to twenty-five.

The army was useless in the crisis. Headed by an incompetent general and by officers who now skulked in their tents, and lacking food and ammunition, it suffered more defeats.

The Vendée insurgents were victorious at Aubers, Beaupréau and Thouars. If Nantes fell and they united with insurrectionists in Brittany, they would have access to England, which had now joined the war against the Revolution. The Girondists, aided by the Royalists, set the whole Rhone Valley from Lyons to Marseilles aflame. They had called in rebels from Sardinia and handed over the fleet and arsenal at Toulon to the British.

Danton did not falter. With passionate oratory he defended the crushing of the Girondist conspiracy, and the Committee of Public Safety sent emissaries to the provinces. They wore the tricolor cockade of the Revolution, tricolor sashes around their waists, and at their sides naked swords. The threatened rebellion dissolved in days. A leader of the Girondists mourned, "The seventy-two departments which had declared for us turned around and abandoned us in twenty-four hours."

Danton devoted every waking hour to the war effort. Seven hundred and fifty thousand patriots were mobilized. By January 1794 the enemies had been pushed off every inch of French soil, the Vendeans were defeated, and their leaders shot. Royalists were ruthlessly suppressed at Lyons, Bordeaux, Marseilles, and Toulon; feudalists and Girondists were savagely massacred at Nantes and Arras.

Two weeks later, his wife having died while he was at the front, Danton married Mademoiselle Gély, a girl of sixteen.

One of the Committee's first steps, after a serious defeat, was to seize Francisco Miranda, its Venezuelan general, as a scapegoat. He was hated by Robespierre and almost went to the guillotine, but at his trial he so moved the judges and listeners that they broke into cheers and carried him out on their shoulders. Later he tried to liberate Venezuela from Spanish rule and was the great precursor of Latin American independence.

Marat, with a wolf pack behind him, having won an acquittal from the revolutionary tribunal, turned the guns of his vituperation on Danton, and redoubled his attacks on the Girondists. On a bright sunny morning in July 1793 Charlotte Corday, a Girondist partisan, took the diligence from Caen to Paris. She was a beautiful, quiet, well-dressed girl, with a classic Greek face, large eyes, and a determined chin. In the morning she wrote to Marat and bought a sheath knife at the Palais Royal, which she concealed under her shawl, then went to his shabby quarters, ostensibly to give him a list of traitors in Normandy. He was seated in his bath. Gloating and chuckling, he listened and told her, "Go on, my child, go on!" She plunged her knife into his heart.

"I have killed one to save a hundred thousand," she told her captors calmly.

She was rushed to the guillotine in the midst of a torrential thunder storm, her red gown plastered by the rain to her body. "She has ruined us," said Vergniaud, the chief Girondist leader, "but she has taught us how to die."

The Revolution had lost all pity for its foes, and official terror gripped Paris. Marie Antoinette was dragged to the guillotine in a cart. After a considerable trial, the arrested Girondists were executed.

Deputy Jean Valazé, when sentenced, slipped off the bench to the floor, as the convicted were shouting, "*Vive la République.*"

"Are you afraid?" said Deputy Jacques Pierre Brissot, leaning over him.

"No, I am dying."

Valazé had stabbed himself. The others went to the guillotine singing the "Marseillaise." Valazé's body was also beheaded. They were dumped in a common grave.

The Girondist leaders were hunted across France. Some committed suicide. The bodies of Pétion de Villeneuve and François Buzot were found in a cornfield, half eaten by dogs. Two others were captured and executed in Bordeaux. Jean Baptiste Louvet de Couvrai, after incredible hardships, reached Switzerland.

"We have killed the tree by pruning it," said Vergniaud, "it was too aged. The soil is too weak to nourish the roots of civil liberty; the people are too weak to wield its laws . . . . They will return to their kings as babies return to their toys."

Once more fear, hunger, and war filled France with anxiety. Toulon and Mayenne also were in British hands. The British, the Austrians, and the émigrés overran the frontiers. Prussia occupied Alsace. Spain invaded in the south. There was no trade. Every port was blockaded. The *assignats,* the paper money, dropped daily in value, and more poured off the presses. The soldiers had no bread, no shoes, and blessed little powder.

While Danton struggled with the problems of government, war and revolt, Robespierre, in an alliance with Louis Antoine Léon de Saint-Just and Georges Couthon, came into full control of the Committee of Public Safety and was sending more people to the guillotine. Among prominent victims was the Duc d'Orléans. For the event he ate a tremendous breakfast and wore his finest clothes. At the guillotine the executioner wanted to take his boots off. "Tush," said the duke. "They will come off easier afterward. Get on with it."

Madame Marie Jeanne Bécu Du Barry—"ex-harlot of a whilom Majesty," Louis XV—blonde, blue-eyed, went shrieking to her doom. Antoine Barnave, a former adviser of the queen, died calmly; the revolutionary mayor of Paris, Bailly, soon followed. "You are shaking," said a bystander. "Yes, from cold"—it was a dismal rainy morning—"not from fear." The head of Rouget de Lisle, the author of the "Marseillaise," rolled into the basket. Comte Adam Philippe de Custine said with good humor, "Fortune is a woman, and my hair is growing gray."

Robespierre was insatiable. The ax fell every hour. Worn out, Danton went to his home in Arcis-sur-Aube to rest. In December he returned to Paris. "I am not a drinker of blood," he exclaimed. "I am tired of this slaughter. Is it never to end? Is France to bleed to death?" On an evening stroll with Camille Desmoulins along the Seine, he cried out: "The river is running blood."

Yet he bowed to Jacobin pressure to accede to the trial and execution of Jacques René Hébert and his followers. Hébert represented the most impassioned faction among the Revolutionists. They went to the guillotine on March 24, 1794. Danton said, on hearing at last that Robespierre, whom he had befriended on many occasions, was plotting to overthrow him, "If I thought that were true, I would eat his bowels out." Camille Desmoulins followed his line and attacked the Committee of Public Safety. "The Tribunals which were once the protectors of life and property have become mere slaughterhouses . . . . Confiscation and punishment have become nothing but robbery and murder."

Danton criticized the Committee's war efforts. He was arrested at midnight, March 29, 1794. Desmoulins, who lived in a room above him, was also arrested. The Convention was terrified, but Louis Legendre, a former butcher who had once denounced the king to his face, spoke up. "Citizens, four members of this body have been arrested during the night. Danton is one of them. He is as pure and patriotic as I am, yet he is in a dungeon . . . . I move that you send for the prisoners and hear them."

Robespierre rose. "We shall see today whether the Convention can crush to atoms a false idol, long since decayed, or whether both the Convention and the French people will be overthrown."

Legendre apologized for his temerity. The deputies hastened to fawn on their new master.

Danton was arraigned along with six others. The prisoners answered defiantly and clearly. "I did not believe," said Danton, "that the Committee, which I created, would become the scourge of humanity." The most eloquent man in France, always able to arouse his audiences to wild emotion, he spoke boldly and sarcastically of the charges brought in by Saint-Just. "A list of lies," he thundered, and denounced the trial methods and his accusers in a voice that could be heard "clear across the Seine." "It will be my obligation to ask the French people to pardon my accusers . . . . You say that I sold myself to Mirabeau, to Orléans, to Dumouriez, but men like me cannot be paid nor bought nor sold." He recited his many accomplishments during and in behalf of the Revolution, how he had been the first at the Jacobin club to call for a republic. The chairman rang his bell. Danton turned on him, "A man speaking for his honor and his life cares nothing for your bell," and he thundered on.

The next day he seemed confused, and when the court paid no attention to his prepared speech of defense, he tore up its pages and scattered the pieces. But the committee members were also in confusion. In desperation Saint-Just went before the Convention and asked them to end the trial. On April 5, at half past eight in the morning, the Convention put an end to further defense. The committee promptly brought in the death sentence. At four thirty that afternoon the prisoners were taken in death carts through throngs that only the week before had cheered Danton. It was a cloudless cool spring day. Desmoulins screamed like a madman and kissed a tendril of his wife Lucile's hair. (She, too, would soon be guillotined.) "Do you not know me?" he shouted. "I am Camille, Camille Desmoulins . . . the first apostle of Liberty."

Danton tried to calm him down. "Don't appeal to the rabble. They are deaf to your eloquence. Leave them alone." He laughed and sang. As they passed Robespierre's house, he pointed and shouted. "You will follow us soon; your house will be beaten down and salt sown in the place it stood." When he arrived in front of the guillotine, he sang in a mighty voice. Just before his head went under the blade, he told the executioner. "Show my head to the people. I shall live in the Pantheon of history."

The guillotine worked day and night as reaction against Robespierre set in. The revolutionary armies rolled the enemy back, while behind the lines the dark remorseless power struggle went on. Thomas Paine who had been made an honorary member of the convention, escaped death by a hair. Francisco Miranda, whom Robespierre hated personally, escaped by the sudden seizure of the tyrant, for within three months of Danton's death, Robespierre himself was sent to the guillotine.

The Red Terror was replaced by the White Terror. The National Convention was replaced by the Directory. It soon imposed the more reactionary constitution of 1795, which wiped out equal franchise. It also instituted public thievery on a gigantic scale.

These antirevolutionary trends were opposed by Filippo Michele Buonarrotti, who founded the Union of the Panthéon, which by 1796 had seventeen thousand members and won converts in the barracks. He was a sort of social democratic St. Francis of Assisi and was to influence social revolt for half a century or more. He did not believe in democracy in a revolutionary period. People long exposed to inequality and despotism could not be relied upon. Power should be firmly grasped by true revolutionary hands. How these could be selected, he did not elucidate. He plotted to overthrow the Directory. One of his chief lieutenants was Gracchus Babeuf, an active conspirator. Young General Napoleon Bonaparte was ordered to dissolve the Panthéon and to suppress the conspiracy. The leaders were taken to Vendôme for military trial. Babeuf and a companion were condemned to death. But Buonarrotti, having been a youthful friend of Napoleon, was ordered into exile. He was held, however, in a Cherbourg prison. Offered a government post, he scornfully refused. Finally released in 1807, he left the country and did not return to Paris until after the 1830 uprising. He succeeded in earning his living as a music teacher. His followers were active in the 1848 revolution, which reestablished the republic.

Napoleon himself overthrew the Directory in 1799, becoming first consul, and three years later, consul for life. In May 1804 he was crowned emperor and soon overran Europe. He plowed up the feudal system all across the Continent. But the Revolution had ended.

It had put land in the hands of the peasants, broken the financial and political power of the clergy and the nobility. It widened the rights of the workers. It paved the way for industry, and the political predominance of the industrialists was well established by the time of the regime of Louis Philippe, after the 1830 revolution had deposed Charles X. Thereafter, Marx and Engels commented, the only revolution that would have any meaning in France would be a proletarian revolution. This, they pointed out, was the reason for the failure of the 1848 revolution and the glory of the unsuccessful Paris Commune of 1871.

[79]

CHAPTER 4

THE REVOLUTION OF LATIN AMERICA

THE SPARKS OF THE FRENCH REVOLUTION, carried on the powerful winds of change, flew over the high wall around the Spanish empire, ignited small local revolts and finally a continentwide conflagration—one of the greatest in the history of the world. Early last century it swept a continent and a half away from Spanish rule.

The living embodiment of the whole movement was Francisco Miranda, the Venezuelan who had escaped the guillotine in France by a hair. He was a true son of the American and French revolutions in both of which he played a military role. His name is inscribed on the Arc de Triomphe in Paris as a leading French Revolutionary general.

Earlier, an officer in the Spanish army, discriminated against because he was a colonial, he had been sent off to the New World, after the Inquisition discovered he was reading the French Encyclopedists, Voltaire, Diderot, Rousseau, Helvétius, and Montesquieu. His large library was burned. Presently in 1783, fleeing from Cuba to the United States to escape trial as "a perfidious intriguer without religion," he met the outstanding men of the new United States, then slipped off to Europe. Harassed by the Spanish authorities, he escaped to Russia, where he became a pet of Catherine the Great, who aided him financially and otherwise until she became frightened by the French Revolution.

While in England, dickering for aid in liberating the Spanish colonies, he became the idol of the Chilean Bernardo O'Higgins and other exiles. O'Higgins was the illegitimate son of the great Irish-born viceroy of Peru and Chile, and was studying in England under an assumed name. Miranda had him read the French iconoclasts and made him the emissary in Spain of the Great American Reunion, a secret organization later to become the Lautaro Lodge, named after a great Chilean Indian leader, killed by the Spaniards. José de San Martín, an Argentine officer in the Spanish army, became a member and founded the order for the first time in Buenos Aires. It was to become the secret power in the new revolutionary governments of Argentina, Chile, and Peru. In Chile, after he returned to his ancestral estate, O'Higgins held secret sessions, disguised as a club of friends interested in gambling, in which the French books proscribed by the Spanish government were read and discussed.

Simón Bolívar, greatest of them all, had a similar background. His boyhood tutor, Simón Rodríguez, had considered the youthful Bolívar a flesh-and-blood model of Rousseau's *Emile*. Bolívar's reading consisted largely of the French theorists about the equality and brotherhood of man. Rodríguez was arrested and found it prudent to go to Europe. Later, Bolívar was sent by his family to Spain and France, where his ideas of New World independence were nourished.

On a second visit to Europe he saw Napoleon crowned. Thrilled, he began dreaming of exalted leadership, of enjoying the plaudits of the multitude. Presently, though, he denounced Napoleon as a betrayer of the Revolution and for a time traveled outside France. On coming back, he finally wrenched himself out of the arms of his beloved Fanny Villiers and returned to Venezuela, secured an army commission, and founded the Patriotic Association, a group of influential citizens, secretly plotting for independence. One of Bolívar's early contributions to Venezuela was a printing press, on which the first newspaper, the *Gaceta de Caracas*, was printed. Soon, after Miranda's revolt failed, he was leading hosts of revolution across the Andes through five colonies.

Spain—both government and church—prohibited the shipment of the works of the French theorists to the New World. Even to have a proscribed book in one's possession meant arrest, torture, confiscation of property, possibly death. But nevertheless they were read by almost everyone who could read. Diderot's descriptions of royal despotism and how it worked were even more applicable to Spanish rule in America. Rousseau was read and quoted with almost delirious enthusiasm.

In Chile, prior to the Lautaro Lodge, numerous reading circles similar to that of O'Higgins were started, such as the Society of Friends of the Country, in which the leading revolutionary Juan Egaña participated.

One of the most notable early Latin American revolutionists inspired by the French Revolution was the Chilean priest Camilo Henríquez, ordained in Lima, Peru, on July 4, 1811. He pronounced a fiery, revolutionary sermon, honoring American independence, and soon had to flee to Chile. "We shall start in Chile, proclaiming our independence. That alone will wipe out the name of rebels given to us by the tyranny." He founded Chile's first newspaper, *La Aurora*. Soon he wrote a memorable poem, *Himno Patriótico* and took up arms. Fleeing to Argentina, he wrote and produced a highly successful revolutionary play, *Camila, of South America*. Returning to Chile, he founded the newspaper *El Mercurio de Chile*, while Spanish troops were still on Chilean soil. He died on the day of final victory for the independence patriots.

A circle in Colombia included such writers and rebels as Francisco Antonio Zea, Camilo Torres, "the Mirabeau of New Granada," and Antonio Nariño, whose life, according to a South American writer was "a hurricane." Nariño published *Seventeen Revolutionary Precepts of World Revolutions* and was arrested in the act of printing his translation from the French of *The Declaration of the Rights of Man*. Sent in chains to Cádiz, he escaped to France, returned to Venezuela, and later became president. Zea, a Spaniard who wrote in a lofty lyric style, founded *El Correo de Orinoco*, Bolívar's paper, when he set up a provisional government at the mouth of the great northern river. Camilo Torres, who later became president of Colombia, wrote pamphlets and manifestos. José María de Salazar wrote the *National Anthem of Colombia*, poetry, and plays.

The Peruvian poet, Mariano Melgar, author of *Letter to Silvia and To Liberty*, was put before the firing squad in 1814.

Everywhere newspapers appeared, many of them revolutionary, and editors were daily jailed from such papers as *El Peruano, La Abeja Republicana, La Cometa*, in Peru; *Papel Periódico, Americano Libre* in Cuba; the most aggressive in Colombia being *La Bagatela*.

The Spaniards had ruled in the New World for three centuries. They had ripped apart the Indian systems, the notable and far-flung

Inca empire, the great Chibcha empire of Colombia and Central America, the Maya-Quiché and Aztec worlds. Governments were destroyed; leaders killed. They endeavored in every way to wipe out the native cultures and implant their own system. They tore down the old temples and palaces and consigned the beautiful Aztec and Mayan codices and all historical and scientific records to the flames. Hundreds of thousands of "books" were heaped in great pyres and burned. The Indian lands were seized; the old communal village life was largely destroyed; the people reduced to serfdom.

In the American colonies and the American West the Indians were mostly killed off, a century-long process of genocide. In the southlands, where the population was dense and the social systems were more elaborate, they were taken over, ruled, and exploited. Many Indians did die like flies under the lash in mines and on plantations, or were decimated by such white men's diseases as measles, and by the white man's firewater, but their culture and way of life survived in vast areas. The American colonists had to start fishing, farming, and other enterprises to earn their keep by the sweat of their own brows, but for a generation the Spaniards and Portuguese lived off the accumulated gold, silver, and wealth of the native peoples. Even the food stored in the Incan *tambos* along the trails lasted the conquistadores for years.

The effort to make the New World over into a replica of their native (Spanish) life, the dream apparently of all conquerors, failed in many directions. The Spanish and Portuguese languages were imposed, in places native languages forbidden, but millions kept on using their native tongues (just as the Anglo-Saxons did in England): Aztec, Zapotec, Mixtec, Maya-Quiché, Chibcha, Quechua, Aimara, Guaraní, and Araucano are still spoken by tens of millions of people.

Little by little the Indians rebuilt their village life. Old idols peeped out behind the saints on Catholic altars and were rented to peasants for blessing their fields. The Spaniards began to eat many native foods—corn, beans, turkey, chili—drinking native pulque, tepache, tequila, and chicha. The gauchos of Argentina and Chile adopted modified Indian dress, and the big sombrero and the sarape became symbols of Mexico. In due time the new independence flag, bearing the eagle and serpent, attested to the vitality of Aztec legends, beliefs, worships, and art already centuries old when the Spaniards arrived—such as those about Quetzalcóatl the Plumed

Serpent. The rising sun on the Peruvian flag is the Quechuas' stellar God, Viracocha.

Within a generation an entirely new ethnic and social group emerged to push for independence, the mestizos, the men of mixed blood, belonging to neither culture. Though held down by myriad regulations, by marriage and property laws, by severe restrictions regarding dress and adornments, they were daring men living by their wits. They became the agile go-betweens of two antagonistic ways of life. Largely they obeyed the laws, the customs, the sexual habits of their own passionate self-willed natures. Cruel, brave, debonair, they often flouted the authorities and lived by their own anarchistic mores and independent ethics.

Many of their women were more beautiful than either Spanish or Indian women. They had more "salt," or flair, and were less bound by the rigidities of the Spanish system, based on the ironclad rules of the Moorish household. Unlike Indian women they were less obliged to toil and lose their good looks at an early age. Some became mistresses, famous in song and legend, such as the beautiful actress Perricholi in Lima, the darling of a viceroy. Such was the beautiful Isabel Riquelme of southern Chile, the mother of the patriot and liberator O'Higgins. Many mestizan women became leaders of guerrillas against Spanish rule. They played a prominent part in the independence movement in the cities and on the battlefield.

Before the final showdown came, the mestizos everywhere had improved their lot. They had become parish priests, although they could rarely advance further in the Church. They had joined the Spanish troops, learning to handle arms and ride horses, otherwise prohibited to them. A few had become petty officers; higher echelons remained closed to them. Some had become shopkeepers, small ranchers, operators of small handicraft industries—textiles, metals, pottery. They made soap and candles, rope and furniture, and carved wooden saints for home and church. Above all they were traders, hardheaded and astute. As such, they became leaders in the independence armies.

On top of the heap—almost—were the Creoles, people of pure European descent, though few perhaps were without traces of Indian, mestizo, or, in Brazil, Negro blood. They were the big landholders; they came to rule the local *cabildos*, or *ayuntamientos*, as the town councils were called, and presently edged into the royal *audiencias*, the Spanish high court, with broad governing powers. A few became governors of provinces; Ambrosio O'Higgins became viceroy. Many bought army commissions and titles. They were closely interwoven with the Spanish colonial system.

Yet even the Creoles resented the petty Spanish bureaucrats who, just because they came from the Iberian peninsula, arrogantly assumed prerogatives both political and social over the Venezuelans and Peruvians and Argentines. The Creoles were superior in wealth, education, and knowledge. As traders, businessmen, and manufacturers, they were irked by the harsh feudal restrictions.

Many came to resent the strict censorship. The only books permitted to be published in the New World were stale and boring theological treatises, poetry, cookbooks, and the like, though toward the end some exuberant geographical and a few revolutionary works appeared, bold essays and poems. Realistic or romantic works dealing with regional customs aroused pride in the local ways of life and awakened national patriotism.

The vessels of England, France, and the United States were largely excluded from Spanish American ports. In Argentina all exports and imports had to be carried over the Andes from Chile, placing an impossible burden on consumers, even though it helped promote native enterprises, otherwise usually forbidden. As in the American colonies, smuggling became a way of life. Everywhere, and particularly in the Caribbean, Spanish officials, unable to check it, connived to line their pockets. Smugglers' warehouses operated openly across the river from Buenos Aires, and the flags of all nations fluttered on the masts of a growing number of vessels, which by law should have been seized. Smugglers are lawbreakers and material for revolution.

The students led the way. As Luis Alberto Sánchez put it in his *Breve Historia de la Literatura Americana*, the rebel students of 1800 became the leaders of 1820 and the governors in 1830. Latin America was living in a heroic new world, and the environment was constantly undergoing radical changes. Tests of local initiative and courage came well before the independence movement. When the British seized Buenos Aires and Montevideo in 1810 at the time of the Miranda expedition in northern Venezuela, the Spanish army ran away; the mestizos (and some Creoles) quickly organized resistance and drove the invaders out. The exploit was celebrated exuberantly by the revolutionary popular songwriter Pantaleón Riverosa. In the *Gaceta*, Estebán de Luca wrote his inspiring *Marcha*

Patriótica, celebrating "the happy dawn of sweet country," and sub-sequently "Songs of Liberty" and odes to San Martín. In Mexico the poet Andrés Quintana Roo of Yucatán inspired independence and was rewarded by having a state named after him. José Joaquín Fernández Lizardi, "the Mexican thinker," founder of the newspaper *El Pensador Mexicano,* was jailed by the viceroy in 1818. He had already written a pro-feminist novel, *Don Quijotito and His Cousin.*

The previous colonial Revolution in the United States pointed the way toward national independence for such thinkers, writers, and fighters. The French Revolution provided the inspiration and ideas, unpalatable though they were to many Creoles. Out of local revolutionary writings came added inspiration for most leaders. The doctrines of fraternity and equality moved them deeply. Miranda and Bolívar abolished slavery, class restrictions, and special privileges of the Church and nobility. Titles were done away with.

But what sparked actual revolt was Napoleon's conquest of Spain, the overthrow of Ferdinand VII, and the imposition of Napoleon's brother Joseph Bonaparte on the throne. At once the Creoles were sharply divided; those desiring the restoration and those supporting Bonaparte rule. Thus the usurpation meant civil war in Spain and in the colonies. The Bonapartists, with France and Spain largely cut off from the New World by the British fleet, lost the colonial battle everywhere. The pro-Spanish Creoles took over the various colonies, aided by wealthier mestizos. The *audiencias* and viceroys soon had to bow to their will or get booted out. It was, at first, a movement to safeguard the patrimony of the Spanish crown. But when Ferdinand VII was restored six years later, and he attempted to introduce far-reaching political and social changes, the New World Creoles, essentially reactionary, fought his regime more virulently than they had French rule. They joined the independence struggle in earnest, not for liberty and equality, but out of hatred for any changes that menaced their positions and properties. The revolution remained largely a Creole enterprise by men desperately seeking to maintain the status quo. Thereby, while achieving independence, they destroyed it.

The situation in Chile was typical. People who had some culture and education resented the monarchy because of the deplorable economic conditions, the lack of freedom of trade with the world, the subordination to Spanish products, doubly expensive because of heavy taxes and high duties. They complained of the lack of schools, the monopoly of all government posts by imported and often inferior Spaniards, the limited opportunities, and the injustice of the courts.

Wealthier native Creoles traveling abroad were impressed by French and English prosperity. From the American and French revolutions they had imbibed the doctrine of the Rights of Man. They secretly read the works of Diderot and the encyclopedists, Voltaire and Rousseau. The ideas of emancipation, as in all the colonies, invaded every home.

The Creoles particularly resented the exclusive Spanish exploitation of the rich mines and dreamed of the day when they could open up the untouched treasures of the Andes. They saw the possibility, long blocked by the despotic rule and the inefficiency of government, of creating a flourishing country. But the slightest show of such ideas or feelings brought stern repression and punishment.

The activities of the Chilean prelate Camilo Henríquez have already been noted. There were others. Two Creole intellectuals, Antonio José de Irisarri and Juan Martínez de Rozas, secretly wrote and circulated the *Catecismo Político-Cristiano:*

The metropolis [Madrid] has monopolized trade and has forbidden foreigners to buy and sell in our ports or ourselves to negotiate with them. This everlasting injustice has caused the most frightful misery . . . . the taxes, duties, levies, and countless impositions [they added] have destroyed fortunes . . . . We are allowed no manufacturing, not even vineyards. Everything we have to buy at exorbitant prices and scandalous prices that ruin us. Everything is planned to allow us only to work in the mines, like good slaves or Indian serfs, which we are in every way, and we are treated as such.

The opportunity for revolt came, as already noted, with Napoleon's invasion of Spain in 1807 and the seating of his brother Joseph Bonaparte on the throne. The Spaniards fought the imposition; his New World subjects fought against the alien rule of the motherland, which was extended to all Spanish colonies. The Creoles mobilized with cries of "Long live King Ferdinand VII," and soon openly talked of independence. By 1809 there were two bands: those supporting Joseph Bonaparte, and those who defied him. The last were also divided into those who wanted permanent independence and those who wished to preserve the colony for Ferdinand when he would be restored to the throne. The second group was made up chiefly of resident Spaniards, the ecclesiastical hierarchy and the army.

At this hour of crisis Chile had an aged governor, the ex-General Francisco Antonio García Carrasco. His secretary, curiously enough, was the illustrious Chilean Juan Martínez de Rozas, secretly seeking independence. He was disgusted at the governor's attempts at suppression and his exiling of many prominent Chileans. On May 25, 1809, the *audencia* meeting at Charcas (Sucre), then part of the La Plata (Argentina) viceroyalty, was replaced by a rebellious Creole junta, which issued a manifesto calling for freedom from Spain in all the Americas. A bloody revolt burst out in La Paz, Bolivia. The royal *audiencia* in Chile, to which several wealthy Creoles had been admitted, feared popular insurrection, which seemed inevitable with the weak vacillating Garcia Carrasco blunderingly trying to run things. They forced him to resign and replaced him with another aged Spaniard, Mateo de Toro y Zambrano, known as "the Count of the Conquest." He was even weaker, but acceptable because he had never mixed in politics. To appease the swirling factions of royalists and angry patriots, he resorted to the dangerous and fatal expediency of Louis XV: He called an open *cabildo* meeting in which he invited some four hundred respectable persons to participate and determine public policy. The patriots brought in people from outside Santiago and set up armed patrols.

The *cabildo*, in an effort to preserve the interests of Ferdinand VII, formed a nine-man Junta de Gobierno, to be presided over by the Count of the Conquest. He had inherited as his secretary Martínez de Rozas, who became the real governor of Chile. The first task of the junta was to organize an adequate military force. It also established freedom of commerce, a move that within a few months doubled the amount of duties collected. But the crucial move fostered by Martínez was to call a national congress. The lid was off. Revolutionary sentiments swept across the land. The royal *audiencia* was suppressed when it attempted to stir up revolt against the junta. The uprising collapsed within twenty-four hours.

The delegates to the national congress were pretty much handpicked by the big local landowners. Its tone was moderate. The deputies swore to defend the privileges of the Church, obey Fernando VII, and support the junta. They hoped to keep alive an intermediary regime until the restoration of the Spanish monarchy.

That this was unsatisfactory to most Chileans was obvious. A young military colonel, José Miguel Carrera, aided by his two younger brothers, sniffed the winds of change and, with his soldiers behind him, stalked into congress in full uniform and took over. He radically altered the representation and set up a five-member Creole governing junta. Martínez de Rozas, then in his home bailiwick, Concepción, in the south, backed the coup and became a member of the Carrera junta. At once he pushed through the most radical measures. The junta was whittled down to three persons: Martínez representing the south; Carrera, Santiago; and José Gaspar Marín from Coquimbo, the north. Bernardo O'Higgins, a congressional deputy from the far south near Araucano Indian country —where he had been managing the estate inherited from his father, the former Spanish viceroy, and promoting secret reading clubs and conspiracy—had refused to serve on the Carrera-imposed junta. Soon Marín also refused. Carrera promptly surrounded congress in December 1811 and proclaimed a military dictatorship. Martínez de Rozas now showed his colors and raised revolt. He was quickly seized and exiled to Mendoza (then in Chile, now part of Argentina) on the other side of the Andes, where he died a few months later.

Actually Carrera was exceedingly radical and progressive for those days. He promulgated a bona fide republican constitution with only nominal loyalty to King Ferdinand, got the United States to send its first plenipotentiary to the new America. He was Joel Poinsett, who imported a printing press and installed the revolutionary priest Camilo Henríquez to edit the *Aurora de Chile*. Later Poinsett gave up his post to fight with the revolutionaries against the Spanish attempt at reconquest.

Carrera ordered free public schools to be established whenever there were as many as fifty families, created the Instituto Nacional for secondary education, founded the national public library, and abolished slavery before any other country in the Americas.

From Peru, where the viceregal regime remained intact, the Spaniards sent out an armed expedition under General Antonio Pareja to reestablish royal authority. It landed on Chiloé Island in the south, recruited more men by forced levies, and marched north, taking Valdivia and later Concepción.

Carrera marched to oppose him. Bernardo O'Higgins, who had been secretly training and arming men on his hacienda, and Juan Mackenna, outstanding leaders, offered their services. Pareja was driven out of Concepción. At El Roble the royalists were defeated by the cool audacity of O'Higgins after Carrera took to his heels. The Santiago junta kicked Carrera out, replaced him with O'Higgins, then moved to Talca to treat with the new Spanish commander Gabrino Gainza. Carrera refused to abide by the junta's order but was captured by the Spaniards, who cannily shipped him north to Chillán. Meanwhile congress replaced the junta and made Colonel Francisco de la Lastra supreme dictator.

The Spaniards moved swiftly toward Santiago, where the patriots put up last-ditch resistance. The invaders' position was not comfortable: Their lines were thin and extended, and winter was coming. O'Higgins' guerrillas harassed them effectively.

A British naval officer arrived, authorized by the viceroy of Peru to negotiate peace—on the viceroy's terms. Lastra signed the shameful Treaty of Lircay, which recognized Chile as a Spanish province. It could henceforth send representatives to the Spanish *cortes.* Spanish troops would be withdrawn, but the Chilean flag was outlawed. Independence seemed lost. But the viceroy refused to accept even the token concessions to Chile and sent in a new army under Mariano Osorio.

Carrera escaped from Chillán and reached Santiago, where he made a second coup. O'Higgins refused to recognize his authority and marched on the capital. But by the time he reached there, Osorio had landed, whereupon O'Higgins put himself under Carrera's command. Together they planned the defense at Rancagua, just south of Santiago. O'Higgins fortified it, but reinforcements promised by Carrera failed to arrive. Rancagua's water supply was cut off, the arsenal blew up, and O'Higgins cut his way out with six hundred men. Not only the battle but the war was lost, and the patriots had to flee across the Andes.

The Spaniards' bloody and vengeful *Reconquista* began. It was the subject of Chile's greatest novel by Alberto Blest Gana. The Spanish Tribunal of Vigilance, headed by the bloodthirsty Captain San Bruno, kept the firing squad busy. A brave young lawyer, Manuel Rodríguez, Carrera's secretary, who had not fled, kept up a daring guerrilla resistance.

O'Higgins and San Martín, the Argentine patriot, set to work in Mendoza to organize an invasion to drive the Spaniards out, a tremendous undertaking. After extensive preparations they crossed through the snow passes, swept down on the Spaniards on the slopes of Chacabuco, and drove on to complete victory in Maipú.

The two conquerors entered Santiago in triumph, and O'Higgins was made supreme director in the Cabildo building, with elaborate ceremonies. That was in February 1817. It would take ten years more to drive the Spaniards out of Chile and off Chiloé Island and end their threat to freedom and independence. Meanwhile San Martín, aided by O'Higgins and the resources of Chile, launched a massive expedition that freed Peru.

Within a few years the friends of freedom took control of the situation in every country except Cuba, where the revolt was put down. Church bells rang out the tidings of final victory all over the continent. Then, when the attempt at reconquest came, as in Chile, bringing marching armies and bloody war, which called for real hardship and sacrifice, the mestizos and Indians began assuming more prominent roles. Even so, the Indians, ostensibly free citizens everywhere, as Bolívar noted, were mostly cannon fodder, still treated, even by the officers of the liberation armies, more like beasts of burden than the free men of the revolution they were supposed to be.

The new constitutions were mostly modeled on those of the United States, not forged out of actual conditions or the revolutionary struggles. The glaring contradictions between governing theory and reality soon shook down the new independence governments on all sides. The visionary idealism, remote from actual economic, social, and racial forces, was to cost the southern republics dearly—a century and more of dictatorships. The characteristics of Spanish feudal rule persisted without the Spaniards. Soon neocolonialism, by England and the United States, took over the so-called republics and joined hands with the feudal reactionaries.

But there was considerable widening of horizons, a degree of new freedom. New industries were born. The colonies traded with all the world. Periodicals circulated. Books poured off the presses: novels, poetry, political essays, works such as Joaquín Fernández Lizardi's great *Periquillo Sarniento* in Mexico. Barnardino Sahagún's great anthropological study, suppressed for three centuries, and the Mayan *Popol Vuh* were published. Peruvian liberator O'Higgins in Chile even attempted some land reform and broke other feudal and church practices. Thus the Indians and mestizos, however much they were still exploited, bored up into the sunlight of new freedoms.

The great achievements of Simón Bolívar, first in Venezuela, following after the earlier failure of Francisco Miranda, provided the great epic of the far-flung revolution. Miranda returned and fought again to drive out the Spaniards, but was again defeated and killed. Bolívar, who had been a young officer with him, for a time was exiled in Jamaica, then returned to struggle on. He set up an independent government at the mouth of the Orinoco River, finally made his long march across the thousand miles of *llanos,* across the Andes to victory in Boyacá, Colombia. His success in Ecuador made possible the establishment of the Gran Confederación of the three northernmost countries of South America.

Much has been written about his famous interview in Guayaquil, Ecuador, with San Martín, who agreed to allow Bolívar to finish the liberation of the continent and gracefully exiled himself in Europe. Bolívar went on in triumph to Lima, Peru, and began the fight to free Bolivia, the first country to start the fight for independence, one of the last to be freed. Bolívar's great lieutenant in that fight was the Ecuadorian liberator, General Antonio José de Sucre, who routed the Spanish army in Ayacucho, high in the Andes. They marched victoriously into Bolivia, then known as Alta Peru, until the liberator set it up as an independent state and renamed it after himself. At this moment Bolívar had become the president of five new republics. He turned the country and the presidency over to Sucre and returned to mend his fences in Peru and the Gran Confederación.

He still dreamed of a great continental confederation of free republics, founded on democracy and freedom. He called for an amphityonic congress in Panama to prepare to build a canal, a canal to be built by all the countries of America, including the United States, to be a symbol of world peace and free commerce, rather than of imperialist aggression and power. His dreams fell to pieces even before he died.

But the succeeding century of the *caudillos* was marked by the struggles of such bold mestizo leaders as José Antonio Páez in Venezuela, who shattered Bolívar's Colombian confederation to bits. Everywhere, from Mexico to Chile, mestizo upstarts seized power. They did not seek liberty, though that was ever their slogan, but to gain control of the state and join the ranks of the wealthy Creole class. Thus the old feudal military system was never shattered and largely persists even today. The old feudal conditions and mentality have never been fully broken except to a degree in Mexico and Bolivia and, of course, in Cuba. Time and human despair have at last caught up with them.

Mexico later went through a far-reaching anticlerical movement, which stripped the church of its wealth, a movement led by the great Zapotec Indian Benito Juárez. But feudal rule in Mexico still existed until after the 1910 Francisco Madero revolt, which stripped away the educational monopoly of the church, broke up much of the large landholding, recognized the rights of labor, and set up a new business oligarchy, in which the country was ruled by the monolithic National Revolutionary party, a veiled form of totalitarianism, which after a long struggle finally won the approbation and praise of the United States government. It was, in short, a hybrid French Revolution.

CHAPTER 5

THE PARIS COMMUNE

THE REVOLUTION that took place in France in 1870 was the by-product of the extensive betrayal of the 1789 Revolution, the sorry condition of the French workers, and the defeat by Germany. The revolutions of 1830 and 1848 had been aborted. But during the intervening periods from the Revolution to 1830, and from then until 1848, a new society and new ideas had taken root. The Industrial Revolution had changed the map of the land and the class structure of the population. The new factories had not yet benefited the workers to any great extent; indeed their miserable wages and long hours made a decent life impossible. Only a few labor unions in Paris and other large cities existed. Not until Flora Tristán (grandmother of the painter Paul Gauguin) toured the Midi a few years prior to 1848, founding her Palaces of the Workers in spite of police harassment, was a national labor organization created. She told of the miserable condition of the workers in the textile mills, the munitions factories, the foundries, and the furniture shops of Lyons, Marseilles, Bordeaux, and a score of other southern French cities.

Fifteen years before as a girl, she had stood in the barricades of July 1830, when the people had driven out Charles X—"the three glorious days" when the workers had repulsed the Royalist forces. The new Louis Philippe government brought few changes. It was feudal and aristocratic but dominated by the new bankers and industrialists who had installed it. "Hereafter the bankers will rule," said banker Jacques Lafitte, a crony of the younger duke of Orléans, who became the king's first mainstay in the government. When the pro-Royalist aristocrats entered the Hôtel de Ville, where parliament met, at their side were the railway owners, the magnates of coal and iron mines and factories. As Octave Festy put it in his *Mouvement Ouvrier,* "The proletariat fought on the barricades, but after the victory the bourgeoisie armed against the workers." The revolution changed only the heads of state.

Disorders became chronic. The frustrated Royalists were troublesome, and raised revolt in the provinces. The Republicans plotted to achieve final victory that would forever end monarchy. But both right and left were badly torn by factions. The church of Saint Germain L'Auxerrois was sacked; the archbishop's palace was burned; and a strike of silk workers had to be put down in blood. In 1834 there were fierce insurrections in Lyons and Paris. A threefold counterattack was made by the army, by the courts—which showed no mercy—and by parliament, dominated by reactionaries. It was true these punitive efforts were paralleled by some democratic reforms, which did little to benefit the workers and peasants.

The revolutionaries hid their fangs in such organizations as the Society for the Rights of Man. The members staged a peaceful demonstration in 1838, which was ruthlessly mowed down by the soldiery—men, women, and children. From then until 1848 novelists, poets, theologians, jurists, attacked the existing order. In 1843 exiled Karl Marx arrived in Paris. Wealthy Claude Henri de Saint-Simon advocated Christian Socialism well before 1830. He believed man's salvation lay in efficient industry and Christian goodness and charity. His followers, commented exiled Heinrich Heine in the *Augsberg Allgemeine Zeitung,* "do not want to abolish poverty but to define it out of existence."

Charles Fourier, a merchant in Lyons, pondered the competition and anarchy of industry, which had ruined him, and believed that cooperative undertakings would provide the solution and bring about the millennium. Society had to be reorganized in phalanxes, living in large hotels of from sixteen hundred to eighteen hundred individuals, large enough to provide emulation, vanity, and concentration of energy. Labor was to receive five twelfths; capital, four twelfths; talent, three twelfths of the products. Free love, seven meals a day, opera, and drama would insure man an average of 144 years of life and a height of seven feet.

His ardent follower Victor Considérant edited the *Phalanx,* to which Flora Tristán contributed, though she did not believe that society could be changed by isolated ideal communities, only by organization of the workers active in society as a whole. Robert Owen of England, founder of the New Lanark benevolent factory system, an inventor and factory owner, the prime mover in the Chartist movement, established an ideal Fourier phalanx in Indiana.

Flora Tristán knew him intimately and admired him. She described his New Lanark utopia, and the Chartist movement in detail in her fine book *Promenades du Londres*. The Reform Bill of 1832, abolishing the rotten borough system and shifting voting strength to the larger cities, failed to remove voting restrictions, so that eligible voters totaled only from 3 to 5 percent of the population. The working class was left out in the cold, and it was almost as miserable and exploited as in France. Flora described the poverty ghettos of London: the prevalence of prostitution, the swarms of street walkers, the houses containing hundreds of girls, the open cribs.

Such leaders as Owen believed that if the workers had the vote, the injustices could be rectified, and with the other Chartist leaders proposed a reform known as the People's Charter, which provided for universal manhood suffrage, secret ballot, annual parliaments, equal electoral districts, i.e., the one-man, one-vote system. Property qualifications for parliamentary candidates were to be abolished, and members were to be paid salaries, making it possible for others than wealthy businessmen and aristocrats to serve. These reforms were considered violently revolutionary, and the Chartists were harshly persecuted by the police. It greatly influenced pre-1848 trends in France. There Louis Blanc, an effective Socialist politician, was closer to "scientific" Marxism. In his 1841 *Historie de Dix Ans*, he divided all Frenchmen into those who possessed property and those dependent upon them for the necessities of life.

The small and larger bourgeoisie, seeking rights and power, forced repeated crises in the Louis Philippe government. Secret societies were formed, modeled on the Italian *carbonari*, each member required to have a rifle and fifty cartridges, very similar to the Jewish resistance, the Z.O.B. so vividly described by John Hersey in *The Wall*, which fought the Nazis in Warsaw. The societies, mostly made up of followers of Filippo Buonarroti, the notable revolutionist who had been jailed by Napoleon on orders of the post-Robespierre reaction, included the students' *Amis de la Verité* pledged to fight for freedom and equality and to hate tyranny; *Droits de l'Homme* ("Rights of Man"), slaughtered in 1838; *Société des Fami-*

lies, and *Société des Saisons* ("Seasons"), led by the revolutionist Louis Auguste Blanqui, who had fought in 1830. Discontent spread, became organized, and presently the workers battled behind street barricades of stones and felled trees. Visiting Ralph Waldo Emerson, having little inkling of what the fighting was about, said it was not worth the loss of a single tree. Louis Philippe fled, and the Second, or "Social" Republic was formed.

The new republic, headed by Alphonse de Lamartine, the Catholic poet, was a combination of Socialists, Proudhon Socialist-Anarchists, labor, and small bourgeoisie. Unprecedented reforms, most of them previously advocated by Flora Tristán, who died in Bordeaux on the eve of the uprising, were carried through: women's rights, the partial abolition of capital punishment, the widening of the suffrage. The most radical proposal was a right-to-work law. A workman named Marche put a pistol to the head of Lamartine until Louis Blanc wrote down the proposed legislation. It was strongly supported by Alexis de Tocqueville, who argued that industrialization of modern civilization doomed an ever-increasing number to misery in the very midst of expanding prosperity. The state must support them. But the republic had no money, and presently exiled all the unemployed to the provinces. It also alienated the peasants by imposing heavier taxes on them. Soon the nonproletarian elements in control sought to disarm the workers. This law-and-order group caused innumerable arrests; a slaughter followed, a bloodbath. The revolutionist Blanqui, just out of jail, was resentenced to ten years.

Louis Bonaparte organized hoodlum gangs, clad in blouses like the later Black Shirt Fascists, to attack Leftist leaders and organizations, and was swept into the presidency by an overwhelming vote. He headed a gang of political and financial adventurers. Reform elements were extirpated. Toward the end of 1851 he declared himself emperor. As Napoleon III, he took over the army and ruthlessly attacked labor organizations and leaders. He maintained his position by military adventurism: the Crimean War, invasion of Southeast Asia, Algeria, Italy, and—the crowning glory—Mexico, where the ill-fated Maximilian was put on a phantom throne.

He opened the doors to corruption, which enriched speculators and get-rich-quick entrepreneurs. His much-favored bastard brother Duke Charles Auguste de Morny was a clever speculator on the bourse. He staged bad plays he had written and fornicated with beautiful women whom he passed on to the emperor, to the annoyance of Empress Eugénie, the granddaughter of a wealthy Scotch wine merchant of Málaga. De Morny projected the 1862 invasion of Mexico in order to collect the fantastic Jecker claim, a deal that was to net him 25 million francs. The Swiss banking house (later French) of Jecker had made a loan to the reactionary Miguel Miramón government, which received 700,000 pesos out of 15,000,-000. This claim had now been puffed up to 70,000,000 francs. The entire court and much of parliament were corrupted by judicially distributed shares. Napoleon was lured by the invasion project, Eugénie even more. It would, Napoleon announced, prevent the territorial and trade expansion of the United States and check the spread of its pernicious democracy and its material greed, a menace for the world. But when the American Civil War was won by the North, and Prussia became a danger in Europe, he had to pull his troops out fast. The foolish enterprise had drained France of wealth and resources.

In 1867 he expected to annex the east bank of the Rhine as a reward for remaining neutral in the Austro-Prussian War, but the Prussian victory was so swift and overwhelming, Bismarck told him bluntly to keep hands off. Nevertheless in 1870 Napoleon found a pretext to cross the Rhine. Prussia moved at once in "defense of Germany."

It would be a calamity even if Germany should win, for France would thereby be thrown into the arms of Russia. Czar Alexander was already licking his chops, believing that the exhaustion of the two major powers would make him the arbiter of European affairs. Karl Marx called it a "race war" that would later lead to the devastation of all Europe by fifteen or twenty million armed men. "History," he said, "would measure its retribution, not by the . . . square miles conquered from France, but by the . . . crime of reviving in the second half of the nineteenth century the policy of Conquest."

The French people were sick of the deaths, the costs, and the blunders of the Mexican war, and fresh war was not popular. The Corps Législatif, as parliament was called, refused to grant credits. The International Working Men's Association—"the First International"—sent out messages to all Europe, calling the war a "criminal aggression." But protests were steamrollered into silence in both France and Germany. Once more Napoleon loosed his blouse-shirt gangs to beat the drums for war. They stirred into life a colossal counterpeace demonstration. The prefect of police forbade further demonstrations by either side.

Marshal Achille Bazaine, head of the French occupation forces in Mexico—there grown fat and wealthy, and having married a sixteen year old Mexican beauty—commanded the army against the Prussians. Its officers had been corrupted by graft and high living. The French forces were quickly shattered at Sedan, and Napoleon was taken prisoner. Alsace-Lorraine was annexed, and Paris, by then stripped of troops, was besieged. Only the queen remained in the palace; she escaped to England. Parliament was too frightened to act. Even the leader of the opposition party fled.

The Republican deputies, composed of bourgeois Radicals, Socialists, and Anarchists, led by Léon Gambetta, met at the Hôtel de Ville, and set up a provisional government, September 4, 1870, and whipped together some forces for defense under General Louis Jules Trochu, the military governor of Paris. It sent a mission to Tours to keep resistance alive in the provinces and maintain contact with the outside world. In October Bazaine cravenly surrendered his entire army to the Germans at Metz. The news aroused popular rage, and on October 21 workers' battalions stormed the city hall and seized members of the government, who were set free after a minor armed clash.

The Germans ringed the capital without serious effort to enter the city and kept up a heavy but intermittent bombardment for nearly five months. The people were then close to starvation. The Paris defenders made numerous brave but ineffectual sorties.

Meanwhile irregular troops attempted with little success to prevent the Germans from overrunning all France. The provisional government at Tours had to take refuge in Bordeaux.

The Paris authorities secured an amnesty on January 29, 1871, until peace terms could be arranged. The Germans waited at the gates of the city for the French to hang each other.

A new National Assembly was whipped together on eight days' notice and met in Bordeaux. It was largely controlled by the Orléans party, mostly large landowners, who occupied 440 of the 750 seats. They were called the Rurals but were "the partners" of the big industrialists. They were rabid monarchists, rehabilitated by Charles X after the 1789 Revolution to the tune of billions of francs. Naturally the Assembly tried to put the whole burden of war costs and the indemnity of five billion francs demanded by the Germans on the peasants. The Paris workingmen angrily insisted that the peasants should be freed from such burdens and from the tyranny of rule by gendarmes and prefects. The Treaty of Frankfurt was drawn up in May 1871.

Indemnity payment of the five billions was postponed while Louis Adolph Thiers, the head of the Bordeaux government, "Chief of the Executive Power of the French government," who moved to Paris, collected two billions, of which he and his clique expected to pocket two hundred millions. The entire levy, despite protests, was to be on the peasants. Napoleon III was formally deposed, and the empire abolished.

Thiers, "that monstrous gnome," was a seasoned politician. He had betrayed the 1830 revolution, blocked every effort to reform the army, and amassed a million francs as minister of Louis Philippe. It was he who had effected the 1838 slaughter of the Rights of Man adherents in the Rue Transonain. Later he hastened to tell the 1848 revolutionists that henceforth he would be faithful to the revolutionary cause until death. He had steadily opposed Napoleon III and his imperialist adventures.

The new foreign minister was Jules Favre, who had fought the Mexican invasion from start to finish, and hence was now popular. Unfortunately he had recently been involved in litigation concerning a forged document by which he had obtained some millions of francs for his Algerian mistress, wife of a drunken official, and his two children by her. Now, named mayor of Paris, he made a vast fortune.

Ernest Picard, finance minister, in 1867 had abetted his brother Arthur in spectacular "black leg" speculation on the bourse, by means of inside information on the disasters to the French army.

General Trochu, though he said it was folly to try to defend Paris, had put up blatant posters stating he would never surrender a stone in the French forts around the city, but on January 8, 1871, he handed them over, along with all weapons. Only the National Guard refused to give up their guns, and when the Germans marched down the Champs Elysées on March 1, it was they who prevented a complete take-over. So belligerent was their attitude that the Germans quickly withdrew almost to their previous positions.

Thiers ordered the National Guard to hand over its artillery, alleging it was national property. Actually it had been purchased by popular subscription during the siege. On March 18 he sent troops to enforce his order. Paris rose as one man to defend them, and the regular army was driven out. That very day the Commune was declared with a thunder of popular acclaim.

The Central Committee of the National Guard, made up by this time mostly of workers, proclaimed that the hour had struck to take over the government and establish "the second republic." "The political rule of the producer cannot coexist with the perpetuation of social slavery. With labor emancipated, every man becomes a voting man, and producing labor ceases to be a class attribute."

On March 26 it installed the provisional Commune of elected municipal counselors in the Hôtel de Ville, and Thiers, then in Paris, and his entourage fled to Versailles with, as the National Guard expressed it, "all his dandies, aristocrats, rich men, wastrels, hangers-on, pimps and whores." The existing Republican machinery, the new Paris regime proclaimed, had remained clogged by "medieval rubbish and seignorial privilege . . . a hotbed of huge national debts and crushing taxes," all based on "place, pelf and patronage." Under Louis Napoleon Bonaparte, a regime of class terrorism and deliberate insult toward the vile multitude, the government became "a national war regime of capital against labor." Once labor had been crushed, he turned the deputies out to pasture and became emperor.

A similar process, it was noted, had taken place in Germany, with Bismarck wielding the bayonets of Prussia. Thus, until the war, there had been tacit connivance between the two regimes.

The members of the Paris Commune, elected May 20 by free unlimited adult male suffrage, were largely of working-class origin. The majority were Blanqui Socialists, who also dominated the National Guard committee, and followers of the Anarcho-Socialist philosopher Pierre Joseph Proudhon, who had died a few years before. Few participants had any knowledge of Marxist doctrines. Otherwise their first move would have been to take over the Bank of France. They had merely gaped at it in awe. They did shoot Jacques Necker, which put an end to his claim against Mexico and the French government.

Most economic innovations were carried out by the Proudhonists, such as setting up workers' cooperatives. But most steps were in contradiction to their anarchistic tenets. Political changes were largely effected by the Blanquists. They believed, being disciples of Buonarrotti, that a small organized group should control the state until the masses could be activated. But now, in control, they advocated a federation of free communes. A grandiose plan was drawn up. Half a dozen other Communes had taken control, the leading ones in Toulouse, Narbonne, and St.-Etienne. Those in Lyons and Marseilles had been quickly crushed by Versailles, aided by the monarchists and Rurals. The most serious mistake the Paris Commune made was not to march on Versailles at once, before Thiers had a chance to secure arms and bring up troops from the interior. A golden moment was lost.

House rents were abolished for a seven months' period. The sale of pawned objects were forbidden, and soon all pawnshops were abolished. The status of foreigners—some had been elected to the Commune—was recognized, for the flag of the Commune was "the flag of the World Republic." The top salary for government officials was set at a modest six thousand francs. All administrative, educational, and judicial posts were filled by direct election, subject to recall. Separation of church and state was decreed on April 2. Church property was nationalized, and government payment of priests' salaries abolished.

On April 5 the Thiers regime began shooting all pro-Commune prisoners. The Commune arrested enemies who had not escaped from Paris to be held as hostages, offering to exchange all of them for Blanqui, whom Versailles had rearrested. He was court-martialed and banished. In Paris the National Guard burned a guillotine in a public plaza amid public rejoicing and demolished the victory column on the Place Vendôme, cast from guns captured by Napoleon I in the war of 1809. It was considered a symbol of national and chauvinistic hatred. The Tuileries and part of the Louvre were burned.

On April 8 the schools were secularized. All symbols, pictures, dogma, and prayers were excluded from the schools—everything that belonged to each individual's conscience.

A census of closed factories was taken, and they were ordered reopened by cooperatives of former employees organized into one big union. Night work for bakers was prohibited. Police registration of workers was ended, cards henceforth to be issued by the twenty ar-

rondissement mayors. On May 5 the Chapel of Atonement, built as an expiation for the execution of Louis XVI, was ordered demolished.

For the first time since 1846 Paris was safe. One could walk anywhere day or night without fear of being mugged. Yet it was practically unpoliced. "The only cannibal was at the gates," a revolutionist remarked. Doubtless the Republicans and monarchists considered that all cannibals were inside the gates.

This condition was not to last long, for Thiers realized that the Commune would soon bring on a nationwide peasant uprising. In the shadow of the German guns still dominating Paris, and with the connivance of German officers, he set to work to destroy the Paris regime. He began bringing up more forces from the provinces—sailors, marines, gendarmes, *mouchards,* Chouans from Brittany, bearing white flags and the red heart of Jesus on white cloth over the chest.

As early as April 7, the Versailles troops captured western Neuilly Bridge over the Seine, but five days later General Jean Eudes was thrown back with heavy losses when he attacked the southern fringe. By then the city was under almost continuous bombardment. This aroused protest in all France and elsewhere in the world, for those days it was considered inhuman to bombard a city and its noncombatants. Thiers airily denied he had bombarded it. He had only cannonaded it.

He asked the Germans to release prisoners to augment his forces, and with them on May 3 was able to take the Moulin Saquet redoubt on the south front. Within a week Fort Issy, already destroyed by gunfire, and also Fort Vanves were occupied. A gradual advance on the western side captured all villages and outposts as far as the city wall. By passing through the German lines, per previous agreement, in violation of the armistice agreement, Thiers's troops were able to make a surprise attack and force their way into the city. Fighting grew more bitter as they pushed toward the eastern working-class *arrondissements.* It took eight days of savage fighting before the defenders were overwhelmed on the Belleville and Menilmontant heights.

Wholesale slaughter began, a mass shooting of unarmed citizens against the wall of the Père-Lachaise cemetery. Many prisoners were herded into concentration camps. En route, generals arbitrarily picked out hundreds to be executed on the spot. A British corre-spondent reported that the wounded were dying amid the cemetery tombstones. Six thousand workingmen took to the catacombs. Poor hungry wretches were gunned down in the streets. In all thirty thousand people, men, women, and children, were shot down; for-ty-five thousand were arrested; and twenty-five thousand managed to flee from the city—a population loss of a hundred thousand.

Even as this terror was going on, the cafés reopened and were full of exultant celebrants drinking champagne and absinthe. The cabinets of elegant restaurants were again the scene of amorous se-ductions.

Marx had been strongly opposed to the Commune revolt, but once it had taken place, he rejoiced and, despite the bloody out-come, hailed it as a victory, indeed a greater victory than had it ac-tually succeeded. It was wrong, he then admitted, to insist that rev-olutionary efforts should not be undertaken even if they had little chance of success. Such confrontation taught the masses and aroused ardent support; they increased the temper and strength of the world movement.

Many years later Lenin declared: "The cause of the Commune is the cause of world revolution, the cause of the complete political and economic emancipation of the toiler. It is the cause of the pro-letariat of the world. As Marx said, it was immortal."

Like most revolutions, it was a by-product of war, of human mis-ery, of social disintegration and corruption. It was powered by hu-manistic, national, and international sentiments. It contained most of the ideas of the Revolution of the Bastille. It taught a historic les-son for all future revolutionists and governments. Paris in itself did not provide a wide enough theater for success. If the Commune had struck out at once at Versailles and had thereby been able to link up with the short-lived Communes in other cities, it might have begun a new era in France. Most of its acts have since been adopted as part of French law, of course. It was too kind at the be-ginning and too desperate at the end. Its weakness did not reside, as its enemies argued, in its democratic and humane efforts but rather in its reluctance to execute them.

Its enemies showed none of the compassionate consideration dis-played by the Commune. The Republicans and monarchists of Ver-sailles, admired as more respectable people, were the ones who did the slaughtering and destroyed the workers with ruthless cruelty. What was more important than either the generosity or the cruelty of either side was the Commune's failure to develop an outstanding and forceful leader.

CHAPTER 6

THE MEXICAN REVOLUTION

THE 1910 MEXICAN REVOLUTION, which predated the Sun Yat-sen revolution in China by two years, was precipitated by the jailing of Francisco I. Madero, the leader opposing dictator Porfirio Díaz in San Luis Potosí in the fall of 1910. He escaped to the United States, issued his Plan de San Luis Potosí, and soon headed a revolt that broke out in many parts of the country.

The San Luis Potosí *pronunciamiento*, which became an important landmark in Mexican history, was a call to arms to overthrow the dictator, establish free elections, and abolish reelection, i.e., put an end to perpetuity in power. Madero's motto, *No-Reelección, Sufragio Efectivo*, adorns all official documents just above the signature—to this day. The Plan de San Luis Potosí was the dynamite that wrecked the Díaz regime, an outworn edifice, and plunged Mexico into fifteen years of bloody revolution, a struggle for far-reaching economic and social change far beyond the simple political formula set forth by Madero.

Its major achievement was that it did end the thirty-year Porfirio Díaz dictatorship, with its notable design of peace (and silence) for the nation, prosperity for the few, and poverty for the masses. Díaz's rule rested on militarism and oppression of the people, on the church, large landholding, and serfdom. In spite of productive growth—new railroads, more international trade—the plight of the people grew worse, along with ostentation and bureaucratic corruption. Fat concessions were granted to a small inner clique, known as Científicos, who alleged to have discovered the secrets of scientific government, based on concepts of Comte's Positivism. They were granted vast areas of land, which they then sold profitably to wealthy Mexicans and to foreigners, particularly Americans. Remaining village *ejidos*, communal lands, were stripped away, and from 80 to 90 percent of the rural population was without property. Horrible slums festered in the cities and towns.

Díaz ruled over all in taciturn austerity, adulated by the great of the earth and by foreign governments from Washington to St. Petersburg. His decorations and medals so weighted down his eighty-year-old body, he found it difficult to stand erect. In the country-side his smart *Rurales* shot first and inquired afterward, if at all. Actually his army was a beggarly abused body of conscripts, badly officered, without power, and no longer loyal. Now the Crusader had risen against him, his forces crumbled quickly.

Madero, son of a wealthy wine-making family, engaged in the smelter business in competition with the Guggenheims, was a strange liberal mystic, who believed in spiritualism, the planchette, or Ouija board, astrology, vegetarianism, and democracy. He was a non drug-using, teetotaler pre-hippy, with a small black beard, wearing pinstripes—an intense, righteous man, hopeful and kindly. His brother, Gustavo, part of his administration, once remarked, "The Madero family has many competent members, but the fool of the family became President." It was a bon mot at a diplomatic gathering, but Madero was scarcely a fool, unless we bracket him morally with Socrates, Jesus Christ, and John Huss, and under more normal circumstances he could have provided Mexico with progressive honest government. In politics fate made of him a sort of Kerensky, balanced between the old corrupt forces and the new revolutionists, between the demands of the United States Embassy and the national needs, too close himself to the old crowd to weed out the Científicos and not fully aware of the colossal forces unleashed by the Revolution. For all his small stature, he had moral grandeur, unshakable integrity, bravery, stubbornness, and he believed in mankind. He was nailed to the cross.

Before his arrest in 1910 he had raised a great following, for he was eloquent. All classes were attracted to his banner. Díaz had announced that Mexico had progressed enough to enjoy free elections. Soon it became apparent that for him free elections meant bayonet elections. He and his coterie were appalled by the enthusiasm the apostle of democracy aroused. The dictator had had no real intention of stepping down. Even in 1911, when lying sick with an ulcered tooth in his Cadena Street house, mobs screaming outside and bullets whining down the streets, he resisted the pleas of his wife, the archbishop, and his trusted, able-but-tricky finance minister José Ives Limantour to resign. "I came in with bullets," he replied gutturally, "and I shall go out only with bullets."

After Díaz's pronouncement of free elections, Madero had been able to campaign as the candidate of the No Reelection party, the first bona fide opposition party in thirty years. He toured the country from Veracruz and Yucatán in the south to Guadalajara and Monterrey in the north. Great enthusiastic crowds turned out to hear him. It was a triumphal tour. New newspapers advocated his election and were duly harassed by the police. Editors were jailed, editions confiscated, but Madero was not seriously bothered, and his popularity rose to an emotional crest. Everybody was reading his *Presidential Succession,* a clear summary of existing abuses, a lucid program for political emancipation and political justice. The social and economic emphasis was not strong, only hints of land reform and improved living conditions. His chief insistence was on honest elections. He assumed that honest elections meant democracy. In the eyes of the masses he had become a prophet, a messiah, and an apostle, observed Edith O'Shaughnessy, wife of the United States Embassy secretary.

By this time nearly everybody, except the privileged, realized that serfdom and land monopoly were not compatible with modern economic ideas. A few saw that the church, which since the great Reformation of Benito Juárez in 1856 had edged back into power and wealth, must again be curbed. This was the age of industry, and Mexico needed more industry. It was the age of the proletariat. Close by, to the north, was the great colossus, the United States, where industry, elections, and capitalism had created a powerful nation of free people—so it seemed to the Mexicans, though nearly all despised American culture and morality. It seemed in 1910 that the hour of true freedom had now struck for Mexico also.

But men have varied ideas of what constitutes freedom, that magic word used by all politicians, who usually bracket it with law and order and national unity, catchwords that dictators also find convenient. But clearly in Mexico the law had begun to stink, especially as the worst violators were the ruling powers. When the avenues of needed change are dammed up, revolt strikes forth, and when it does, there are few limits to men's ideas of freedom. New horizons opened up as soon as the battle was launched.

A few years before, in 1907, the Flores Magón brothers, anarchists in Los Angeles, California, attempted to start revolt, but it was nipped in the bud when they were jailed by the United States. Ricardo Flores Magón finally died in Leavenworth in 1922. Anarchism was not an unknown word in Mexico. The first labor leaders, when a few unions struggled into existence, were followers of the anarcho-syndicalist doctrines of Spanish labor leader Juan Grave. During the Madero revolution the labor unions adopted the red-black banner of anarcho-syndicalism, and it is still draped over the closed door of establishments wherever workers go on strike. Every strike is 100 percent effective. No "scissor-bills" and no strikebreakers ever get in, not even the owner or the manager.

The response to Madero's call to arms was nationwide. Clearly it was the end of an epoch. Díaz and his associates were thoroughly discredited. Armed bands sprang up on every hand. City after city fell quickly before revolutionary assaults. Telegraph lines were cut, trains ambushed or derailed, track torn up. When Madero, having crossed back into Mexican territory, captured Ciudad Juárez on the border, with the aid of Pancho Villa, Pascual Orozco, and numbers of American adventurers, from the crack troops of the army, and took the dictator's most competent general prisoner, the end was near.

Authorized emissaries of Díaz consulted at the customhouse with Madero and signed a pact by the light from their automobiles, which deposed Díaz and set up Francisco De la Barra, a cabinet minister, as provisional president until elections could be held. The news sped south, and a mob of five thousand surrounded the dictator's home on Cadena Street. The soldiery fired into crowds everywhere. The dictator was stubborn, but at last, late in the afternoon, he signed with a shaking hand and was whisked off to Europe never to return.

Madero entered Mexico City in triumph and was duly elected in November. His mild reforms failed to satisfy the people, yet infuriated the reactionaries and American Ambassador Henry Lane Wilson, close to large corporations with interests in Mexico, all of whom plotted to overthrow the new regime. Revolution is always very sinful. It always irritates the most respectable people. Madero was caught between two powerful grindstones. He could neither meet the demands of the underdogs nor deny them. Nor could he satisfy the demands of the oil interests, the mine owners, the refiners of ore. Hostile to him was the might of the United States government, concerned not with the fate of the Mexican people but the comfort of American investors, so long favored by Díaz. If personally a saint in conduct and sacred dedication, Madero could not measure up to the mighty forces unleashed, and in politics he was a frustrated between-worlds man.

There was no peace. The Indians certainly had their own ideas. They wanted the restoration of the village *ejidos*, the last of which had been stripped away by the Porfirio Díaz crowd. They wanted serfdom abolished. They wanted land and water and schools. This became the slogan of rebel Emiliano Zapata in the south, who, by the time Madero was seated in the palace, had swept through seven states, burning haciendas, killing *hacendados*, handing out hacienda lands to the peasants. Everywhere the peasants began moving in on the big holdings and settling in mountains and valleys long sealed off, unutilized. The same slogan was later adopted by Pancho Villa in the north, the ex-bandit who came to lead large armies.

Zapata grew ever stronger. A serious pro-landholders' revolt in the north was headed by turncoat General Pascual Orozco. Madero's able old-style army general, Victoriano Huerta, able, alcoholic, and gross, aided by Pancho Villa, put down the revolt promptly, but Huerta also put Villa before a firing squad. He gave in to the importunity of Raúl Madero, brother of the president, and sent the guerrilla leader off to the Mexico City penitentiary, from which he eventually escaped for a time to the United States. Despite these successes by the government, the uproar continued great in many parts of the country. Stability went out the window. Madero was menaced on all sides. At one time he admitted that two hundred armed bands were operating. He tried to rehabilitate the regular Díaz army, to the wrath of his own followers, and finally tried out land reform, but too late and too little.

Félix Díaz, nephew of Porfirio, headed an unsuccessful revolt in Veracruz. He was to have been shot, but Madero had him brought to Mexico City and pardoned him. Early in 1913 Félix Díaz got a new band together, tried to storm the palace, and finally holed up in the Ciudadela, the arms factory and arsenal. Victoriano Huerta, now head of the army, mounted artillery on the roof of the tall YMCA building and started a senseless artillery duel across the houses and streets of the capital. The dead piled up in the streets unburied. The event was called the *Decena Trágica,* the tragic ten days.

Ambassador Wilson, backed by the diplomatic corps, finally arranged a truce. He arranged much more; he arranged for a hand-picked cabinet to be installed when Huerta took over power. The proposed treachery, it turned out, was to spill a river of blood across Mexico.

On February 19 Gustavo Madero was seized in the El Globo café, dragged out, and murdered. The palace was taken over, and the high red-backed presidential chair was riddled with bullets. President Madero and Vice-President José María Pino Suárez were arrested. Wilson voiced satisfaction at the restoration of law and order. Madero and Suárez signed their resignations on the promise they would be given safe conduct out of the country. Madero's wife pled with Wilson to see that her husband's life was saved. She was given little satisfaction. Wilson told the diplomatic corps, according to the Cuban ambassador, M. Márquez Sterling, "Mexico has been saved. From now on we shall have peace, progress, and prosperity. I have known the plans to imprison Madero for three days!"

A few days later, on February 22, on a dark night in a narrow street behind the palace, the two executives were murdered, apparently by the guards transferring them from the palace to the penitentiary.

All Mexico gasped with horror and shame. For most of the country, despite the numerous revolutionary groups loose in the country, Madero was popular, a Moses who had led the land out of the night of dictatorship. The entire nation sprang to arms.

Like many another, Ambassador Wilson had not realized the powerful revolutionary forces in the land. To believe that they could be so easily quelled or turned aside was little short of lunacy. To imagine that a fat drunken general of the old regime could restore order and justice, or what Wilson may have imagined to be justice, was a figment based on some secret contempt for the Mexican people.

Ruthless and murderous, Huerta did try to restore order. It was too late. President Woodrow Wilson, who took office soon after, had a dream of democracy, and he was determined to make that dream come true, not only in Mexico, but, as it turned out, in the entire world. Ambassador Wilson was yanked home, but Huerta did not take kindly to the President's schoolroom sermons, especially as he had the definite backing of the Lord Cowdry oil and railway interests, which he favored at the expense of American interests, now less enthusiastic for the new government than at the beginning. When professorial tactics failed, Wilson moved the Marines into Veracruz to cut off ammunition and supplies.

In the end, caught between the Marines and the large rebel armies converging on the capital, Huerta in turn had to flee the country. The constitutionalist armies of the leader of the anti-Huerta movement, Venustiano Carranza, and his outstanding general, Alvaro Obregón, entered Mexico City in July.

By then there were too many bigwigs with armed forces, and the cohorts of agrarian leader Zapata took over the capital. He was quickly joined by Pancho Villa and his fifty thousand men. From then on, for years, a bloody seesaw jolted Mexico with its wild and uneven movement and countermovement.

After retaking Mexico City, Carranza attempted to settle matters by calling a national convention. It soon got out of control and was moved to Aguascalientes, north in Pancho Villa territory. There proceedings were dominated by the Villistas and Zapatistas, who refused to recognize Carranza as provisional president. They appointed their own man and marched to Mexico City, installing him in the National Palace.

Carranza was forced to retreat to Veracruz, which the Marines evacuated. There he signed a national idle lands law. As in Madero's case it was too late and too little. Nevertheless by March 1915 he reentered the capital to rule over a badly disorganized country. Zapata's watchfires burned close by, visible from the National Palace, in the hills of the Anahuac Valley above Mexico City. In Washington schoolmaster Wilson continued to remind Carranza of his duties.

In all this mélange of revolution and counterrevolution one could discern various strands of thinking: anarchism, Marxism, liberal democracy, anti-imperialism, nationalism, antinationalism, and internationalism. But the biggest demand was for land, water, and schools. Even before Madero was killed, Zapata had issued his famous Plan de Ayala from his home village in Morelos, providing for the restoration of the village *ejidos*, or communal lands. Carranza's piecemeal legislation fell far short of Zapata's more radical demands.

Carranza was not a reactionary, though for years he had been a

Porfirio Díaz governor, of Coahuila, a northern state. But he was to the right of most revolutionary elements; furthermore he was arbitrary and brooked no opposition. He was something of an enigma behind his dark glasses and enormous white beard. He lost the support of organized labor when he shut down the Casa del Obrero, the first national labor headquarters, modeled after the Labor Palaces founded by Flora Tristán a century before in France. In due time it was replaced by the Mexican Regional Confederation of Labor (CROM), so named to indicate that it was merely part of the worldwide dominion of labor. The newer business elements had their own hopes of profiting from the nationalistic tenor of the revolution. The generals had their own ideas, mostly of easy loot and power. The Indians clung steadfastly to their hopes of village communalism.

The new ideas came out of the very entrails of Mexico, ideas deep in the hearts and minds of the most illiterate. But there were also magazines, newspapers, pamphlets, and books galore. The most widely read volume was probably that of Madero, *The Presidential Succession,* but more penetrating, also widely read, was Andrés Molina Enríquez's *Los Grandes Problemas de México,* which had appeared in 1909. Far more powerful than Madero's book, it broke new ground in economics and politics and above all in the problems of land tenure. An able but less-known book, not published until 1916, was by the anthropologist Manuel Gamio, entitled *Forging the Fatherland.* It advocated reconstruction of the old Indian culture and its great monuments, such as those at Teotihuacán, Mitla, etc. Thus the revolutionary slogans and proposals soon raced far beyond the Madero position.

The various revolutionary demands finally found articulate and organized expression in the Querétaro Constitution of 1917, adopted under Carranza's administration, while the John Pershing punitive expedition was still on Mexican soil, a fact that undoubtedly deepened its antiforeign nationalistic tone and the curbs put on foreign investments. That the expedition remained there while the convention was in session in order to influence its provisions seems more than likely. Secretly and openly the United States State Department protested against the sections that proposed to nationalize Mexican oil. Pershing moved out soon after the constitution was adopted.

The document was hammered out in Querétaro during 1916 and

early 1917. Though Zapata did not participate, many of his followers were delegates, and the final land provisions were practically a reiteration of the Plan de Ayala. The Socialists of General Salvador Alvarado of Yucatán, who had helped save Carranza by sending millions from the treasury of his government-owned henequen industry, the Reguladora de Henequén. This Socialist take-over had caused the United States to boycott his government and his henequen, needed for United States harvest fields. Present at Querétaro, too, were the leaders of the so-called Red Batallions de Veracruz, which had stood by Carranza in the struggle against Huerta and at the time of his retreat from the capital. Carranza adherents were numerous. Villa had been pretty well defeated by then, but his followers were subject to arrest, so none of outstanding merit was present.

In general the consensus was liberal, democratic, the final version still following the traditional models provided by the American and French revolutions and the tripartite division of governmental powers. However, within that framework were introduced some highly revolutionary concepts that had deeply moved Mexico. The state was conceived of, not as an aloof instrument for preserving order, the hands-off role provided by the American Constitution, but as a dynamic instrumentality for promoting economic and social welfare —a positive rather than a pacific neutral role.

A number of tendencies came through strongly. It was anticlerical, anti-big-landholding, anti-American. It was prolabor, pro-peasant, pro-Indian. It reestablished the Indian communal land system and provided for the return or setting up of village *ejidos*. Measures toward the elimination of foreign ownership were inserted, providing for 51 percent Mexican ownership of all industries. No foreigners could own property within a hundred kilometers of the frontiers or within fifty kilometers of the coast. All foreign property owners were subject to Mexican laws, and had to agree not to appeal for protection by their home governments. Mexican subsoil, that is all oil and mineral deposits, were nationalized. All ownership of lands and waters had originally been vested in the nation by Spanish law, and the new constitution gave the government the right to "impose upon private property such restrictions as the public interest may require." This is the right of eminent domain exercised in varying degrees by all governments, but rarely defined so precisely. All this was rooted in traditional Spanish law, but it frightened most foreign

[*115*]

owners and investors, though they have since managed to devise means of bypassing much of the restrictive legislation.

This document, in force in Mexico today, embodies the various revolutionary ideas regarding land, Church, and labor reform. Madero's original demand for effective suffrage and no reelection was included. Article 123 spelled out a thoroughgoing labor code. It provided three months' separation pay, plus an extra month for every year of employment. Wage claims in full were given priority in cases of bankruptcy. Article 130 took all education, except for religious seminaries, out of the hands of the Church, and nationalized all Church property including the churches, though they were left nominally in Church hands, except for a few that were closed to become national monuments.

Various states passed more severe laws, such as limiting the number of priests and the length of time church bells could be rung. Governor Tomás Garrido passed a law making it obligatory for priests to marry. Not anticlerical at all, he commented: "I merely want to make their children legitimate."

Carranza, who disliked many provisions, nevertheless accepted the final document and established it by decree February 5. He was duly elected president under its provisions in 1918. He showed little energy, however, in enforcing the program it set forth.

The country remained far from pacified. Zapata clung to his Plan de Ayala, refusing to lay down his arms until full land reform was carried out. He was finally tricked into ambush and murdered by General Pablo González in 1920.

Pancho Villa still operated in the north, and Carranza's army was so corrupt it made little effort to suppress him. Army officers made deals with him to sell ammunition and supplies to his forces. Only the central portion of the country was pretty well controlled by Carranza.

In the 1920 elections Carranza tried to impose a civilian as president, his Washington ambassador "Meester" Ignacio Bonilla, favored by the United States. Carranza placed the rival candidate, his great general Alvaro Obregón, under house arrest. Obregón escaped to Iguala, where he was joined by Luis N. Morones, head of the Regional Confederation of Labor. His close friend Plutarco Elías Calles, governor of Sonora, seceded and raised revolt. He had the backing of Obregón's faithful Yaqui Indian soldiers. Other generals joined the uprising and converged rapidly on the capital.

Carranza had to abandon Mexico City, a hurried, fantastic flight in twenty-three commandeered trains, filled with troops, guns, and ammunition, loot from the palace, seventy million gold pesos in chests. Officers brought along their mistresses, rarely their wives, with birdcages and cosmetics.

The last train was wrecked just beyond nearby Guadalupe Hidalgo. Progress of the other trains was slow. They were attacked by guerrillas. Here and there torn-up track had to be restored under sniper fire. Finally, in the state of Veracruz, Carranza had to abandon the trains and take to the hills. He and his entourage, including most of his cabinet, took refuge the first night in an Indian mountain village, where they were welcomed by an apparently friendly guerrilla. The president was murdered in the night, riddled with machine-gun bullets.

Alvaro Obregón marched into Mexico City and staged a monster victory parade that lasted from early morning till nightfall. It was a hot day, and he rode with his shirt sleeves rolled up, wearing suspenders. A new era was inaugurated that May 1920—the so-called Revindicating Revolution took over.

Adolfo de la Huerta was installed as provisional president until elections for Obregón could be held in November. He was quickly successful in reestablishing order, putting down or buying off guerrilla leaders. He instituted some notable reforms. A period of more constructive effort was at hand. In the north, Villa made a pact to lay down his arms in return for cash to pay off his *dorados* and a personal gift of the big Cantillo hacienda in Chihuahua, where he settled with a large group of his followers and carried on the peaceful pursuits of a wealthy *hacendado,* of the sort he had fought against and destroyed. He, in turn, was assassinated toward the end of Obregón's term of office, just before Plutarco Elías Calles was elected. The country was firmly in the control of its more moderate revolutionary leaders.

Obregón's administration, however, was far from calm. His efforts to implement the constitution led to serious confrontations with the Roman Catholic Church and the United States government, which refused to recognize him unless he pledged himself not to nationalize Mexican oil. He refused to do so.

He consolidated his power over the army, organized labor and the agrarians. The generals were lavishly subsidized. He even paid their huge gambling debts—at least in one instance. He made Luis N.

Morones a powerful force, and membership in CROM jumped from fifty thousand in 1920 to twelve hundred thousand in 1924. Strikes were almost always settled in favor of the workers. He more or less took Antonio Díaz Soto y Gama, who had been Zapata's intellectual mentor, and his peasant confederation under his wing, set up state agrarian commissions, and cautiously doled out nearly 3 million acres of the three hundred million still owned by the *hacendados.*

He was particularly interested in education, which he put in the hands of the brilliant José Vasconcelos, a former intellectual adviser of Pancho Villa. Vasconcelos laid stress on the cultural heritage of the Indians, though he was deeply aware of Spanish literary traditions, and he issued a series of Spanish and world classics. He had a concept of the creation in the New World of a new "Cosmic Race," a blend of peoples, Spanish, Indian, and Negro, which would gain the multiple heritage of all its components, hence would be superior to all other races.

He built up a new type of rural school called the Casa del Pueblo, to teach not merely the three R's, but also music, dancing, art, sports, and scientific farming. Many teachers were driven out by the local priests, inciting their congregations to violence, but the Casas del Pueblo were set up in the most remote villages in the mountains where in some instances nobody spoke Spanish.

The minister was a good patron of the arts and put Diego Rivera, José Clemente Orozco, and David Siqueiros to painting the walls of public buildings, and thereby set in motion the great school of Mexican revolutionary art. Carlos Chávez, a musical genius, composed new types of music, in which Indian dissonance was blended with traditionally Western forms.

In January 1923 in northern Mexico, four archbishops, eight bishops, and the pope's apostolic delegate dedicated a memorial to Christ the King, with great pageantry before a vast concourse of people. It was so patently a violation of the constitutional provision that prohibited performing religious ceremonies (or wearing the religious habit) in public that Obregón had to act promptly. He deported the papal nuncio.

Obregón's oil policy threatened to bring war between Mexico and the United States. However, conferences were held on Bucareli Street. After much negotiation the Mexican government agreed not to make the new laws retroactive. This salvaged nearly all American holdings. Obregón was duly recognized in August 1923, and soon thereafter the United States rushed arms to him, long-barreled rifles originally intended to be sent to Kerensky. The consignment was to help Obregón quash a revolt by ex-President Adolfo de la Huerta. Actually the oil controversy was far from settled and became even more serious after Calles took office in 1924.

Backed by Obregón, the army, and Morones of the CROM, Calles was elected and duly sworn into office in December 1924. He was determined to enforce the church and oil provisions of the constitution.

This powerful iron-jawed man, a former schoolteacher who had organized the workers of Cananea, the copper mines and refinery, was to rule for ten years, six of them through provisional presidents (after Obregón's assassination in 1928) and put his stamp on Mexican affairs more decisively than any previous revolutionary president. He called himself a Socialist; he was already a millionaire general as well as a Socialist. He led the Revolution to its most notable achievements, organized the National Revolutionary party, which still rules the country. He established firm order, which still prevails. And he also led the Revolution to its most ignominious surrenders.

Morones was made minister of labor, and labor membership increased to 2,250,000 by 1927. Morones became the Czar over nearly all commercial life. He waxed fat and wealthy. Diamonds glittered on his fingers. He had fine homes and many automobiles. Woe be it to any employer, and also any workers, who did not bend the knee. Labor gained a bit in wages and some fringe benefits.

Calles' minister of agriculture was the ex-bullfighter Luis León, who flaunted his bedizened mistresses in public cabarets. But by 1928 some 7,500,000 hectares were expropriated and handed over to the villagers. The farmers on the *ejidos* and on small properties were provided with seeds, fertilizers, and tools—though much of these benefits went up in the smoke of graft.

In January 1926 all the archbishops signed a protest against the 1917 constitution, which they claimed wounded the most sacred rights of the church. Plutarco Elías Calles at once accused the hierarchy of treason and deported all foreign priests, closed all church convents and schools. In July he ordered all priests to register with the government, as other professionals had to do. The church went on strike, refusing to perform the usual rites of baptism, confession, consecration, or to deliver any Masses. Vast hysterical crowds gathered to try to obtain last-minute baptisms and confessions and hear the last Mass. People stuck stickers in their windows, "Christ is King." A Cristero revolt broke out in Jalisco and elsewhere. A train to Guadalajara was ambushed, and most of the passengers were killed. All trains thereafter were garrisoned with troops. The government force, under Secretary of War Joaquín Amaro, retaliated with a ruthless scorched-earth policy in northern Jalisco.

The oil controversy moved to a new impasse. Secretary of State Frank B. Kellogg, a shaky man called "Nervous Nellie," whipped up much anti-Mexican sentiment in behalf of the American oil companies against the "Communist" in the Mexican National Palace.

But American sentiment was deeply divided. Calles was canny enough to hire good propagandists on the American scene. It seemed insane to wage a battle simultaneously against two such powerful enemies as the church and the United States government. But thereby he also won allies on the American scene.

The American Protestants and their churches came out strongly on Calles' side in his conflict with the Roman Catholic Church. The ranks of American finance and business were also divided. The bankers were more interested in getting their loan money back than in fighting for the oil companies—the properties chiefly of Doherty, Sinclair, and Mellon interests were involved. Doherty and Sinclair were on the hook for the Teapot Dome scandal, and Senator Albert Fall was being sent to jail for a bribe delivered in a little black bag. Smaller business interests were upset by the bad effects on trade. City councils, chambers of commerce, and other respectable organizations were issuing resolutions and protesting to the United States government. The United States was having plenty of trouble with Sandino in Nicaragua, to whom Calles sent four boatloads of arms, and wild opinion was whipping up against American imperialism and marine intervention. The epithets of Communism hurled against Calles by Kellogg and President Calvin Coolidge scarcely cleared the air. The matter came to a climax when Calles ordered the oil companies to exchange their holdings for fifty-year leases. Pre-1917 holdings were specifically included.

President Calvin Coolidge drew back from the brink and rushed down Dwight W. Morrow of the House of Morgan as ambassador to smooth things out. He moved in with a fanfare of publicity for his ham-and-egg breakfasts with President Calles—a very heartening symptom for the American public if not for Mexicans, who had never enjoyed ham-and-egg breakfasts.

Morrow and Calles hammered out an oil agreement, which pretty well met the Mexican position. If the oil corporations mumbled in their beards, the bankers were pleased by arrangements for the repayment of the Mexican debt. What was more shocking for Mexicans was the agreement to expropriate no more land unless it was paid for in cash, not in bonds. It meant that the land distribution program of Mexico, the main drive of the Revolution, was brought to an almost complete halt. The church question was also settled by secret negotiations in Veracruz. Apparently the Revolution was over, and the twenty years of turmoil had been mostly in vain.

But the United States was uneasy over the threatened return of Obregón to power. He had had the constitution altered to permit his reelection. However, he was assassinated in 1928 by the religious fanatic José Toral, egged on by the mother superior of a clandestine convent and a shadowy priest never apprehended. Toral and the nun were sent to the Islas Marías penal colony off the Pacific Coast for twenty years. They were married there.

After the assassination Calles forced all revolutionary elements into the National Revolutionary party (now the Institutional Revolutionary party), ostensibly representing workers, peasants, and soldiers. However, other parties were not forbidden, thus a pro-Catholic, and Communist, and a Labor party still exist; but the monolithic official organization runs all public affairs, monopolizes nearly all public offices. Actually power has remained largely in the hands of the unruly revolutionary army, though its role has steadily diminished, as gradually the new bourgeois, largely United States influenced, increasingly takes over the state. With the suppression of a short-lived revolt by Saturnino Cedillo, revolutionary general of San Luis Potosí, and the subsequent Escobar revolt after the assassination of Obregón, Mexico has remained largely at peace, until the serious student uprising of 1968.

The Revolution made one last effort. General Lázaro Cárdenas of Michoacán, elected president in 1934, moved boldly to carry out the revolutionary and constitutional principles. He nationalized the oil companies when they refused to abide by a National Labor Board ruling, and put that industry, along with the nationalized railroads, into labor union hands; he pushed the agrarian program rapidly to near completion, distributing some forty million acres—more than had been distributed all told during nine previous administrations.

Fearing new tensions with the United States, Cárdenas transmitted power to the arch-Conservative President Manuel Avila Camacho. Since then the country has moved steadily to the right. The Church has recovered much of its political influence and prosperity. Restrictions on foreign ownership have been set aside or evaded.

Many gains have remained intact. Serfdom and debt slavery have been abolished. Labor has become part of the new oligarchy, retaining many prerogatives, but strikes have been pretty much outlawed, and less amenable labor leaders, such as the heads of the railroad federation, are in the penitentiary, half a dozen with the equivalent of life sentences. A Bastille attempt to free them by the student rioters in September 1968 was averted. Legal university autonomy was brutally violated by the army in the University of Morelia on a flimsy protest, similarly in the north, and the soldiery soon occupied most of the country's higher institutions. The result has been the resignation of university heads and weeks of rioting in the streets, with sniping, tear gas, and deaths, revolt so serious that it has jeopardized the stability of the Díaz Ordaz administration. There are ninety thousand students in Mexico City National University alone, plus even more secondary and vocational school students.

Freedom of assemblage has been curtailed, especially reunions favoring Castro or opposed to American imperialism. Thus far freedom of the press has been pretty well guaranteed, though some arrests of editors have been made, and *Política,* one of the world's great news magazines, was forced out of business by the end of 1967. Today editors, fearing government pressures, are cautious. There are seven thousand magazines and newspapers in Mexico. Most are dependent upon official favors for newsprint. Most are subsidized by this or that ministry. Thirty-five percent of all advertising is paid for by United States corporations. Independent papers find it difficult to survive.

Yet the country has prospered with much new industry and considerable American capital. The native industrial class has expanded, and profits have steadily increased. Mexico City has become a great modern metropolis of four million people, though its slums and shacks have spread out faster than the great new sky-scrapers and apartment dwellings—the story of all Latin America, and of much of the Third World.

Marxists and Leftists today sneer at the 1910–1940 Revolution, even though it definitely altered the structure of Mexican society. There is little argument, if one accepts it as a bourgeois or capitalist welfare revolution. Leadership was largely taken over by the generals, then by the new industrialists and the elite nouveaux riche. Nevertheless it was carried out by the people and provided real gains for the peasants and workers.

Except for a considerable middle-class growth, living conditions have not been vastly improved. Token public housing has been built, but half of all Mexican families—and they are large—live in one room, and 80 percent have no more than two rooms. Stability is threatened by one of the largest population growths in the world. New production scarcely keeps pace. By the end of the century, at the latest, Mexico will have a hundred million people, compared to seventeen million when the Revolution began. Not much additional land can be put under cultivation; hence land distribution, even if carried out once more, cannot meet the problem of providing food for the new cities, let alone the entire population.

Mexico stands at the crossroads. Which will it take? Militarism? Democracy (badly undermined)? Another revolution?

CHAPTER 7

THE OCTOBER REVOLUTION: AN EMPIRE IN CONVULSION

DURING SEPTEMBER AND OCTOBER 1917, Petrograd, capital of all the Russias, was dreary with bitter cold rain driving in across the marshes from the Gulf of Finland. The magnificent city of Peter the Great turned into a slough of mud, and every building was tracked with slime from big boots. Nobody bothered to clean up. The terrible Russian winter was approaching. Already it was dark by three o'clock; gray daylight never showed till ten next morning. There were a few scattered street lights on the main avenues, only from six in the evening to midnight was electricity provided in homes. The Kerensky provisional government, which had taken over soon after the czar's downfall the previous March ("the February Revolution"), was too pinched for fuel, and it feared German Zeppelin raids. Municipal services had broken down, and the streets were piled with garbage that stank in spite of the cold. It was a pre-epileptic Dostoyevsky nightmare.

It was a dangerous filthy city now, full of reckless starving people, prowling the black streets for food, ready to steal, mug, or murder. Its population of nearly 2,500,000 had been augmented by 200,000 deserters from the front lines of a mismanaged war now collapsing, who slept ragged, cold, and famished, in the squares and streets. Sullen, drunk, brawling, threatening, they fought for every crust, and apartment dwellers were obliged to stand guard every night with loaded rifles. The mild-mannered unarmed city militia, which had replaced the czar's ruthless Gorodoveye as police, were unable to cope with the robbery and thuggery. Occasionally a crowd—there were always aimless half-dazed crowds—caught some thief and stamped him to death.

In the daytime the war derelicts sat in solid rows—hearts thirsting for vengeance and peace, stomachs hungering for bread—along the broad Nevsky Prospect, from the massive Admiralty on the Neva to the vast Aleksandr Nevsky Monastery on the inner Neva. They squatted there in the shadow of Romanov splendors: impressive banks, insurance offices, and fashionable apartments, the great Kazan cathedral with its replica of St. Peter's colonnade and its Florentine Ghiberti portals, the municipal Duma beyond the Stone Bridge and opposite St. Catherine's, the magnificent Yeliseieff Palace facing the Moika Canal (an exclusive club for the nobility), the florid Stroganoff Palace, and other regal residences of the grand dukes and lordly merchant-traders who long ago had carved dominion and wealth out of the swamps and black forests. Here movies, theaters, cafés, fine restaurants, somehow still flourished. The war outcasts brooded in the thick moving mist and sold contraband weapons, toys, knickknacks, cigarettes, propaganda leaflets, sunflower seeds, and old rags.

In narrow Znamenskaya Square, farther out in front of the main railroad station, there was always mad chaos: swarms meeting returning loved ones or fighting tooth and nail to board trains, soldiers moving out grimly, often not knowing to where, deserters flocking in. The jammed mass was repeatedly crushed against the wall, then bounced back like a released squeezed sponge to shatter in deafening din upon the tangle of carts, vans, and decrepit tramcars in front of Trubetskoi's brutal statue of Alexander III, reminder of the Romanov dynasty that had ruled Russia with Byzantine splendor for four hundred, bloody, cruel years—a regime now swept away forever in reckless war, defeat, and chaos.

Other deserters and smeary urchins peddled newspapers—the Bolshevik *Rabotchi Put*, the Menshevik *Dien*, the reactionary *Russkaya Volia*—along the Fontanka Canal Bridge or the Liteyna Prospect intersection, shouting out government edicts, counterproclamations of the Soviet Military Revolutionary Committee, of the municipal Duma. The military commandant periodically threatened to round up all deserters and ship them back to the front—something everybody realized couldn't possibly be done. The renegades knew all about fighting and death now—nor would the soldier Soviets permit it, nor would the twenty-five thousand restless sailors of the Baltic Fleet at Kronstadt fortress on nearby Kotlin Island. The entire Petrograd garrison of sixty thousand men now leaned toward the Bolsheviks, and Kerensky could count on only twenty thousand armed cadets (Constitutional Democrats) and fierce cossacks—not that they loved the young radical lawyer from the Lena, but they despised and feared the Bolsheviks. Growing desperate now, Kerensky was bringing in "Czarist" Yunker regiments and elite students from the war colleges, in the hope of restoring the balance of power and shoring up his crumbling position. The hungry shivering city sank deeper into lawlessness and hopelessness.

Regular residents, though housed better than the deserters, found life well-nigh impossible. Even at bandit prices, there was little kerosene for cooking, heating, or lamps, and candles cost forty cents apiece. A load of wood cost two weeks' wages. The daily bread ration—some weeks there was none—was down to four ounces. Sugar was as precious as diamonds, and a pound of tasteless candy cost considerably more than a day's wages. Coffee sold for thirteen rubles a pound. To buy each item, it was necessary to stand in line for hours, in the incessant rain (later in the snow). People spent the better part of each day, from before dawn on into the afternoon, in this frustrating fashion, shivering in thin clothes, often coatless, many with feet wrapped in dirty wet rags or burlap. A pair of shoes cost three months' wages.

Such was the deplorable state of the capital of all the Russias seven months after the February Revolution, born of a swift hour of terrible defeat and slaughter. This was the great millennium that generations of martyrs, poets, musicians, and writers had dreamed about. Millions upon millions of people were nearly breadless, and the fifteen million soldiers along a thousand miles of icy front were rarely supplied.

Yet the dark shivering city was not without gaiety. The well-to-do could patronize the *maradiors*, or "ghouls," who were still speculating, profiteering, and black-marketeering. Corruption had reached plague proportions under the czar, when many officers were in the pay of the German enemy, and whole divisions had been sent out to fight without food or shoes or guns. Under Kerensky the cancer had spread.

The czar had been weak and vacillating. He had been kept in place toward the end solely by the nobility and tradition, not because of his talents. The czarina was hysterical and superstitious. Both were under the sinister spell of the black monk Grigori Efirnovich Rasputin, a lewd, illiterate, cunning peasant. Several nobles finally assassinated him.

A wild February surge of workers, led by the cadets, and the Social Democrats, had forced the czar to abdicate. The Duma, still clad in uniforms obligatory under the czar, took over supreme power. Food depots were raided. The speculators, thriving and enjoying themselves, shouted loudly, whenever army deserters raided a food warehouse, that the soldiers, millions of whom had perished, were "cowards and traitors" or "robbers."

The moderate Pavel Nikolayevich Miliukov, cadet leader—a group which Trotsky called "sober-minded political champions of capitalism—" had been too radical for the British foreign office. Aleksandr Feodorovich Kerensky, more radical, soon took over. The old vices flourished even more. Gambling casinos were jammed from dark till dawn, stakes often running to twenty thousand rubles. Never so many prostitutes paraded the Nevsky, Gorokhavaya, and Voznyesenski Prospects, or around the dark red Winter Palace and the dark red general headquarters beyond its imperial victory arch. Girls swarmed in every café, with furs and glittering jewelry, not all of it false, some of it perhaps from rich bourgeois homes, looted when owners had been hauled in for sundry crimes against the Revolution.

In spite of the trouble and uncertainty, there were still numerous splendid balls and dinners. Social life continued much as always. The ladies still held simpering afternoon teaparties, though guests now brought their own sugar in little bejeweled gold boxes and half loaves tucked in their muffs. The movies were always full, an occasional British or American film, but mostly Italian cloak-and-dagger melodramas of elegant lords and ladies and adoring serfs, strange diet for a land shaken with revolutionary turmoil. Theaters, too, were going every night, including Sundays. Karsavina was appearing in a ballet at the Marinski, and people would go hungry to see her dance or hear Chaliapin sing. At the Alexandrinsky, the palatial theater on the Nevsky Prospect—where the out-front statue of Catherine the Great now held a little red flag in her hand—Vsevolod Emilievich Meyerhold's production of Count Aleksei Konstantinovich Tolstoy's *Death of Ivan the Terrible* had been revived. The Krivoye Zerkalo was staging a lavish version of Arthur Schnitzler's *Reigen.* At the Troitsky Farce Theater, angry monarchists broke up the burlesque *Sins of the Czars.*

The contents of museums had been shipped to Moscow cellars for safety, but the galleries staged many exhibits. There were many lectures on art, literature, music, philosophy. Above all, a fever of talk, for many people had not dared be free with their tongues under the czars; all Russia had suddenly turned into a lashing sea of babbling tongues—debates, speeches, harangues, day and night—on street corners, in cafés, factories, clubs, schools, union headquarters, and barracks, often around great caldrons of cabbage soup, *kashka,* black bread, and five-kopek tin cups of hot tea. Every night on the banks of the Fontanka the enormous gloomy Cirque Moderne amphitheater, lit only by half a dozen naked bulbs, each on a single wire, was packed with soldiers, sailors, and workmen listening to firebrands, sometimes as many as ten thousand of them. No other language has such rhetorical magnificence as Russian, and the sonorous periods rolled forth in endless exhortation everywhere. Ideas bubbled, fermented, steamed, exploded—as the country marched, or rather jerked and plunged, toward a new destiny.

Scores of little newspapers had sprung up in every town and city to voice the creeds of as many factions. Millions of pamphlets spewed forth. Never had there been greater demand for books, even though most of the population was illiterate—mostly good books, on economics, politics, world affairs, philosophy, biology; the writings of Gogol, Tolstoy, Turgenev, Dostoyevsky, and Gorky. All Russian culture had joined the revolutionary torrent.

Many new reprints and pamphlets came from Smolny Institute, the former Taurida Palace. This vast edifice, with smoke blue, gold-rimmed cupolas, on the wide Neva at the eastern edge of the city, had been the elite convent school of the czarina, but was now headquarters for the Tsay-ee-Kah, the central executive committee of the all-Russian Congress of Soviets, the elected people's parliament, made up of nearly a thousand feuding delegates. Here were the executive committees of government coalition parties, also of the nongovernment Bolsheviks; of soldiers, sailors, trade unionists, and peasants. Here tons of pamphlets and books were printed and sent forth—whole trainloads every day, though rolling stock could not be found to send food and clothing to the front. Little food or clothing was available anyway.

In the face of swelling clamor for peace, Kerensky—originally a

Duma member for the Populist Socialists (*Trudoviki*), a minuscule nationalistic group of small shopkeepers, teachers, and kulaks—was struggling to keep Russia fighting, striving to please the western Allies from whom he was receiving money and arms. Arms were being hurriedly manufactured for him in the United States, where the Revolution had sent chills down spines, lest Russia be rendered *hors de combat* and the war would therefore become a long-drawn-out agony, victory uncertain. Yet to keep Russia in fighting trim was an incredible hope, based on Allied ignorance and on Kerensky's own poor measurement of the Russian temper. The front-line soldiers had had little equipment to begin with, and for them the war was little more than a ghastly rout. The country was bleeding from all its pores. In the Ukraine, nationalist bourgeois groups had set up an independent counterrevolutionary government. Kerensky had managed to separate only five districts from its control.

Though he was strongly backed by the Oborontsi—all the bickering moderate socialist groups—he was being crushed between extremes. The bourgeoisie and aristocracy shuddered at the slightest reform and prayed for German invasion, while the Bolsheviks demanded immediate cessation of hostilities, full socialization of the land and factories. Kerensky vacillated between reform and repression. He had crushed a fruitless police-provoked attack on Taurida (Smolny) Palace, led by the Bolsheviks, in July. Most of the leaders were in jail in the Kresty or in the Fortress of St. Peter and St. Paul (Leon Trotsky, Madame Aleksandra Mikhailovna Kollontai, Lev Borisovich Kamenev) or in hiding (Lenin, Grigori Evseyevich Zinoviev).

On July 18 the bicycle battalion Kerensky had brought into the city had sacked Mlle. Kshesinskaya's palace, which had belonged to the dancer who had been a mistress of Czar Nicholas II, but which was being used by the military organization of the Bolsheviks.

At the same time Kerensky had stopped land distribution to the extent possible and tried, without much success, to throw the peasants off the estates they were seizing through all Russia. Meanwhile the war front was crumbling. His shaky coalition of Socialists, cadets, bankers, merchants, and manufacturers was confused and faltering, angry, bitter, impotent, and quarrelsome toward each other. They only succeeded, wrote Trotsky in his *The Russian Revolution* in making the confusion "worse compounded." On July 17 Kerensky

[*130*]

brought in "trustworthy" troops, the Volhinya Guards. But in November they marched at the head of the revolutionary anti-Kerensky forces with banners proclaiming, "All Power to the Soviets."

In September General Lavra Georgyevich Kornilov, son of a Siberian cossack, and Kerensky's supreme commander, led his fanatically loyal "Savage Division" of Tekke Muhammadan tribesmen from Central Asia and other regiments on Petrograd to take over the country and continue the war, a "rightist" military putsch secretly abetted by several of Kerensky's own cabinet ministers, particularly the Socialist B. V. Savinkof and the cossack A. M. Kaledin—as Trotsky put it, soaping the rope to tie a knot about the throat of the Revolution.

Only yesterday—in February—the cadets had led the people to overthrow the czar, now they were asking the cossacks to put down the people.

In the shadows of the Kornilov putsch were the czar's dreaded Okhrana secret agents, willing now to commit any crime for pay, and the footpad "Black Hundred"—nationalists, scheming in every sewer and in the richest dwellings against the provisional government, striking in the dark with kidnappings and assassinations. This group of reactionary terrorists had originally been created in 1905 by the czarist secret police, utilizing criminals and outlaws. For a time these terrorists published *Zhivoye Slovo*, edited by A. M. Umanski. They more or less followed the line of strong government and the extreme right, known as the Defensists, or Prizyov party. Presumably they were financed by St. Petersburg bankers and industrialists. As Lenin put it in his October 29–30 Letter, the Black Hundred crew was a branch firm of P. P. Ryabushinsky, Pavel Miliukov, and company. Ryabushinsky was one of Moscow's wealthiest businessmen and industrialists. However the chief leader, G. G. Zamyslovsky was a furibund anti-Semite. He was a plaintiff in czarist days in a notorious suit to prohibit the Jews from using Christian blood for ritual purposes. He was also a member of the third and fourth Duma, or parliament, under the czar.

The reactionary threats brought the quarreling Tsay-ee-Kah factions of the elected people's parliament together in a panic of desperate defense. The Bolshevik leaders were released from prison to help fight the menace. They came out of jail and hiding as heroes and prophets—though Lenin, taking no chances, fled to Finland and on his return hid out in the Wiborg factory district, wearing workman's clothes and an absurd wig as a disguise. The Petrograd garrison was determined to stop Kornilov and his "savages."

The showdown never came. The general was suddenly arrested by the soldiers' committee of one of his regiments. He escaped and later led the first White army in the south. Conservatives sneered that the whole business was a phantom revolt, a figment of Kerensky's febrile imagination, a ruse to buttress up his shaky position.

But his headaches multiplied. The frightened Tsay-ee-Kah demanded immediate reconstruction of his government. He fought this, formed a new coalition, including the cadets, but as evidence of their pro-Kornilov treacheries piled up, he dismissed all rightists, making no replacements, and governed with only five ministers.

The "Dogs' Deputies," the Bolsheviks, won sweeping control of the all-Petrograd Soviet, and dark, bitter, relentless Bronstein (Trotsky) became its president. Similar Bolshevik successes were chalked up in elections in Moscow, Kiev, Odessa, and other cities and towns. Where they did not win, they set up rump soviets. Revolutionary passion was rising faster than the leaders could lead. Only Lenin and Trotsky, the steel-hard Bolsheviks, rode the full tide and prepared to strike with the hot blade of the aroused people.

Stalin, editing *Pravda,* till Kerensky suppressed it, also Zinoviev and Kamenev, dragged their feet, temporizing. But Trotsky's vibrant oratory and Lenin's knifelike sarcasm struck down all opposition in the Petrograd Soviet and in the party executive committee. Lenin flayed Stalin, and the future dictator quickly changed his tune. For a time Zinoviev and Kamenev were isolated in the party councils. Lenin and Trotsky forged their group into a unified striking force. The Tsay-ee-Kah suddenly discovered they feared Lenin worse than a Kornilov.

Ignoring the Tsay-ee-Kah, the Bolsheviks boldly called for a new all-Russian Congress of Soviets to meet in Petrograd on November 2, that is to say, October 20 by the unreformed Julian calendar then still in use in Russia, instead of the later Gregorian calendar adopted by England and the American colonies in 1752. The opening was later put off to November 7 (October 25).

"We will no longer participate in a government of treason to the people," shouted Trotsky, and the Bolshevik representatives at Lenin's insistence withdrew from Kerensky's Council of the Republic, already sharply split into irreconcilable factions, snapping at each other in savage differences of theory and methods. Soon the Bolshevik delegates left the municipal Duma also.

The Bolshevik leaders raced from factory to factory, staging impromptu rallies: Kamenev, a little man with a pointed red beard and Gallic gestures, shouted, "The Provisional government must resign. Only the Soviets can rule." At the unfinished government munitions factory on the Schlüsselburg Prospekt, slender Anatoli Lunacharsky, with his sensitive artist's face—he was a playwright—called out to ten thousand black-clad workmen, from his high perch on a red-draped scaffolding among the picked guards under a dark windy sky, "The enemy is betraying the revolution, ruining the country and the army, paving the way for another Kornilov."

G. T. Petrovsky, a Ukraninian, slow-voiced, relentless, answered, "If they dare lay their hands upon the organizations of the proletariat, we will sweep them away like scum from the face of the earth."

Soldier and sailor orators exhorted the monster meeting of workers and peasants and soldiers to move forward shoulder to shoulder. Many were now as hungry as the deserters, for factory after factory was closing doors for lack of materials—or was deliberately shut down, some claimed, by provocateurs.

"All power to the Soviets" was the new rallying cry. Constant consultations were held with N. V Krylenko, a squat, tartar-faced soldier always smiling; with F. M. Dybenko, the blond, bearded giant with candid blue eyes and almost infantile countenance, leader of the Kronstadt sailors' Soviet, whom Madame Kollontai loved for his transparent eyes and smooth cruelty. In rooms 10 and 18 at Smolny, the Bolshevik councils and committees maintained round-the-clock activity. The Petrograd Soviet and its Military Revolutionary Committee, planning insurrection, were in constant session. Propaganda was intensified—millions of pamphlets, speeches, even appeals to the cossacks to join their brothers, the people.

Peace! Land for the peasants! Factories to the workers! *At once.* "At once"—that was the rub. Other leftist factions favored these proposals, but said that the economic ruin of such a sudden transition would lay Russia wide open to German invasion.

Already Bolshevik M. I. Skobeliev had drawn up his famous *nakaz*, or peace demands on the Allies, which had sent a shiver of ice through the chancelleries of Paris, London, and Washington.

The Bolshevik leaders were hotly denounced by Kerensky and by the Conservative prime minister—Bonar Law—of England where the king was parleying with the exiled head of the czar's general staff, whose gross incompetence had already cost the lives of so many million Russians.

At the same time word seeped through to Petrograd of a secret peace parley in Bern, Switzerland, of the Allies with the Germans and Austrians to make peace behind Russia's back. News came from France that, at the behest of czarist officers, artillery and machine guns had been turned on ten thousand encamped Russian soldiers sent there by the czar, because they were setting up soldiers' committees. Of those who surrendered, two hundred were executed in cold blood. Such things were not known in the censored press of the West, but they became known in Russia. "The smoke of our revolutionary conflagration makes the eyes of our Allies smart," said the conservative paper *Novoye Vremya*.

The Russian clamor for peace and the hostile attitude of the Allied press, damning Russia for the inadequacy of her war effort, got under Kerensky's skin. In a press interview he burst out: "The Allies ask why the Russians have stopped fighting. . . . Where was the Balkan fleet when German battle-ships attacked us in the Gulf of Riga? . . . Why aren't the Russians fighting? . . . Because the masses of the people . . . are exhausted, and because they are disillusioned with the Allies." It hit the Russian papers, but was suppressed by the United States State Department.

In Russia the great ground swell was cracking the crust everywhere. Along the thousand-mile front, millions of miserable soldiers talked of nothing but peace. Everywhere the officers were prisoners of soldiers' committees, kept on tap merely for technical help in battle. But more and more officers were being murdered by their own soldiers. Their committees sent back anguished appeals: "Comrades! We are starving here at the front; we are stiff with cold. We are dying for no reason!" Great tides of deserters moved across the face of the land, hungry, demanding, menacing—"voting with their feet," as Lenin put it. More deserters streamed into overcrowded Petrograd, shouting, "Peace! Peace!" Several hundred people stamped a soldier to death for stealing bread. But, every side street off the main avenues was unsafe.

More and more peasants were burning manors, killing landlords, seizing land. Spontaneous strikes broke out; Moscow and Odessa were convulsed. Transportation was shattered, cutting off bread to the urban masses. Cossacks slaughtered striking miners in the Donetz Basin—thirty thousand were out—but got no coal mined. Cossacks and the elite Yunkers, the student officers corps, slaughtered town soviets en masse, and more towns turned pro-Bolshevik. Official and military terror was digging its own grave—rapidly.

At Smolny Institute, the "dark people," the underdogs, during late October converged for the forthcoming all-Russian Soviet congress to open, it was believed, on November 7, and boiled about waiting for the seventh—burly bearded soldiers, sea-rolling sailors, workers in black blouses, long-bearded peasants. They jammed into the big downstairs refectory to attack caldrons of steaming cabbage soup with greasy wooden spoons and snatched up propaganda leaflets from the long tables. At night it was necessary to step over long rows of them sleeping in the corridors, snoring in spite of the constant thunder of soldiers' and sailors' boots along the wooden floors, or the roar of victory from the all-night sessions of the Petrograd Soviet, presided over by Trotsky, or the brawling roar from the meetings of the bewildered Tsay-ee-Kah, where the parties bickered over the insistent demands of the Bolsheviks for peace and land for the peasants. The impending new all-Russian Congress of Soviets, likely to be dominated by the Bolsheviks, hung over them, over the Kerensky government, over all the land, like a black lightning-rent cloud.

On November 3 the Bolshevik Central Committee met behind closed doors. Lenin, still wearing his workman's clothes and wig, moving his delicate hands like a cat's tail, called for the overthrow of Kerensky and the setting up of a workers' and peasants' revolutionary government. Trotsky, tearing himself from his duties with the Petrograd Soviet, wagged his sharp beard, fire in his dark eyes. Both argued for insurrection *now*—to be timed for the all-Russian Congress of Soviets. They must present the congress with a fait accompli, for the Bolsheviks might not even have a majority. Zinoviev and Kamenev again argued against any insurrection. Worker and soldier delegates grew red-faced, demanding no delay. Madame Kollontai—slim, dark, attractive, an ardent theoretical, and sometimes not so theoretical, advocate of free love, whose only true love was the Revolution—seconded them in a passionate speech. Stalin, sniffing the wind direction of the brush fire—he never openly op-posed Lenin—said, "Unless we act, the counter-reaction will. The time is ripe."

Though Lenin and Trotsky stood shoulder to shoulder, Lenin usu-ally harped on broader strategy; Trotsky was, for the moment, more concerned with immediate tactics. In the October issue of *Prosvesh-cheniye* (*Education*) Lenin quoted a long paragraph from Marx about the French disturbances of 1848, "Never play with insurrec-tion unless you are fully prepared to face the consequences of your play. . . . The forces against you will have all the advantages of or-ganization, discipline and habitual authority." Once started, the in-surrection should take the offensive. "The defensive is the death of every armed uprising." Daily successes were essential. Vacillating elements would always look for the safer side. "In the words of Dan-ton, the greatest master of revolutionary policy yet known, 'Bold-ness, again boldness, and always boldness.' "

The article began with the statement that actually the impending Soviet revolution had nothing to learn from the French Revolution:

The guillotine only frightened, only crushed active resistance. For us that is not enough. The Soviets have to crush not only *active* resistance but also *passive* resistance which is more dangerous and harmful. This has to be done by putting the capitalists into new state services. Poor families would oust them from their palaces. By universal bread cards, the Bolsheviks would establish the rule "He who works not, neither shall he eat."

Trotsky especially was aware that a general strike at this juncture might be unfavorable for the Bolsheviks, for the party did not con-trol the central labor committees, only shop committees. In any case, as a coup it might hamper revolutionary mobility as much as that of government forces. The leaders of the railroad employees and the telegraph operators, the most strategic of all, were dead against the Bolsheviks. As for a mass uprising, the people would merely be exposed to slaughter by the cadets and cossacks, of whom Kerensky now had twenty thousand in the city. The tactic had to be that of quick daring with well-planned insurrection, swift blows by small groups of experts and trained men.

As early as October 15, 1917, Lenin had set November 7 as the last feasible day for the insurrection to achieve, "All Power to the Soviets." On October 21 he called for the recall of all Bolshevik members from Kerensky's pre-parliament, an effort to forestall the power of the Soviet. To participate, he had insisted all along, had been an error. "Don't hang on to the coattails of the conciliators. Go into the streets for the struggle for power."

In a letter to I. T. Smilga of the Central Committee on October 10 Lenin talked of bringing in forces from the Finnish front. "There's no need to retire to the Gulf of Finland," insisted Trotsky, "merely to march back and take objectives in the city." Technical experts were required to start a revolution—here he saw eye to eye with Lenin, and was merely implementing Lenin's earlier suggestions. The secret was to operate in a small space with small trained groups of militant workers and technicians to isolate and paralyze the government and its forces—a minimum of head-on fighting. The city should retain outward normality; people should go about their ordinary business, to the factories, cafés, restaurants, theaters, as on every other day. Capture the state; the government would be severed from its body.

Once Trotsky pointed at the reeling mishmash deserters and pedestrians, the snarled traffic along the cobbled muddy streets, the people hanging to the lumbering old steam tramcars, sides and rear, like Spanish moss. "There is our general strike. There is our mass uprising. Our best ally is the chaos and confusion that already exist in the city," Curzio Malaparte, the Italian poet and Fascist, reported him as saying. In his brilliant but superficial *Coup d'Etat: The Technique of Revolution*, Malaparte, being chiefly interested in the overthrow of government by a surprised military stroke, cooks up a radical difference of viewpoint between Trotsky and Lenin. Apparently he neglected to read Lenin's exhortations all through October, his insistence on the seizure of strategic points, which he named. Trotsky, with help from a former czarist officer, was merely the one who worked out the details and actual organization for the quick blow of November 7, but in every respect it corresponded to Lenin's suggestions. Lenin's over-all plan was far more grandiose, and he favored a mass uprising, which, of course, eventually came once Petrograd was taken.

Using his fertile imagination, Malaparte goes on to say that Lenin regarded Trotsky thoughtfully—this Semitic Trotsky, a former Menshevik and latecomer to the Bolshevik ranks, who had become overnight the most passionate and daring of them all. "I am not of the Twelve," Trotsky had said once, when a jealous comrade had taunted him about his belated turncoat fervor. "I am more like St. Paul who was the first to preach to the Gentiles."

Lenin, according to Malaparte, was anxious to arrest Kerensky. "Kerensky," Trotsky snapped his long fingers disdainfully. "Why bother, just take away his pants."

Lenin may have remembered a taunt flung at Trotsky a few days before in the Petrograd Soviet by one of the Mensheviks, when Trotsky had been advocating death for the bourgeois and all the Kerensky traitors. "The guillotine leads to Napoleon." Trotsky had snapped back, "I prefer Napoleon to Kerensky." Lenin was a phenomenal judge of men, their strength, weakness, usefulness, their value and danger to the cause, and perhaps at this moment he was thinking—as later Felix Edmundovich Dzerzhinsky, Stalin's hangman, said openly—"Trotsky loves Napoleon more than Lenin." Perhaps Lenin, with the destiny of his party on the razor's edge of victory or ignominy, foresaw this dark, sharp hero of the hour as the future creator of the new Red army. Would that lead him, like Napoleon, to march across the face of Europe—to world revolution? A military affirmation of the new proletarian Russia, a Russia now prostrate and bleeding but ere long to be the powerful Russia of tomorrow? There is no proof Lenin was thinking any such thoughts of Caesarism, though he looked forward to worldwide revolution.

Actually the man who did the most to implement the basic ideas of insurrection held by Lenin and Trotsky was the brilliant, ever-smiling V. A. Antonov-Ovsyenko, secretary of the Petrograd Revolutionary Committee, a former czarist officer turned revolutionary and exiled by the czar, now returned. His collar was usually dirty, his face unshaven, his long hair in a tangle to his shoulders. His faded blue eyes seemed lifeless; he had a thin unhealthy face, but he had a tremendous analytical mind, was a fine mathematician and an expert chess player, and a passionate fire drove him to tireless Herculean effort. Day and night, in a little room above party headquarters, he pored over maps and blueprints of Petrograd and its services, working out objectives for small numbered units. He divided the city into districts (*raions*), each to be isolated and controlled by seizure of strategic points. Post and telegraph offices, power plants, bridges, and railway stations were to be taken over promptly.

A thousand workers, sailors, and soldiers—workers from the Putilov and Vilborg factories, sailors from the Baltic fleet, and soldiers from the Latvian regiments—were carefully screened and selected to be trained. Antonov-Ovsyenko ordered them out in broad daylight to practice revolutionary exercises; little unarmed groups sauntered into post offices, barracks, and across bridges, where they sized up how best to handle the soldiers on guard when the hour struck. Smooth rehearsals were staged at the post office on Ulitza Swayazi and at the Moscow terminal halfway out the Nevsky Prospect. In spite of the hostility of the leaders of the trainmen and telegraphists, much of the rank and file had lined up with the Bolsheviks, and trained experts were recruited to accompany the designated units and to control all train movements and operate the telegraph system once it was in the control of the revolutionaries. Plans were made for the seizure of railroad stations in Petrograd, Moscow, Warsaw, and in between. F. M. Dybenko head of the sailors' Soviet, selected members who, with engineers and engineroom workers, mastered the network of underground water and gas mains, the electrical power and telegraph system, all the trunk and local lines. They even explored the drains under general headquarters. If necessary the whole general staff could be blown to kingdom come. All this was merely a detailed elaboration of Lenin's statement early in October.

Publicly Trotsky, though knowing every detail of Antonov-Ovsyenko's plan and the date for the general assault, kept vehemently denying up to the very hour of the strike that any *vystoplenne* (insurrection) was being planned. He said that such talk was merely a dirty attempt by the reactionaries to wreck the forthcoming all-Russian Congress of the Soviets. *They* were the ones planning a coup. Had not the cadet General N. N. Dukhonin called for a restoration of the monarchy? The counterrevolutionists were hatching their conspiracy right in Kerensky's Council of the Republic. It would be a failure, for the government had lost all authority and strength; it was powerless. And such a betrayal of the people would be the *lutte finale* (last fight) for Kerensky, since the Soviet now had the loyalty of most soldiers, sailors, workers, and peasants.

Things moved toward crisis as early as October 30, when the Petrograd garrison (sixty thousand troops) refused to take orders any longer from the provisional government, only from the Petrograd Soviet via its Military Revolutionary Committee, set up the day before as a result of a decision of the Bolshevik party's Central Committee meeting secretly on October 28, at which Lenin and Trotsky had been present. There was reiterated the resolution of early

October for insurrection as soon as possible, the only dissenters then and afterwards being Lev Berisovich Kamenev and Grigori Evseyevich Zinoviev. The Petrograd Military Revolutionary Committee was to gain enormous power and become the instrument of the entire revolt. On receiving word of adherence from the Petrograd troops, it sent commissars to all sections of the forces to prepare and coordinate future action. Trotsky ordered the workers of the Sestroretsky small arms factory to issue five thousand rifles to the Red Guard. The order created panic in government and reactionary circles. Maxim Gorky in his paper *Novaya Zhizn* (*New Life*) prophesied the collapse of all cultural life and talked gloomily of the approaching end of the world.

Kerensky thundered brimstone and fire but invited representatives of the Petrograd garrisons to join his general staff. This suggestion was set aside by Kerensky's own minister of war. Red soldiers were then instructed by the Bolsheviks to seize arms and ammunition at the major Kronversk arsenal. The adhesion of the Petrograd soldiers, who were resisting Kerensky's efforts to send them off to the front, sealed Kerensky's fate, Trotsky later said in *Lessons of October*. The more dramatic events of November 7 were mere mopping-up formalities. The battle was already won.

Already the government was "hanging in the air, no firm ground under its feet." Smelling disaster, Kerensky resorted to classic police power methods. He ordered elite Yunkers to guard the edge of the city and concentrated on protection of government buildings and the government personnel. These were not the initial Bolshevik objectives, which aimed to bypass the police power, so that his defense of them merely furthered the Antonov-Ovsyenko–Trotsky plans.

At the important Marinsky Palace on the Moika Canal (where the Council of the Republic—the pre-parliament—sat) Kerensky's cossacks now paced with their tall black *chapkas* rakishly tilted over one ear. At the Winter Palace, cadets in long green coats were lined up at the main entrance behind machine guns and two 75-centimeter guns. Inside a large Yunker detachment planted machine guns on the sills. In the rear, inside the Neva River entrance, a fanatic death battalion of women, pledged to give their lives to Kerensky, was bivouacked. Other guards were placed around the municipal Duma at 33 Nevsky Prospect, about general headquarters and its great triumphal Roman arch, and about Taurida Palace, not far from Smolny itself, all defending places the Bolsheviks had no intention of attacking first. The city militia blossomed out with pistols in bright new holsters, and mounted cossacks patrolled the main streets. Armored cars nosed slowly up and down the Nevsky through the milling crowds, sirens blaring. On November 4 martial law was declared. But in the *Rabotchi Put,* early in November, Lenin again wrote boldly, "All Power to the Soviets or an uprising. There is no middle course."

A few days later Trotsky went to speak at an open-air meeting of the Semyonovsky regiment, considered the chief support of the Kerensky government. They listened to Trotsky, and shouted down Kerensky's ministers, who also came to talk to them, and declared themselves for the Revolution. On November 5 Trotsky went to a meeting in the Modern Circus of the Cyclist Regiment of the Fortress of St. Peter and St. Paul. Five months earlier it had attacked the Bolshevik headquarters. Now with only thirty dissenting votes, it declared in favor of the assumption of authority by the Soviets. Other cyclists, called hurriedly to Petrograd by Kerensky, sent representatives to interview the Petrograd Soviet, then came over to the side of the Bolsheviks. These were not isolated examples.

In the Council of the Republic in chill unheated Marinsky Palace, Kerensky delivered long eloquent addresses, defending his war policy, demanding economic recovery, denouncing the Bolsheviks bitterly. At one point he shouted, "I am a doomed man," and wept; then in a flaming diatribe he said he would never give in to the hated Bolsheviks.

On November 5 the pre-parliament debated foreign policy. The rows of Bolshevik seats—some fifty members—had been empty for days, but all foreign diplomats, except those from Italy, were present. Kerensky's war minister was hissed, for some factions had come around to the Bolshevik peace position. Delegates from front-line regiments were bringing back word that if decisive steps for peace had not been taken by November 15, the whole army would leave their trenches and march to the rear.

As recriminations were tossed back and forth, two more companies of long-coated Yunkers swept down the Morskaya, singing their crashing czarist chorus in the damp bitter wind. Still bigger forces of militia were deployed.

In the stale twilight, news vendors hawked papers, which the milling crowds snatched for anxiously. Whole brigades of paste-pot men were slapping up fresh posters on the walls: appeals, threats, diatribes; proclamations from the government, the Tsay-ee-Kah, the Socialist parties, the Duma, the army commander, the peasant and trade-unionist groups. "Support the government!" "Down with the government!" "All Power to the Soviets!" Everywhere groups were arguing, debating, occasionally fighting. The crowds flowed on and on into the night.

The next night, November 6, the insurrection would occur. Lenin had sent final word. To wait even another day, he insisted, would bring disaster. Only the select few of the Bolshevik party knew the actual plans or the date; only the Petrograd Revolutionary Military Committee, and the chosen squadrons. But this night and all day on the morrow, the circle of those in the know would widen, as additional forces were called upon.

A last meeting to go over the plans. Antonov-Ovsyenko reeled in dizziness from lack of sleep, but his head was like a buzz saw. Present were Krylenko, smiling flat-faced as usual; Dybenko, combing his big blond beard. Posters and communiques were ready. The pro-Soviet garrisons were instructed to mobilize in the barracks for orders. Factory shop committees had been called to meet at midnight. The head of the Factory Shop Committee was handing out orders to forty delegates (and more would come) for 150 rifles for each Bolshevik-controlled factory. Some factories, on their own initiative, already had stacked-up piles of rifles. Messengers and couriers waited to carry instructions across the city to shock troops, trusted garrisons, and factories—each message a call to life or death combat. Toward midnight the Smolny Guards, now wholly Bolshevik, were strengthened, and additional machine-guns were planted at the doors. Strong contingents guarded the inner and outer gates, and patrolled nearby street corners. The gun carriages could be heard rumbling. It had become a fortress.

In another room Trotsky was addressing the Petrograd Soviet, which had been holding day and night sessions. He and Kamenev, V. Volodarsky, and others sometimes spoke eight hours at a stretch. The place was dense with cigarette smoke and the smell of bodies. Now and then someone would shout, "No smoking!" pointing at the signs, and the delegates would roar out, "No smoking"—and keep right on smoking. Sometimes they would drop on the floor for sleep, then suddenly stand up and again join in the discussions and the cheering. Trotsky, fresh from the secret planning, once more denied vehemently that no *vystoplenne* would occur unless the government interfered with the all-Russian congress of the Soviets.

Toward midnight a messenger appeared with word that the Fortress of St. Peter and St. Paul had run up the Red flag. Another brought word that a regiment of troops being brought in by Kerensky had stopped the train, shouting, "All Power to the Soviets."

Kerensky ordered all soldiers except cadets and cossacks to their barracks, threatening courts-martial. A company of Yunker artillery jingled under the Arch of Triumph to the general staff building. He appeared again before the pre-parliament of the republic in Marinsky Palace and delivered a long, almost incoherent speech, denouncing the incendiary speeches of Bronstein-Trotsky and attacking Lenin, "He is a state criminal whom we are trying to find."

At that moment Lenin, still using his disguise and muffled in a greatcoat, shuffled into Smolny in heavy workman's shoes. Even inside, he kept on his wig.

Over at the Marinsky Palace, Kerensky continued his passionate address. A copy of the Petrograd Soviet's order for the soldiers to be ready, mobilized in their barracks, was thrust into his hands. It was almost his own decree. "Treason!" he screamed, reported John Reed, American journalist, "An attempt to raise the populace against the existing order. . . . Those . . . who dare lift their hands against the free will of the Russian people," are betraying the war and "must be liquidated." He stepped down, pale, wringing with sweat, and swept out with his retinue of long-coated officers.

But his tearful oratory—and next to Trotsky he was the most eloquent man in Russia—fell on a frightened, divided assemblage. From the center to the left a roar rose against him. Why had he brought rightist elements into the government? Why had the government failed to heed any of the popular demands? Why had it drifted into this impasse? Why had the government not energetically proposed peace to the Allies? And in this hour of crisis, Kerensky's own pre-parliament passed a resolution censoring him.

Angrily he summoned the Menshevik and Socialist leaders to the palace. They cringed before the white heat of his words. He tendered them his immediate resignation. They stammered that the resolution merely embodied suggestions; it was in no sense intended as lack of confidence.

Already Antonov-Ovsyenko's squads had taken up positions, mounting machine guns in buildings at important intersections. A colonel led a company of Yunkers to the Free Mind Club to arrest the editor of *Rabotchi Put.* An enormous mob threatened to lynch the Yunkers. The colonel begged that his men be taken to the Fortress of Peter and Paul for safety. This was done.

Before dawn the telegraph agency telephone and post office were easily occupied by the Bolsheviks' squads. The telegraph office had been guarded by fifty police and cadets, and the girls had come out in opposition to the Soviet. Three of Dybenko's sailors in civies walked in with hand grenades under their coats. A few shots were fired from a machine-gun corps previously installed in a building across the street. As the guards rushed to repel attack, the sailors threw their grenades behind them. Confused, appalled by the wounded, the guards made no further resistance, and Bolshevik sailors quietly moved in with machine guns.

Toward morning the doors of the Military Hotel on Isaac Street, where the Yunker top officers lived, were locked. All they could do was pace the lobby, biting their nails. At the power plant and sub-stations Bolshevik shock troops merely marched up and reported to the officer on guard that they had been sent to take over in case there should be an insurrection. The state bank was occupied at dawn. The gasworks and railroad stations, where for days watchers had kept close track of all troop movements, were smoothly seized without fighting.

Nobody, not even Kerensky, not even most Bolshevik leaders, knew for sure what was really happening, whether the program had succeeded. Citizens went about their business as usual.

Nearly all barracks declared at once for the Bolsheviks. The few that did not were isolated by cutting light and telephones and stopping all messenger service. Adjacent buildings were manned with machine guns.

At 3 A.M. a commissioner and workers reported that the government had suppressed all Bolshevik papers, Red Guards—"the valiant Vohynia regiment"—were sent to break the seals, and the papers went to press as usual. The Red Guards in turn closed down all other newspapers.

Not even the members of the Tsay-ee-Kah were aware of the putsch being made. Even before they met that night, the Minister of Justice and Religion, A. Karteshev, had been picked up on Milliony Street near his home after a session at the Winter Palace of the provisional government and had been whisked off to Smolny and held prisoner in the cellar.

The big hall at the Smolny filled up that night of November 6 with an enormous, humming, buzzing mass of workers and soldiers. It was midnight when A. R. Gotz, leader of Kerensky's Social Revolutionary party, called the last meeting of the Tsay-ee-Kah Soviet to order. Theodore Dan, Menshevik leader, wearing a shapeless sergeant's uniform, rose to speak. By then the hall under the big chandeliers was blue with cigarette smoke, the smell of unwashed bodies and rancid bear grease.

He painted a gloomy picture. The enemy and famine were at the gates and blood stained the streets of the capital. (He did not know that Kerensky's militia chief had already been captured and shot.) John Reed and Trotsky described the scene.

"If the Bolsheviks start anything," shouted Dan, "that will be the end of the Revolution." The counterrevolutionsists would precipitate "riots and massacres."

Cries of "Lies!" "Shame!" shook the walls.

"Your elected Tsay-ee-Kah has full power to act, and it must be obeyed . . . . We are not afraid of bayonets, and our party will defend the Revolution [i.e., Kerensky] with our bodies. Now concerning our policy about peace . . ."

A roar of laughter interrupted him. "It was a dead body long ago."

"Today the Council of the Republic ordered the surrender of land to the people and the institution of immediate peace negotiations," he persisted.

"Eleventh-hour repentance," Trotsky retorted sarcastically, amid a roar of applause. Too late . . . late by a day . . . late by weeks . . . eight months too late. Trotsky mounted the tribune amid thunderous applause, his pointed dark face wreathed with a malicious smile. "Your committee . . . is comic . . . . The peasants are already taking the land as we told them to."

A resolution was introduced to set up a committee of safety. "A trick," shouted a Bolshevik delegate. "The Tsay-ee-Kah is dead and doesn't know it."

As if to affirm this, the delegates surged to their feet and sang a funeral hymn. And so, toward dawn, nervous over the sound of gunfire in the city, the Tsay-ee-Kah resigned for all time. The new all-Russian Soviet Congress of workers and peasants would convene the following day.

Opposition leaders ran around Smolny in circles or hurried to the Marinsky or to the Winter Palace. "What has happened?" "The

devil knows—*tchort mayet.*" One leading Menshevik was more positive, "The Bolsheviks won't be able to hang on to the power more
than three days. Let them try—that will finish them for good."

The streets were not quite as safe on the seventh day. Snipers
shot from roofs, and boots rang on the cobbles as Red Guards ran
to smoke them out. Barricades had been flung around the Marinsky
Palace and the Moika quay—boxes, barrels, bedsprings, a wagon,
piles of lumber, and firewood. "Run along home, all of you." Along
the Nevsky passed autos full of arrested Kerensky officials, including several members of the Tsay-ee-Kah. Down the Vosnyesensky
Prospect, moving toward the Admiralty, Red soldiers came marching in—from as far as the eye could see.

At one o'clock in the afternoon of November 7, Trotsky, in the
name of the Petrograd Military Revolutionary Committee, informed
the Petrograd Soviet that the Kerensky government no longer existed. All authority was being exercised by the Military Committee.
"On the third floor in a small room," wrote Trotsky in his *The Russian Revolution,*

the Military Revolutionary Committee was in permanent session. Hither
flowed all information regarding the movement of troops, the frame of
mind of soldiers and workers, the propaganda in the barracks, the
doings of hooligans; the conferences held by the bourgeois politicians,
life in the Winter Palace and the intentions of the former Soviet [Tsay-
ee-kah] parties. Our information came from every quarter and included
workers, officers, house porters, Socialist Cadets, servants and fashionable ladies. Many brought only ridiculous nonsense. [From there, too,
flowed out the orders for further action.] The members of the Committee had not left Smolny for the last week. They slept in snatches on
sofas, constantly awakened by couriers, cyclists, telegraphists, telephone
bells."

The most anxious night was that of November 6 to 7.

We were informed . . . that the government was summoning the artiller-
ists . . . and the ensigns from the Peterhov School . . . . By telephone we
ordered detachments of trustworthy military guards to bar all entrances
to Petrograd and send agitators to meet the detachments summoned by
the government. If they could not be kept back by reason, then arms
were to be used . . . . A portion of the Cadets from the Oranienbaum
Training School did however get past our barriers in the night, and we

followed up their further movements by telephone . . . . An order was issued to put down ruthlessly every Black Hand agitator, to use arms at the first attempts at street programs and to act if necessary without mercy.

Most points were captured without firing a shot and without victims. "The crew of the *Aurora* informed the Committee they had been ordered to leave Petrograd waters. We countermanded the order." They were to be ready to use all forces in behalf of Soviet authority.

What had happened to Kerensky? About the time he whirled away from Marinsky on the sixth, a cordon of soldiers took charge of traffic flowing in from the three avenues toward the Admirality. All cars, official or private, were waved toward the Winter Palace, but at the Kazan Cathedral they were stopped and shunted back out the Nevsky. Half a dozen sailors came swinging along with rifles and joined the soldiers. Their hat bands bore the gold lettering of the leading cruisers, *Aurora* and *Zaria Svobody*. Both had Bolshevik crews. So Kronstadt was coming—twenty-five thousand strong!

But it was well into the night before Kerensky realized how serious the blow was. At 4 A.M. he left the Winter Palace and stayed at staff headquarters, sending orders to cossacks, Yunkers, and cadets. All were unable to move. "Stay at your posts and defend the conquests of the Revolution," he commanded. Proclamations were hurriedly prepared . . . New martial-law severities . . . Dismissal of the Petrograd Commandant . . . Save the Fatherland . . . Citizens. . . .

At 9 A.M. Kerensky fled—for the front to hunt for troops that would follow him. His car ran out of gasoline. Some was borrowed from the English Hospital.

In the Winter Palace the ministers carried on, still guarded by cadets, Yunkers, and women cadets. The same Shveitzari attendants, still in the czars' uniforms, blue with red-gold collars and brass buttons, politely took the hats and coats of any visitors who managed to get in. The women soldiers were stationed in the back, "Where," said one minister, shaking his head, "they would be less likely to get hurt. A grave responsibility." The women had grown hysterical and were less willing to defend the palace now that their adored leader had fled. The Yunkers, the "student gentlemen" officers, were in the great state salons in front overlooking the gardens, their rifles stacked under the gilded cornices and enormous chandeliers. The floor was littered with dirty mattresses, cigarette butts, bread crusts, and French wine bottles filched from the cellars, now empty. Disheveled, unshaven, red-eyed, they pointed machine guns out the long dirty windows at the square. No attack came. The officers were unhappy and worried. The rank and file could switch over, but they would be thrown out, most likely shot. Still, they intended to fight. They swore not to give in to the dirty rabble, not until their next to the last bullet was gone. Each had a golden bullet he would fire into his own heart. Some, very likely, would use them. Day faded into another anxious night.

Bicycle soldiers rode up to general staff headquarters, bringing orders from the Fortress of St. Peter and St. Paul, whose guns loomed on the hill on Vassily Island, to surrender or be shelled. The new Kerensky commander—Count Aleksei Nikolaevich Tolstoy—the generals, and the colonels talked and fumed. Finally the staff turned the place over to the Reds and withdrew to the Winter Palace.

At six o'clock that evening, according to Malaparte, Antonov-Ovsyenko staggered haggard and pale, but smiling, into Lenin's office at Smolny. "It's all over," he said.

Unable to believe that the battle was really won, Lenin still clung to his wig. There had been no attack on general headquarters, nor on Taurida, nor on the Winter Palace. "The members of the government . . ." he began.

"All points taken have been heavily reinforced. Barricades have been set at all the city gates. The bridges over the Neva are in our hands."

Rumors that the Bolsheviks had taken over the city, that Kerensky had fallen, brought great crowds surging down the Nevsky in the early twilight. At the Winter Palace they recoiled. It was brightly lit, and the cadets in their long green coats were still lined up behind their cannon and machine guns. The crowd dispersed. People went back to the cafés, to the movies and theaters, or to their own crannies.

From noon on, the Red Guard forces had begun throwing a tight ring around the Winter Palace. The square and gardens filled up with Red soldiers and sailors—before both the Admiralty and the palace. "We're waiting," said one officer. "There are women in there. We can't shoot them. We are dickering with the Cadets."

But at seven o'clock, when the unlit squares had become dark, desultory firing began. Bystanders scattered, drifting back to the Nevsky to the shops and cafés. Theaters were open as usual. Never had the thoroughfare been more jammed. The whole city congregated there. There was an anxious but almost festive air. The uniforms of red soldiers wove in and out, fraternizing, talking. A few armored cars nosed along slowly, up and down, up and down. The czarist names had been painted over with big red letters of the Bolshevik party and the Petrograd Soviet. At Stroganoff Palace Bridge over the Moika Canal, Red field guns were now in place behind more barricades.

Out at Smolny Palace, at both outer and inner gates, the guards had lit big bonfires against the biting chill. The Petrograd Soviet was just winding up its week-long day-and-night sessions. The provisional government no longer existed; the government of soldiers, workers, and peasants, headed by Lenin, had been born. The dictatorship of the proletariat had arrived. Amid thundering ovation, Lenin yanked off his false wig. Bald-headed, he prophesied world-wide social revolution.

Downstairs under the great chandeliers every seat filled, the aisles jammed, the windowsills occupied, the newly elected all-Russian Congress of the Soviets was preparing to open its session. There on the platform (as a courtesy) were the defeated leaders of the old Tsay-ee-Kah, including Gotz, hollow eyes glaring. Once more the great hall filled with smoke and the stench of bodies. Then came the heavy boom of cannon, and the delegates looked anxiously toward the windows. The heavy boom kept on and on steadily. Not a salute to the new congress, that was sure. Had Bolshevik control of the city broken down into civil war right on the hour of victory? Soon word came that the Winter Palace was being attacked.

Dan, still in his tousled surgeon's uniform, head of the outgoing Tsay-ee-kah, rang the bell at 10:40 P.M., and silence fell.

"At this very moment," he began dourly, "our party comrades are in the Winter Palace under bombardment, sacrificing themselves to carry out the duty placed upon them by the Tsay-ee-Kah."

The cannon boomed again, as the *Aurora* opened fire from the Neva. The hall shook with confusion. Once more Dan's voice rang out. "I declare the first session of the Second Congress of the Soviets and Soldiers Deputies now open."

A presidium was elected—fourteen Bolsheviks, eleven oppositionists. But all the Socialists, Mensheviks, and the Gorky Internationalist declined to serve. They were replaced by one Ukrainian Soviet delegate. It became an all-Bolshevik presidium. The old Tsay-ee-Kah officials stepped down from the platform, but stayed in the hall. Their places were taken by Trotsky, Kamenev, Lunacharsky, Madame Kollantai, V. P. Nogin, and others. All were greeted with thunderous applause.

Four months ago they had been a despised, persecuted sect; now the central government of Russia was in their hands. Could they hold it—could they consolidate it, enforce their authority across the far reaches of the steppes? The Caucasus? Siberia? The Ukraine had set up an independent government. And if the Germans marched in? The Soviets took up their duties now amid the booming of cannon, the crash of artillery, the spat of guns. Uneasily again the delegates looked toward the windows.

Menshevik J. Martov jumped up, screaming hoarsely, "Our brothers are being shot down in the streets." Pandemonium. Screams. Recriminations back and forth.

The minority demanded that a delegation be named to negotiate with all Socialist organizations. Passed.

A soldier announced that the all-Russian peasant delegates were outside but refused to participate unless formally invited in and given votes. Accepted by unanimous vote.

More minority delegates spoke angrily, charging Bolshevik treachery. A fait accompli had been perpetrated behind their backs. Each such speaker then led his followers out of the hall. Once or twice it looked as if they would not get out with their lives, but shouts rose, "Let them go! Let them go!"

A natty officer with a brown goatee, claiming to represent the Fifth Army Soviet, said the army was not properly represented. Anyway, this congress was uncalled for. Soldiers jumped to their feet. "You speak for the officers, not the soldiers."

"The place to fight is not here but in the streets," he replied. "We have been betrayed by a conspiracy." He led a small front group from the hall.

A leader of the Jewish Bund jumped up, eyes flaming behind his thick glasses, and shook his fist with rage. "What is taking place in Petrograd is a calamity. The Bund will leave this Congress." He was hooted down and cursed as he led fifty more delegates from the hall.

Lev Borisovich Kamenev banged the bell. "Get on with our business." Trotsky spoke next, pale, cruel, full-voiced. "Let them go! They are all just so much refuse that will be swept into the garbage heap of history."

The slow drum of cannon kept on. There was general firing now, snipers all along the Nevsky. People were scattering, running stooped, ducking into doorways. At the Catharina Canal Bridge, the Red Guard blocked a large well-dressed crowd marching determinedly four abreast. Some were delegates who had stalked out of Smolny, led by the white-bearded mayor of Petrograd. By his side walked Kerensky's minister of supplies. (We reconstruct the scene from John Reed's *Ten Days that Shook the World*.)

"You can't pass," said the guard.

"We are going to the Winter Palace, where we will die with our comrades if necessary. Let us by."

"You cannot pass," the sailor repeated, scratching his head.

"We shall pass. Will you shoot down unarmed people?"

Perplexed, the sailor shook his head. Another Red sailor stalked up angrily. "We'll spank you, that's what we'll do. And we'll shoot you if we have to. Now go on home."

They fell back. The major mounted a box and waved his umbrella. "It is beneath our dignity to be shot down in the street by these street sweepers. Let us return to the Duma and discuss how we can save the country and the Revolution."

Still in a column of fours, they marched back along the Nevsky.

Down at the Winter Palace in the dark of the Kazan cathedral and the Admiralty gardens, all firing stopped. The cadets had vanished, and the Yunkers offered to surrender. A great mass of Red soldiers surged forward, pouring under the Imperial Arch. There, fearing last-minute treachery, they paused uncertainly, behind the big Alexander Column, commemorating the spot where an earlier czar had been assassinated. They moved forward again, clambering over high barricades of firewood.

The Yunkers tossed their rifles and machine guns out the windows. The palace doors stood wide open, light streaming forth, not a sound. The soldiers burst in with wild shouts, not bothering to arrest the cadets. They tore down tapestries and curtains and tablecloths. One big fellow strutted about with ostrich feathers in his hat, a big bronze clock in his arms. Crates were broken open, and greedy fingers made off with tableware, dishes, gold-rimmed plates. Two soldiers, wearing rags on their feet, ripped the leather upholstery off carved Spanish chairs—for shoes.

"Comrades," a voice rang out clearly—one of the Red officers (again we follow Reed's version). "Don't take anything. This is the property of the people."

The loot was snatched from their hands. Objects were thrust back into the broken crates. Guards were posted to prevent more thefts. The soldiers were herded out by a Red officer and his soldier aide with drawn pistols. At the doors those who had not already escaped with plunder were searched and allowed to keep only their personal possessions.

The Yunkers were brought out by threes and fours. Shouts went up. "Provocateurs! Murderers of the people!" But each was released after taking an oath he would not take up arms again.

Meanwhile upstairs, officers and soldiers had burst into the gold malachite room where Kerensky had had his quarters. Most of the cabinet members were huddled there. The papers before them indicated their state of mind; the beginnings of proclamations, each crossed off or abandoned in midsentence, pages filled with doodlings. All were searched and led out by Red guards with fixed bayonets. All were in civilian dress, except N. M. Kishkin, the commander. The Red soldiers in the corridors watched the little procession darkly. It passed down the marble stairs, through the stately paved hall, out into the cold dark square. There the crowd wanted to lynch them. More soldiers had to be called. There was shooting, but a company of sailors got them all safely to the Fortress of St. Peter and St. Paul.

Presently the women's death battalion was marched out the back way to the Neva boulevard. They had been found huddling in the dark behind locked doors, completely hysterical. At the Pavlovsk barracks, they got rough treatment: three were raped; one committed suicide. They were taken to the Helsinki train to be sent to a woman's camp outside the city.

The city fell into quiet, like a tired old man. The streets were empty, save for the soldiers and sailors, the deserters and Red Guards, warming themselves around big bonfires.

Back in Smolny, the great all-Soviet Russian congress continued. The names of the captured ministers were read off, amid laughter for some, angry hoots for others. A big bearded peasant rose, enraged. "We Socialist Revolutionaries demand their immediate release! . . . Those comrades risked their lives fighting the Czar's tyranny. Why have they been flung into prison in the Fortress of St. Peter and St. Paul, the age-old tomb of liberty?"

Trotsky calmed the unexpected uproar, sharp, cold, biting. "They and Kerensky's adventurers plotted to crush the Soviets. Did they ever handle us with kid gloves?" With a triumphant shout, he added. "We will die before we will give up what we have won. What is needed now is work . . . work . . . work."

A commissar came in, covered with mud, breathless. "The Tsarkoy Selo garrison [a suburb of Petrograd] is guarding the gates of the city for the Soviets!" Wild cheers broke out. "The Third Cycle Battalion, ordered into Petrograd by Kerensky, has refused to shed the blood of its brothers for the bourgeois and the landowners!" More cheers.

Once more an opposition delegate, a Menshevik Internationalist (the group to which Trotsky himself had belonged until recently) demanded a committee to seek for a peaceful solution.

"Victory is the only solution," bellowed the crowd.

The Internationalists stalked out. "Renegades," Kamenev shouted after them.

At 5:17 A.M. on November 8, Krylenko staggered to the platform waving a telegram. "Comrades, the Twelfth Army from the northern front greets the Congress of Soviets and takes over the front in its name."

Pandemonium broke out. Men, weeping and cheering, embraced each other in mad joy.

At 6 A.M. the meeting adjourned. Some delegates slumped down on the floor to sleep; others lay down along the corridors; a few went out into the cold darkness past the bivouac fires. Dawn had not yet risen over Russia.

Tomorrow and tomorrow? Some saw it as the birth of a new great Russia. Some saw it as the final road to ruin. That road, few doubted, would be long and hard and bloody. Some of the bitter answers were soon forthcoming.

Trotsky negotiated peace with the Germans at Brest-Litovsk, a humiliating cession of Russian territory, for which in the end the Germans would pay dearly. It did not bring peace. He had to march into Poland. He expected the Polish workers and peasants to rise up to greet him. He learned, the hard way, that Polish nationalism was stronger than class hatred.

Soon in the Ukraine and in Siberia, White armies rose up, aided and abetted by Russia's former allies, whose troops marched in to burn Odessa, to threaten to overthrow the Communist regime. The United States invaded northern Novgorod and, with the Japanese, eastern Siberia. White army commander, Admiral Aleksandr V. Kolchak, advanced across Siberia, looting, killing. At Tomsk, which was surrendered by the local Soviet on promises of safe conduct, he sliced every prisoner to mincemeat. But he soon broke before the thrust of Trotsky's army and local resistance.

The Soviets finally won on all fronts, but were left with bitter hard suspicion, never again trusting foreign imperialism and Western democracy. Lenin died. The dictatorship of the proletariat became the dictatorship of Stalin.

Perhaps dictatorship was the only way the country could recover and survive, not necessarily the Stalin variety, though his emergence seemed to be inevitable. But every country eventually pays a higher price for the suppression of freedom, of ideas, the thwarting of independent creative talent. It is a price Russia had been paying for centuries. To succeed, its Revolution had to tear up the old feudal order by the roots. But some age-old traditions, both good and evil, could never be destroyed. Some such have wrapped their strong tendrils around the new way of life. Great technological and material gains have been made, and the lot of the masses has been improved in many ways.

CHAPTER 8

THE MARCH ON ROME: THE BLACK SHIRT REVOLUTION

ISRAEL ZANGWILL, the noted Anglo-Jewish writer, arrived in Florence, Italy, the night Mussolini's Black Shirts took over the city—October 27, 1922. Angrily he refused to show his papers to the Fascist guards in possession of the railway station and was taken under arrest to the revolutionary headquarters on the Piazza Mentana near the Arno (from which the Socialist Engineers' Trade Union had been violently ejected) into the presence of Commander-Consul Tamburini.

An enemy of violence, Zangwill shouted his opinion of all revolution and of Fascism in particular. Tamburini knew no English, "but would hardly have understood . . . the stranger's liberal and democratic sentiments even had they been expressed in Italian"—so wrote Curzio Malaparte, the young poet, second in command of the Florence Black Shirts. Called to translate, Malaparte knew all about the distinguished prisoner and did his best "to translate into polite Italian, observations which could not be pleasing to the ears of a Fascist." His chief, scarcely "an idyllic character from Theocritus or a member of the Fabian society," was enraged by the prisoner's offensive manner.

Tamburini took a deep breath and said bitingly, "I doubt very much if you have translated accurately what he said. English is a counter-revolutionary language. Even its construction, it seems, is Liberal."

As Malaparte took Zangwill to his hotel, the Britisher was unable to believe this was a bona fide revolution: shops were open; smiling people were calmly going about their business. "In Paris in 1789," he observed to his escort, "there was a revolution not only in the minds of the Parisians but in the streets."

Malaparte replied, "The technique of revolution has evolved greatly in modern times."

Benito Mussolini and other Fascist leaders were well versed in the modern literature of violence and seizure of the state. Mussolini, an ex-Socialist expelled from the party in 1914, was steeped in Marx's art of revolution, and he frequently jeered at big-bearded Socialist leaders Giacomo Maneotto Serrati and Filippo Turati for not reading their Pierre Joseph Proudhon. He was well read in anarchist and syndicalist direct-action literature: Mikhail A. Bakunin, Georges Sorel, Juan Grave. The Italians Vilfredo Pareto and Enrico Corradini provided philosophical *ragione* for nationalistic violence. Benedetto Croce's refinement of the moral validity of "violence within limits" had become a repeated justification for the Black Shirt strong-armed methods that had kept Italy in an uproar for two years with raids on Socialist and trade union and cooperative headquarters and newspapers. The Fascist leaders were also students of the Trotsky–Antonov-Ovsyenko tactics for the seizure of Petrograd.

In speech after speech, well before the Fascist coup, Mussolini had openly mocked at the weak succession of governments, bragged how he intended to take over Italy, and told the exact steps he would follow. A "modern" revolution, he said, could not be made against the army. The army had to be cajoled or neutralized. Nor was frontal attack on the state's police power contemplated— only minor fracases. It was essential to maintain an outward aspect of normality.

And so it was in Florence on the final day—as it had been in Petrograd. The *carabinieri* (the police) had all been concentrated to guard the city prefect in the Palazzo Riccardi (once the residence of Lorenzo the Magnificent). All wires were cut, machine guns sneaked into adjacent buildings. The various barracks were in a similar dilemma. There was no general disorder.

The preliminary phase had been the Fascist gang tactics all over the country, as later in Germany the Brown Shirt violence and terrorism, sabotage and secret arson, such as the Reichstag fire, blamed upon the Communists. The organized Black Shirt *squadri* had had two years of experimental training—not a single week as in Petrograd. Opponents had been intimidated by armed raids, arson, and murder. People had grown accustomed when firing started to dropping on their stomachs in the street or ducking into doorways. Otherwise, paying little attention, they went about their affairs. They were psychologized into accepting violence as daily diet and accepting the inevitability of Fascist victory. They actually felt relief when the trouble was over and their liberties had been destroyed, glad to be able to breathe in peace.

As the Fascist raiders grew bolder and more murderous, the government's countermeasures grew more feeble. At first Black Shirts were sometimes arrested and brought into court; but as government resistance weakened, the gangsters came to enjoy the financial backing of landlords and industrialists. Some bands came to be well paid, thirty lire a day per head, with big bonuses for successful forays or the murder of designated labor leaders. Most, however, were idealists, frustrated youths, largely ignorant that their movement was heavily financed by war speculators, particularly the flamboyant Perrone brothers; by bankers, particularly the big church-owned bank; by the owners of *Il Messaggiero*, and other important dailies; and by the big Anzaldo steelworks.

Italy was a sick postwar country in economic collapse with hordes of unemployed. War-victory had been more a defeat than triumph. The First World War had been unpopular, opposed throughout by Italy's major party, the Socialists, except for lip service by some leaders. The Italian soldier was sullen, resentful, unwilling to fight, and the number of officers shot in the back was relatively greater than on the Russian front. The terrible defeat of Caporetto (which provided Hemingway with a theme for *Farewell to Arms*) proved how little stomach the Italian troops had for fighting, how inadequately they were equipped, and how incompetent their officers. As in Russia, war fed the country into the maw of revolution and counterrevolution.

The Italians had bungled badly. Betrayal by their erstwhile allies at the peace table deepened the utter frustration. Though unwilling to fight, the Italian people had had great faith in Woodrow Wilson's Fourteen Points, and in Milan he was greeted with the greatest clamoring crowd in the history of the country—a million cheered him. The people of Italy, as of Europe, were behind him, not behind Vittorio Emanuele Orlando, Georges Clemenceau, or David Lloyd George, and he could have imposed any peace he desired.

Frightened, repelled by the popular acclaim and its revolutionary implications, he betrayed one after another of his Fourteen Points. He came to be as execrated as he had been admired. For the Italians the Versailles Treaty was gross betrayal. England and France were granted vast accretions to their empires; the new Yugoslavia was favored over Italy, which had suffered ten million war dead. Weaker allies, such as Italy, the Arabs, China, were "double-crossed," even despoiled. The subsequent Treaty of Rapallo was humiliating to Italian leftists as well as rightists and nationalists, such as Gabriele D'Annunzio, the novelist who occupied Fiume. It completed the ignominy when actual hunger was stalking the peninsula.

Labor had fought for its rights. Part of it was inspired by the Russian Revolution. In 1920 the Syndicalists began seizing factories. Many people feared Italy might go Communist. That it did not do so was due more to the ineptitude of the Communist leaders—at whom both Trotsky and Lenin jeered—than any effort of the Fascists, not yet in action. Their teeth were also pulled by the clever concessions made by aged Premier Giovanni Giolitti, who played this long tricky gamble with militant laborism in a last-ditch effort to save traditional parliamentarianism and the royal establishment.

His brinkmanship stirred fascism to life. Soon Black Shirts were raiding against both Communists and Socialists, against militant peasant land seizures in the south, promoted by Don Luigi Sturzo, leader of the Catholic *Partito Popolare*. Labor and peasant headquarters, labor libraries, schools, and newspapers were attacked and burned. Strikes were put down with clubs, knives, and guns. Even Catholic priests were attacked. In Florence, a Dante centennial celebration, with marching priests, monks, and nuns, was broken up with Black Shirt clubs and whips, because the church had the temerity to try to monopolize Italy's major "nationalist" hero.

Who composed these armed gangs? First of all, jobless young veterans, particularly the *Arditti*, or shock troops, from the front lines, the elite of the Italian army, who had really tried to fight. Now they saw victory snatched away and the country ruined by the greed of the more powerful Allies and "the international bankers." Ruin also resulted from the ineptitude of Italy's own traditional politicians, by the war profiteers, "the sharks"—the *pescecani* —and by radical labor.

The gangs were also made up of Anarcho-Syndicalist elements from the labor movement itself, followers of Sorel's doctrines of direct action and violence. They were more militant than the Socialist or Communist unions. They stemmed from the early split in the First International, which had seen Mikhail Aleksandrovich Bakunin and Peter Alekseyevitch Kropotkin harried forth by Marx. They hated Marxists worse than capitalists.

Thirdly, the most numerous among the Black Shirts were the militant unemployed middle-class youths, caught in the postwar squeeze between powerful organized labor, with its growing demands in a country with a shattered economy, and the big industrialists growing paunchier. The middle-class Black Shirts hotly denounced "the sharks" whose "only patriotism was for quick corrupt profits." There were few jobs for these middle-class youths emerging into the labor market; their families—the *piccola borghesia*— were going bankrupt. Aiding their movement, ironically, were the very profiteers they hated.

But they did not attack the Anzaldo steelworks. They raided working-class *trattorie*—with black-jacks and bullets. They overturned peasant carts in the markets when prices seemed too high. They careened through labor-controlled towns or working sections of larger cities, firing indiscriminately at men, women, and children in houses and on streets. They seized elected labor officials, beat them, made them drink castor oil, and resign. They stampeded movies with false shouts of "Bomb!" often with tragic consequences. The bombing of the Diana Kursaal Theater in Milan was a sort of early Reichstag fire. They burned the new million-lire Socialist headquarters there and others everywhere. They destroyed *La Umanità Nuòva*, the leading Socialist paper. Preliminary seizures of post offices and public buildings were staged, usually by the *mutilati* or war-mutilated, whom the government dared not fire upon lest it lose public sympathy. The Fascist slogan became "violence to end violence," a variation of Woodrow Wilson's slogan "the war to end all wars," not so different from the present-day slogan "waging war to defend peace."

In their idealism, compounded with deep resentment and economic frustration, the Black Shirts conceived that their terrorism was a necessary surgical operation to save Italy. Most of the western world, because of fear of Communism, applauded them.

The deadline came: the seizure of Florence, Pisa, and Bologna in 1922. Visiting Britisher Zangwill, seeing a normal city except for a few lorries of Black Shirts, was unable to believe that the Fascists had really taken over Tuscany. Mussolini was being pictured as Caesar crossing the Rubicon, and Zangwill told Malaparte sarcastically that the great Swedish statesman Count Axel Oxenstierna had stated in his memoirs that *Caesar* was originally a Carthaginian word, meaning "elephant." Were Mussolini's tactics as clumsy and elephantine as Caesar's?

"There will be much rhetoric of that style tossed about during the next few days," Malaparte replied. "Mussolini had nothing to do with the political methods of Caesar Borgia or Machiavelli," he insisted. "Gladstone and Lloyd George learned much from Machiavelli and Sulla and Julius Caesar," he added, with the comment that Zangwill would have to forget about ancient Rome and Renaissance Italy if he wished to comprehend what was happening in Italy. There was nothing antique about Mussolini. "His plan of insurrection is wholly modern. Against it, the Government will have nothing . . . but police measures," the customary implements of bureaucratic and military minds. Traditional police action was impotent against modern technical revolt.

Zangwill still scoffed, declaring it was merely a smoke-screen deal cooked up between Mussolini and the king, a farcical token revolution, which neither police nor army intended to oppose; that Mussolini was already scheduled to be smoothly inducted as head of a traditional parliamentary government.

This seemed born out by next morning's *Nazione*, which announced that the king's aide-de-camp General Arturo Cittadini had hastened to Milan to confer with Mussolini, to ask him to head a new government. Actually Cittadini was with the king; there was no truth in the story. Zangwill was utterly shocked when Malaparte informed him that on orders from Italo Balbo, top Fascist general, he himself had led Black Shirts to the paper to force it to insert the false notice. The Black Shirts were distributing the paper, particularly to the armed forces, so that they would be too confused to sally forth and fight. "Cunning as well as force is justifiable," said Malaparte.

(If nothing more, this should prove a warning to later historians who so often base their accounts on contemporary newspapers.)

Tuscany was the chief channel through which forces to take Rome had to be funneled. By taking over there, in one blow, Mussolini had broken Italy in two, dividing the strong Socialist-labor north from the *Giolitti* and Catholic parties, the peasants in the south. The south was apathy and poetry, but excitable and unpredictable. The hungry peasants there were seizing land. One Fascist goal was to set aside the recent Viscocchi law, which had opened up idle lands to peasants—the Gracchi and ancient *Leggi Frumentari* all over again, now, two thousand years later. Thus Tuscany was the bridge insuring victory. With the Appenine crossrange at their backs, the lines of communication firmly in their hands, the Black Shirts had an open road to Rome.

Whether Mussolini was aware of it or not, much of Rome's early history was being repeated with due variations, even part of the Risorgimento, which had unified modern Italy. The Duce, or leader as he was called, was northern Italian, son of a blacksmith. He himself had the husky, stocky build of a blacksmith. He was also a renegade Socialist and had studied revolutionary theory and practice. Above all, like Corradini, he was not only versed in Sorel, the Anarcho-Syndicalist philosopher, but he had also read Marx and Lenin and had studied the process of the Russian Revolution. The war and the peace had disillusioned him with regard to the old-fashioned politics of the Italian Socialists Serrati and Turati.

For his own purposes he stood the Marxian doctrines and verbiage on their heads, making an amalgam of nationalism and mirror-glass socialism, even before Hitler's day. Italy, he declared, was a proletarian nation, fighting for its rights, especially territory and colonies—*Italia Irredenta*—a place in the sun. As such it had to fight the capitalist nations, especially England and the United States. He presented his ideas with striking imagery in nationwide speeches for several years before the march on Rome. He set forth in detail, step by step, exactly how he would take over the state. Authority did not listen. The people did. Day after day he built a military state within the state.

His immediate strategy was presented at the party convention at Naples on October 24. There the Fascists announced, "We are the state, the nation, the New Italy, the Fourth Rome. We are Italy supreme in the Mediterranean." The only shift in tactics was the overture made to the Blue Shirt Nationalists, the *Sempre Pronto* ("Always Ready"). It was more a mobilization than a convention—the disciplined march of Mussolini and his staff, the *"Princes* and the *Triari"* (the leaders and upper-echelon followers). The display of uniformed helmeted cavalry, the bicycle squadrons, the gold medalists, the legions, the *Balilla,* Boy Scouts, all elements were uniformed, helmeted, carrying blankets and rations. Only labor syndicate adherents marched drably. More in keeping were the trucks and sanitary services.

"We are," orated Mussolini, "at the point where the arrow parts from the bow or else the tightly drawn cord snaps."

The issue, owing to the failure of the government to heed Fascist demands, had become one of force, "which in the end decides." In that field the victory would certainly go to the Black Shirts. There could be no more delay—"It would murder the future."

It was raining in Rome on the morning of Saturday, October 28, the day set for Black Shirt mobilization for the seizure of the capital. The major Black Shirt forces in Tuscany were led forth, bound for Rome, the night previous, by Tamburini; others were streaming through Florence from Cremona, Bologna, Ferrara, Venice, Milan, Genoa. But in Rome, as in Florence, there was no special hubbub. Early in the day, without resistance, the Black Shirts had taken over newspapers, telegraph and post offices—"the ganglia of the nation"—à la Trotsky. The Black Shirts ordered police to their barracks and took over traffic control on downtown streets. A motortruck, filled with Black Shirts, rolled down Via Due Macelli and Corso Umberto, calling out, "Up with the tricolor!" At once, red, white, and green banners were flung free in the rain from office and apartment windows. On street corners appeared typewritten notices ordering full Black Shirt mobilization at midday. Martial law orders came from the "quadrivirate" in Milan (the Fascist directorate), as the military revolutionary committee called itself. It consisted of Michel Bianchi of the general secretary; General de Bono, commander of the Black Shirt militia; Captain DeVecchio, a D'Annunzio legionnaire from Fiume and the original organizer of the militia; and aviator Italo Balbo, planner of terrorism before and after the coup. He and De Bono were later implicated in the assassination of Socialist Deputy Giacomo Matteoti, and they not only went unpunished, but were honored.

How the word *quadrivirate* echoes the long record of violence down the Italian centuries—though actually Rome produced only triumvirates.

The directorate proclaimed: "The hour of decisive battle has sounded . . . . Today the Black Shirt Army reaffirms the since-mutilated victory [of four years ago] and, striking fiercely at Rome, returns the victory to the glorious Campodoglio."

"Fiercely"! Little seemed to be happening. Few people on the rainy streets. Wine and coffee sippers, shivering under wet awnings in the almost deserted sidewalk cafés, stared out at the dismal rain, muttering "Que scherzo!" ("What a farce!") Where was this Black Shirt revolution? Only fluttering handbills. Only a few Black Shirts wandering around aimlessly like wet cats, with cudgels, table legs, knives, an occasional gun, hoodlums seeking a fight, not finding any. A more determined group swung along singing, "*La Giovanezza, la Giovanezza, Primavera di bellezza.*" But this wasn't spring, only chilly wet autumn. Now and then they stuck out their arms in a stiff semaphore robot salute, shouting "*eje . . . eje . . . eje . . . alalà,*" the old battle cry that Caesar's legions flung against the Gauls of northern forests!

The quadrivirate circulars read, another echo of ancient Rome:

From this day, the *princes* and *triari* are mobilized. Fascist martial law enters into full force. At the command of Il Duce, the military, political, and administrative powers of party control have been assumed by the secretly acting Quadrivirate with dictatorial powers. The Army, the supreme safeguard of the nation, is not to participate in the struggle . . . . Fascism does not march against the agents of public force, but against the imbecilic and deficient political elements, which, during four long years, have not known how to govern the nation.

[The Fascists would] impose discipline [and] aid all forces which will augment economic well-being. The working people . . . have nothing to fear from Fascist power. Their just rights will be loyally guarded . . . . We call upon Supreme God and the spirit of 500,000 dead to testify that one sole impulse inspires us . . . to contribute to the salvation and greatness of the patria . . . . Fascists of all Italy! Be Roman in spirit and strength. It is necessary to conquer, we shall conquer.

If Zangwill had been puzzled by events in Florence, Rome was even more mysterious. Where do revolutions happen? Where was the government? Where were the army and police? What was going to be done?

Neither army nor police had taken over Fascist headquarters on the Piazza Barberini, the first essential step in any decided government resistance. There, only a few grumpy-eyed Black Shirts stood guard with cudgels. They feared they were missing "fun" elsewhere. The author spoke to them. "The ammunition works at Terni have been seized," they said. "Twenty thousand Black Shirts are camped five kilometers out on Via Nomentano with cannon and machine-guns . . . . Sixty thousand more are coming south from Tuscany . . . ."

What *were* the government forces doing on this crucial day of downpour? At the Quirinal Palace—nothing, not even an extra guard. Anyway, the king was supposed to be at Gombo, his vast estate on the Ligurean seacoast, enjoying himself in the warm sands. He had just got his name in the papers for having heroically rescued a shipwrecked fisherman at the mouth of the Arno. What was he doing to save the shipwrecked nation?

At the Quirinal, the minister of war rolled up in an enormous limousine, black as a funeral hearse, stepped out leisurely, apparently worried about nothing. At Montecitorio, the Chamber of Deputies, two olive gray uniforms, as on every other day of the year, but not a single representative on hand to debate the threat to the people's institutions. At the Supreme Council of State in the old Palazzo Spada alla Regola in the squalid Tiber quarter, just a vacant vista through giant portals to the stone courtyard and rain-drenched gardens. In the piazza, a few smudgy *bambini* sailing straws between the cobbles, but not a single *Guardia Regia,* not a single policeman, no cock-feathered *Bersaglieri.* No Black Shirts either. Not a stir.

Only at the ministry of interior, where the cabinet, falsely rumored to have resigned early in the morning, was in session, two companies of soldiers stood, soaked and shivering, hashed into futuristic polychrome by the iron grilling of the gate and the slanting rain. But not a Fascist. Not one.

Where do revolutions happen? Where do governments take a last stand? And how? In the Piazza della Pilota, workmen were leisurely installing barbed-wire entanglements, and government machine-gun lorries with red-white-green-striped turrets were stacked idly in the wet, unattended. But two hundred white horses hung their heads in the rain; two hundred dismounted cavalrymen crouched, guns in hands, in surrounding doorways, not overly worried, just uncomfortable. Waiting? Waiting for what? Not a Black Shirt in sight.

In the adjacent courtyards of the Palazzi Venezia and Pamfili-Doria other small cavalry detachments were waiting in the downpour. Waiting for what? The Fascists? For orders from rotund Premier Luigi Facta (also rumored to have resigned)? Waiting for the decision of the king?

In Piazza Venezia in front of the long white surge of granite steps to the super-atrocious semicircular monument backed against the side of the Capitol, twenty double-decker green buses were lined up against the east curbing, dismal, rain-stained, in the empty square. Who had ordered them off the streets? The government? The Black Shirts? No one seemed to know.

Noon passed. The mobilization deadline. But nothing happened. Nothing changed. Were both sides holding back pending secret parley? Or was it because Italians, like other people, don't like rain?

Night fell. Out on the Via Nomentano perhaps twenty thousand were still encamped, a dreary night for them. But out there near Mons Sacre, the seceding plebs had camped twenty-three hundred years ago. Class war, it seemed, was not so new a thing. Militarism was not new. Civil disorder was not new. Struggles for human rights or for control of the all-powerful state to destroy human rights were not new.

Over that same road had marched the legions of the conquering Caesars, coming back arrogantly from the frontiers to seize Rome, the Eternal City, the Heart of the World. And it was on that road in 1870—the year before the Paris Commune—that the troops of the House of Savoy had marched in to batter down the walls of Porta Pia, to found a new nation and a new dynasty. But where was the king of Savoy at this vital moment?

Actually he had come back to Rome. He had had to pass through Pisa, already taken by the Black Shirts, and must have crossed the bridge over the Arno held by them. After that he had skimmed freely over the coast highway through Livorno (Leghorn), Cecina, and small tourist towns. In the Quirinal, where he arrived toward morning, he found Premier Facta waiting with the resignation of the cabinet.

Facta was a pudgy well-meaning stopgap after the downfall of Sforza, Nitti, Giolitti—a man neither respected nor disliked by the political factions. He had no stomach for a fight. And so, at the moment when the gangster revolution was hammering at the gates, there was no forceful personality to whom the king could turn. As Don Luigi Sturzo, clever leader of the Catholic Popular party, had remarked some weeks before, Italy had had sixty-eight different governments in seventy-two years. This final debacle was merely a culmination, an aggravation of a half-century failure in representative government. The day of reckoning had come now to an Italy shaken by dubious war-victory, betrayed by her powerful wartime allies, and beaten down to economic disaster. There was no way now—or so it seemed—to save parliamentary government as one could a drowning fisherman.

But the little king made a last-ditch effort. He patted Facta on his pudgy shoulder and asked him to do his best to save the government—and the crown. Neither the king nor Facta believed the Fascists could be stopped. It was too late. But a government has to make some show of self-respect.

And so Facta ordered a few hundred cavalrymen and machine-gun lorries to the Piazza della Pilota and heavier contingents to the city gates and the Tiber bridges. Later that morning Facta prepared a martial-law decree in answer to the Fascist decree. He denounced "seditious manifestations . . . in all parts of Italy" that threatened "to throw the country into the greatest disorder." Public order had to be maintained at whatever cost. He forebade assemblages of more than five persons, ordered all buses, streetcars, and private vehicles off the streets, and closed down theaters and movies. His effort was hours late, months late, years late. And if the government did succeed in blocking the Fascisti, might it not then be faced with a resurgence of Communism? Or chaos?

The king refused to sign this desperate decree, perhaps realizing it was unenforceable, or else beset by the vacillation that overtakes leaders at critical moments, or perhaps secretly determined to make a deal.

The street-corner Black Shirts cheered the king's action as a victory. Rainy Saturday in Rome thus passed into Sunday without any test of force. On the bright rainless Sabbath that followed, a proclamation came through from Mussolini in Milan.

The political authorities—somewhat surprised and greatly terrified—have not been able to cope with our movement, because a movement of this character has no limits and still less can it be beaten down . . . . But the victory cannot be mutilated by eleventh-hour compromises . . . . The government must be completely Fascist . . . . Fascism wishes to rule, and it will rule.

It was rumored that the king, dickering behind Facta's back, had offered Mussolini a cabinet post, which had been scornfully declined. He had then offered him the premiership, provided he would set up a broad coalition government. This, too, was scornfully declined. Thus the false rumors, spread days before in Florence papers by DeBono and Malaparte, ironically had become the truth.

At 10:30 that Sabbath a gang of Black Shirts smashed Nitti's paper, *L'Epoca*, on Via Tritone. Furniture, subscription lists, records, were burned in the street, and the presses smashed. One Black Shirt was carried out dead from touching a high-voltage wire. Labor papers and others were also destroyed.

The Fascist dribble into Rome became a torrent, wholly unopposed. Hordes gathered at concentration points, particularly in the Piazza Barberini—where once the historian Sallust had looked down from his gardens as human liberties were trampled by Pompey and Julius Caesar. The Black Shirts were coming in by bicycle, motorcycle, auto, truck, train, airplane, and on foot; they carried guns, clubs, and knives.

Among them marched the Blue Shirts, the *Sempre Pronto* ("Always Ready") the ultra-ultra nationalists, whose heroes had been Corradini and D'Annunzio. D'Annunzio had ridden his white horse into Fiume in defiance of the Versailles Treaty and the new state of Yugoslavia. Mussolini, perhaps jealous of the poet-novelist's fame and drama, said that Italy had first to become strong before it could embark on adventures to recover *Italia Irredenta*. In due time, he promised, Italy would recover all Trieste, Corsica, Tunis, reestablish its influence in the Near East, take its share of Africa. He sympathized with D'Annunzio's flamboyant patriotism, but said sarcastically that the way to remake the state was to strike not at the periphery but at the center. "First it is necessary to take Rome." And, of course, the Blue Shirts followed joyously behind the final putsch. Many girls—the percentage of pulchritude was high—swung along in tight blue or black sweaters or blouses and tam-o'-shanters. Some carried guns or knives.

[*167*]

Civilian throngs began to gather, curious, apprehensive, not overly talkative or excited. It took many Black Shirts now to police a lane down Via Tritone and along the Corso for hurtling autos and trucks with Black Shirts and Blue Shirts clinging to sides, rear and top. Other contingents marched by on foot with the swinging stride and an exaggerated arm swing that was de rigueur. Occasionally they gave the *"eje . . . eje . . . eje . . . alalà,"* arms grimly outstretched in the ancient salute, eyes fish-glazed, faces dummy-set, an air of the smug self-satisfaction of brainwashed soldiers at parade moments. Now and then exaltation broke through, and they burst into the rollicking *"Giovanezza, Giovanezza,"* even smiled back when greeted by applause. Most watchers just stared as if this were something strange and remote from their lives—remarkable, for Italians are quick to display joy or hate. But the war and postwar period had created a great national trauma—a universal weariness.

The Black Shirts had the run of the city. Not that existing authority had been entirely replaced. The *carabinieri* and *Guardia Regia* (the special corps set up by Nitti) still made a token show of maintaining order. On the Street of Four Fountains between the Via Quirinal and Santa Maria Maggiore Church (the ceiling decorated with the first gold brought from the Americas) a group of Fascists ripped off the iron shutters from a gun store and reemerged with stolen rifles—like bumblebees out of a shaken nest. Gray-helmeted soldiers, rifles at the thigh, raced downhill, nailed boots ringing and sparking on the cobbles. Across the street, attendants of the Teatro Quattro Fontane stood ready with steel hooks to ring the shutters down if things got ugly. But the soldiers merely shooed the Black Shirts on their way.

At four o'clock the *Giornale di Roma* issued an extra. The king had appointed Mussolini prime minister—without conditions. The diminutive "French" king came out on the Quirinal balcony to read the proclamation to a swarm of deliriously screaming Black Shirts and apathetic civilians. The little king's enormous military cap, its visor almost down to the tip of his nose, barely showed above the stone balustrade. All Rome swirled into the streets in a mood of vast relief, almost gay and carefree, not for love of the Black Shirts but for the banishment of uncertainty.

By morning (October 30) more rain was driving over the towers of Rome, rattling on the balconies, gurgling in the rain pipes under the red-tiled eaves, staining the old walls of Trajan and Diocletian and the ancient Forum of the gladiators and lion-tossed Christians.

Once more the streets were almost empty. *Giornata triste!* Grim October in Italy whirled to its grave, shrouded now in the black robe of Fascism. The heavy boots of Caesarism had trampled down the Italian democracy. The marching boots, of course, were headed straight for World War II—though the memory of forty million dead was only four years stale. But the democracies sighed with relief that stability had been assured to Italy. If the democratic politicians read or understood Mussolini's speeches, they would have known that he represented world disorder. Except, there was contempt for Italy as a world power; it was too weak to be dangerous. They could not foresee Mussolini's legion thrust into Albania, the horrors of Guernica in Spain, the brutal attack on Ethiopia, the breaking down of the League of Nations and its replacement by world anarchy. World War I had been the first major effort of the peoples of the great democracies to commit suicide. Its end-products were the Russian Revolution, the rise of Fascism and Nazism, the smashing of democratic republicanism in Spain. The second suicide attempt, World War II, was brought closer by the marching feet of the Black Shirts—Communism, Fascism; militarism would be spread still wider across all the earth.

The wily Cavour had said, when he created a new Italy, setting a French dynasty on the throne, "It has been Italy's glory to have known how to constitute herself a nation without sacrificing liberty or independence, without suffering the dictatorial grasp of a Cromwell."

Now the dictator was here. The Fascist peace had been signed with clubs and guns; the drama was apparently finished for Italy—but certainly not for the world. Despite all the effort of the king to coat Mussolini's armed victory with the lacquer of constitutionality and law, political democracy was dead. "We have buried corrupt Liberty," Mussolini gloated. "We shall trample on its prostrate body again and again." And so a new era had begun—as in ancient Rome with the dictatorship of Sulla.

On the evening of the thirtieth the Black Shirts celebrated their victory. The rain over, they broke into the Rome headquarters of *Avanti,* the Socialist daily previously wrecked in Milan, and staggered out under great loads of books and furniture to fashionable Corso Umberto for a victory bonfire. The royal guards looked on indifferently as the loot was heaped on muddy stones, tracked with three days of marching and countermarching. Flames leapt into the twilight sky near the medieval Palazzo Doria. Under the shifting feet of the dancing, gibbering crowd, the heat curled back torn title pages: Max Stirner, *The Ego and His Own;* Trotsky, *Our Revolution.* The Black Shirts were burning their own gods! And at the head of the state now was the ex-Marxist, secretly financed by the frightened industrialists and bankers of Milan. So was Italy saved!

In short it was a "bona fide" revolution. It brought changes and even some needed reforms. And it stopped the land seizures. Many important Americans hailed Mussolini because he made the railroads run on time. He was the savior of Italy—for the people who counted. But it was not better technology, merely the use of bayonets which for a time any good railroad man will respect. Basically it was counterrevolution, which often wears the face of real social revolution. Indeed, both may be marching relentlessly down the same highway of history, not that history always takes the desirable course; it is merely an inevitable movement made by fallible men, with nudges from Nature. Both often march backward into the unknown future. History has had its prolonged darker periods.

It was National Socialism—though not yet so named. Mussolini used many of the classic Socialist catchwords. Repeatedly he insisted, as noted, that Italy had to fight for its place in the sun against the rich capitalist nations. He echoed the reiterated theses of Enrico Corradini:

Just as the methods of Socialism are strife and the general strike . . . so must the methods of nationalism be war or preparation for war . . . . The Nationalist idea is the greater one; instead of class, the whole nation; instead of the bourgeoisie, the world—the international struggle for markets, colonies, navies, and armies.

Really nothing new. This had been the game of the respectable governments of Western Europe for centuries. The newcomers of Italian nationalism merely called a spade a spade. But Italy had neither the will nor techniques nor resources to play again that power game in which it had already lost; it was merely the vainglorious beginning of a new march of death—such as larger nations had often made, are still making.

For the moment Mussolini was surprisingly tolerant of old forms. Il Duce even went through the formality of a vote of confidence from parliament. The National Chamber was permitted to reopen November 16 in traditional Montecitorio. But the deputies—except for Socialists and Catholics in hiding—had to walk single file through a narrow lane of close-rank Black Shirts, rifles at their chests. A few deputies faltered, perhaps out of last-minute shame and humiliation and fear.

Mussolini did not mince words. "The Italian people have imposed a government above and beyond any designation of Parliament. I leave it to the melancholy fanatics of ultra-constitutionalism to discourse more or less lamentingly on that fact. . . . The Revolution has its rights." He warned that with three hundred thousand troops at his back, "resolved to do anything . . . mystically ready" to obey his order, he could have "punished all those who defamed and attempted to throw mud at Fascism. I could have made this gray hall a bivouac for my bands. I could have closed Parliament and constituted a government purely Fascist." But the people needed their "toy"—parliament—he added insolently. The king, too, for the time being would be allowed to continue since "it is necessary for the people to feel that not all has fallen." In every revolution—this he had said a year earlier in Milan—a second wave always overwhelms the first. "In the Fascist revolution there will be no second wave."

Vain boast! Nothing ever stops that second wave. Neither King Canute, nor Caesar, nor a Mussolini. It would be delayed, but it came with the new World War, which Fascism helped precipitate. And the mutilated body of Mussolini would dangle from a telegraph post, like the liberty he had trampled. Not that Fascism would really die in the world. It would merely be draped for a time in new slogans, in new countries.

Suppressions and persecutions were not long in coming. Socialists Turati and Serrati found themselves in prison—odd bearded men of an earlier, more hopeful era. Matteotti was assassinated. Writers who declined to join the Fascist Writers' Corporation were hustled off to Lepanto Island prison for ten, fifteen, years—as for instance, Renzo Rendi, correspondent for a Chicago paper. Labor headquarters were smashed everywhere. For the sheer joy of shooting recklessly, that first night of October 30, the Black Shirts pumped machine-gun bullets for hours into the empty headquarters of the Provisional Roman Confederation of Labor and at lights in adjacent houses. The contents of the confederation's headquarters were burned in Croce Bianca Street, across from the Roman Colosseum.

Fascist police units were established in factories, either as secret stooges or brazenly parading between the machines with swinging blackjacks.

One initial step was the abolishing of the Commission of Inquiry on War Expenditures, scheduled to report to the king before December 31. Mussolini made any publishing of its findings punishable by imprisonment and a minimum five-thousand-lire fine. Involved here was a duel to the death between old financial interests (including the great Jesuit bank) and the Perrone brothers, worst of the wartime speculators. Il Duce did not intend to bite the hand that had fed him. Immediately he bailed the brothers and the Ansaldo steelworks out of the threatened postwar bankruptcy and put them in charge of the new Fascist Banco Nazionale di Credito, partners in a new enlarged government-private steel enterprise—"necessary for national security."

Elections were duly held, but the outcome was as certain as the rubber-stamp confidence given Mussolini by the cringing deputies of the National Chamber. The Black Shirts dragged nonvoters to the polls by force to provide the appearance of a free voting contest.

Over parliament was superimposed the organ of the "Corporate State," the new *Consiglio di Corporazioni,* made up of professionals, industrialists, bankers, labor men, and peasants. Had such a body been at all democratic, it would have been an organic reform with more vitality than strictly geographical representation, which mostly brings lawyers to the surface, for the state would be run by specialists and by people doing the actual work of the world. But only Fascist organizations were allowed to participate.

The third phase of Fascist rule—and this was put off for some years—was the recovery of *Italia Irredenta.* Since the issue never was forced with either Yugoslavia or France, the Black Shirts vented their patriotism on captive Austrians and Slavs in frontier areas, beating them and administering castor oil, destroying foreign-language newspapers and schools. Not that Il Duce forewent saber-rattling. He shook his fist repeatedly at France and England and sometimes the United States before great crowds in front of the Palazzo Venezia. But it was against weak little Albania that he made his first courageous thrust; then against Ethiopia, the last free country of Africa, aggressions that cost him dearly. It was a rowdy fist-shaking at the League of Nations, already half destroyed by the

great powers and plunged into the maelstrom of international anarchy, without knowing how to swim. Then he went adventuring in
Spain along with Hitler. He railed at the strong and bravely attacked the weak—as even greater powers do.

By then the second wave was almost due. It brought the occupation of Italy by German storm troopers who also had to bail Il Duce
out of defeat in Greece. In spite of Mussolini's posturing and new
goose-stepping drills, Italian troops did not want to fight, they had
no morale, nor did they have the equipment for modern war. They
weren't worth an empty peanut shell. Yet he had thrust Italy into a
futile death struggle, utterly disastrous, as the ally of Hitler and the
Japanese warlords. The counterwave rose to its death crest when
Italy was invaded by the Allies. Mussolini was overwhelmed, torn
apart savagely by Italians he had so long persecuted and derided.
The king went down also, if less ignominiously—belated retribution
for his earlier weakness. All *Italia Irredenta* and more were lost.

It had taken twenty years for the wave to gather its force—and
crash. During those twenty years the creative life of the Italian nation had all but been extinguished. Saber-rattling had drowned out
music. In the land of Leonardo vulgar sign painters had daubed up
walls with cheap slogans instead of imperishable frescoes. Dull,
bootlicking writers had had their fifth-rate work published by the
state, while their betters lived in fruitless exile or in prison. The
lives of millions, of a whole generation, were distorted.

Such is the nature of counterrevolution.

CHAPTER 9

THE SPANISH REPUBLIC

THE 1931 REVOLUTION in Spain was the product of war, outdated imperialism, and world depression. It was the belated result of the collapse of what in its day had been the greatest empire in history. As in Cuba, later, it was a hundred years in the making. The change-over was an attempt to catch up with the modern Western world and to join in the prevailing European system, which still stopped at the Pyrenees. Spain was a feudal anachronism.

Montesquieu noted in the middle of the eighteenth century that the Spanish monarchs had accumulated great stores of gold and silver but had failed to make a great people. The collapse of the empire, following the victories of San Martín and Bolívar, had saddled the Iberian peninsula with wreckage and an enormous crew of parasites from overseas; bureaucrats and arrogant proconsuls, nearly all inept wastrels, had come home to ride on the backs of their own people, since they could no longer drive their spurs into colonials. Spain was also overloaded with defeated generals, colonels, majors, captains, and soldiers, and the military retinues who, having no other haven, came back to live off the state and tax monies and strut through the streets like peacocks in medieval bespangled uniforms. Few native priests or nuns or monks had been permitted in overseas dominions; nearly all were Spaniards, and these, too, came home to make all Spain seem like a religious convent and church-yard. This extra burden of nonproductive people, converted into parasites, drained Spain of prosperity and the means to progress—added burdens in an era of national disaster and decline. The lot of ordinary Spaniards became miserable; the peasant could scarcely breathe; poverty widened, and beggardom was scarcely hidden by the exaggerated pomp, splendor, and braggadocio. The dawn-to-dark church bells could hardly drown out the moans of misery.

The loss of Cuba and the Philippines in 1898 was the echo of the long din of earlier overseas disaster. After the first stunned awareness of this final shame, a group of young intellectuals wished Spain to revamp its life and thinking by becoming a bona fide part of Europe. It must turn its back on further imperialist adventures, adopt political freedom, accept modern enlightenment. By joining in the economic and cultural life of Europe, Spain could be resuscitated. They managed to bring about some parliamentary reform, a few liberal laws.

They smelled fresh disaster when Spain joined with France in 1912 in the partition of Morocco. To ape the worst evils of Europe would merely drain Spain once more of its strength and resources. This was not true Europeanization but Africanization. It was turning toward the dark, not the light. The glory of Spain did not lie along the path of a fresh imperialistic adventure that would merely accentuate Spain's backwardness and poverty and governmental oppression. But the powerful idle generals, the corrupt bureaucrats, and the churchmen saw the Moroccan adventure as a chance to take new spoils and to justify their existence.

They were nearly all rusty blunderers. By the early twenties, thanks to the strains of international rivalries caused by World War I, by arrogant aggressions and mismanagement, revolt was aroused in the Rif, the eastern half of Morocco, in the summer of 1921. It was led by Abd-el-Krim, the wealthiest man in the region, whose father had had lucrative business deals, particularly in mining concessions, with the Germans.

The long-robed *harka* galloped down the hills, and in three days every Spanish post in the Rif had been wiped out, culminating in the July seizure of Anual. Sixteen thousand Spaniards were slaughtered, and General Silvestre committed suicide. "He was a good soldier," said Abd-el-Krim mildly, "but he lacked political sense." Three thousand panic-stricken survivors fled across the burning sand to Melilla, where they found little food and no supplies. Even water had to be brought over from Spain. Later four million pesetas had to be paid out to ransom prisoners, considerably less than the Bay of Pigs ransom money, but a great deal in days of Spanish national bankruptcy. The Rif became a republic overnight, and Spain fought a losing battle, with ever-mounting disaster in the rest of

Morocco, all of which, except for one coastal corner, came under the control of Abd-el-Krim.

Parliament held investigations that turned up shocking details of corruption and incompetence. The soldiers, treated like dogs, had lacked uniforms, shoes, food, medical care. It was the typical story of nearly all war, not often disclosed except after crushing defeat. The trail of double-dealing led on up to the palace, to the throne itself. Two generals were ordered tried. The government fell. Popular wrath mounted. Even the market women jeered and spit at the civil guards. Premier Eduardo Dato Iradier was assassinated.

The disclosures were never completed. The generals were extricated and the parliamentary system overthrown by the coup of General Miguel Primo de Rivera, backed by the army, the king, and the Catalan industrialists. He was a strutting overdecorated general, not without energy and competence, who had no roots in the people, but a mighty talent for absurd and magnificent rhetoric. So Fascism came to Spain.

To save the day Primo de Rivera rushed to Morocco, where he made magniloquent speeches about the greatness and the civilizing role of Spain. The Spaniards were driven out of holy city Sheshuán and every post, with a slaughter almost as great as that in the Rif, though many evacuations were bought and paid for. At the last the Spaniards were aided by their old enemy, Raisuli, but Abd-el-Krim took the fat man prisoner. The guns of the patriots pounded into Tetuán itself. More soldiers had to be rushed in from the peninsula, most of them unable to shoot a gun. By costly withdrawals Primo de Rivera finally salvaged the northwest corner of Morocco and a strip along the Atlantic coast. He then returned to Spain under triumphal arches announcing a great victory, a practice as old as Rome. The homeland, in any event, is conquered.

The republicans gathered in the *tertulia* (literary café circle) of Ramón del Valle Inclán, the Galician novelist, and moaned about the ill fate of the land, wrung their hands, and did nothing. The wizardlike novelist raked his fingers through his long gray pointed beard. Manuel Azaña, then an employee in the department of justice, and others drank their cups of *gordo grande*—five centavos— black coffee or sipped manzanilla. There, whenever not suffering too badly from neuralgia in his shoulder, came plump Indalecio Prieto, the future premier, in those days leader of the central wing of the Socialist party; Martín Luis Guzmán, Mexican writer, then editor of *El Sol*, Madrid's leading daily; the poet Pedro Domen-chino; occasionally also Alvarez del Vayo, correspondent of *La Na-ción* of Buenos Aires; and his brother-in-law, Alvarez de Albornoz; in fact, most of the future bigwigs of the republic.

Across the avenue in a sleeker café the students gathered more noisily every evening. Their discussions were more practical. They had just been ridden down in the streets by the soldiery. These youths were apparently the only brave persons in the country. They had just shocked even sympathizers by sawing up a bronze univer-sity statue of the king, shipping the arms, legs, hands, head, torso, all over the country, in imitation of a recent shocking homosexual murder. The students had begun to carry guns and use them. That was in 1929. By 1930 Primo was so shaky and so unpopular that the king, in a last-ditch effort to save his throne, dismissed him and put in discredited General Damasio Berenguer, who called local elec-tions. In April 1931 the republican slogan was "Your vote must be an arrow in the heart of the monarchy." It was. The vote was over-whelming for the republicans. Everywhere the people shouted, "Down with the King." The republicans won almost two to one.

Toward mid-April, Azaña and a little group of republicans walked calmly past the guards in *Gobernación* (Government Build-ing) and unfurled the flag of Caballero freedom on the roof, announc-ing the establishment of the republic. They named a provisional cabinet, headed by Niceto Alcalá Zamora, a conservative landholder. Azaña became minister of war; Indalecio Prieto, finance; Largo Ca-ballero (head of the Socialist General Works Alliance), minister of labor. General José Sanjurjo, head of the all-powerful civil guard, declared in their favor, and the guards added the violet ribbons of the republic to their uniforms. Peace was thereby assured. By 9 P.M. the king had fled by auto into France, never to return.

Not a drop of blood was shed—not then. The only casualty was a frightened Jesuit priest who jumped out of a window. But blood was bound to flow once the monarchists and conservatives, generals and clericals, got their breath, and blood did flow in torrents. The people were not to win their freedom so cheaply. But for the mo-ment they danced in the streets, and guitars thrummed all night long. Everywhere violet banners, violet dresses, ties, flags, signs, ap-peared.

The new Cortes, elected June 29, was made up of right, 42 seats; center, 130; left (including 114 Socialists) 291. It showed great en-

ergy. In August the religious orders were dissolved. General Berenguer was condemned to twenty years imprisonment for high treason. By October suffrage was granted to women. In November
Alfonso XIII was found guilty of high treason. In January all Jesuit
properties were confiscated. By September the estates of the gran-
dees were taken over.

A new constitution was adopted, and Niceto Alcalá Zamora was
again named President; Azaña, secretary of war. The constitution, a
liberal democratic document, scarcely leftist, declared that Spain
was "a democratic republic of workers of all classes organized as a
regime of Liberty and Justice." War was renounced as an instrument of national policy. Church and state were separated, subsidies
to the church halted, and freedom of religion and civil marriage established. Civil rights were set up, but the articles—ten to twenty—
that established local autonomy were only partially implemented.
Article Thirty-four established freedom from censorship. But rightist and leftist papers continued to appear with many blank spaces,
indicating continued censorship. New human rights enraged the reactionary elements without disarming them. The army was slightly
reduced but not restructured.

From 1932 on, serious difficulties appeared. Spain, like most
countries, was suffering from deep economic crisis. In August General José Sanjurjo seized the city of Sevilla, and was driven out, arrested, and sentenced to death, but escaped to Germany. Strikes
swept all the provinces. In 1928, under the dictatorship, there had
been only 96 strikes in all Spain and less evil economic conditions.
By 1930, when Primo was ousted, there were 402, and by 1933, 1,499
with 620,000 unemployed. Production was declining, and prices
rose 24 percent. Iron ore output was less than half that of 1929. In
Biscaya less than a fourth of the mines were operating. Coal output
was dropping badly.

Factionalism developed in the government parties. The Communists attacked the administration relentlessly. The Socialists gave
only grudging support. Azaña was forced out in September 1933.
The Fascists (the Falange)—led by José Antonio Primo de Rivera,
son of the deposed dictator, backed by millionaire Morocco war-
speculator Juan March, who had been put in jail—were active and
merged with the Juntas de Ofensiva Nacional-Sindicalistas (JONS).
They broke up workers' meetings, smashed strikes, and presently
killed political opponents. Important also was the Fascist-type Reno-

vación Española, led by the ex-monarchist Antonio Goicoechea and José María Gil Robles, an editor of the clerical *El Debate*. Gil Robles formed a strong clerical and landlord coalition, the Popular Action party, and it won 62 seats in the December 1933 election—part of a rightist bloc of 207, as compared with a centrist 167. The left representation had declined to only 99 deputies. The Socialist vote had been cut in half. The republic was in the hands of its enemies.

Right-wing republican Alejandro Lerroux, secretly leagued with Gil Robles, became premier, followed soon by Ricardo Samper, Basque nationalist. Disorders grew. In April 1934 Gil Robles staged a Fascist parade in Asturias and a mass meeting at the Escorial, the monastery near Madrid. This was answered by a twenty-four-hour general strike, which for the first time drew the Anarcho-Syndicalists, mostly in Catalonia, into a united front with the General Workers' Alliance. A mass meeting of a hundred thousand persons was staged in Madrid. But the People's House (labor headquarters) was closed by the police, and hundreds of workers were jailed.

On October 3, as bitterness grew, the Gil Robles Fascists were brought openly into the government. A general strike was called, fighting broke out in Biscaya, León, and Madrid. Open insurrections began in Asturias and in Barcelona, where the curtailment of autonomy, granted in part at the outset by the republic, was abolished, thus arousing not only the Anarchists, Socialists, and the Andrés Nin Trotskyites, but nationalists of every class. Automobiles and government buildings were seized. A militia of ten thousand workers was organized. The evening of October 6 the Catalonian Republic was declared. By the following day it had been suppressed in blood.

The Asturias Commune, chiefly headed by mine workers who organized a militia force, lasted from October 5 to 19. In Oviedo the banks were seized. Guerrilla warfare wiped out soldiers' garrisons throughout the province. The government, not trusting the regular army, brought Arab troops and the Foreign Legion in from Africa. After bitter fighting, an armistice was declared October 19. The arrangements were soon violated by the government forces. Villagers were butchered.

Spain entered a period of martial law. The firing squads went to work on the streets and plazas. Thirty thousand prisoners filled the jails. Prieto fled to France. Azaña, Largo Caballero, and others were put on trial. Catalan leader Luis Campanys and his associates were condemned to thirty years. Azaña was acquitted. But leaders of the Asturians' revolt were condemned to death. Agrarian reform was abolished. The economy went from bad to worse, perhaps a million and a half unemployed. Exports dropped.

Throughout Spain, some thirty-five thousand Socialists, Anarchists, and Communists were jailed. But the country was now aroused. The elections of February 1936 produced a more pronounced swing to the left. The Communist vote had grown from sixty thousand to four hundred thousand, and sixteen deputies were elected, as compared to one in 1933. The Popular Front, led by Largo Caballero, obtained 268 seats; the center and right, 205. Thirty thousand people walked out of jail.

The Falangists, or Christian Fascists, were determined not to accept the electoral verdict. José Calvo Sotelo, associate of Gil Robles, decared, "Democracy in Spain will always lead inevitably to Communism." The Fascists, monarchists, clergy, and landholders set out to destroy democracy, an effort soon abetted by all the great powers, as Europe shaped up for World War II.

Manuel Azaña replied to Sotelo's threat, "There is no danger of waking up one morning and finding Communism ruling the country." No Communist formed part of his government. "There is great need," he added, "for social justice in Spain, and my purpose is to prevent the accumulation of great wealth by a few individuals while many suffer from hunger and poverty."

The restored republic declared a general amnesty, restored civil rights, and reformed the judiciary; gave semiautonomy to Catalonia, provided land for eighty-seven thousand peasant families, or half a million people, disbanded the more overt Fascist groups and purged Fascists from the police. Primo de Rivera II, head of the Falange, was arrested. Monarchist and pro-Fascist generals were reassigned to outlying provinces. They began smuggling in arms. But capital, to the tune of millions, flowed from the country. The big landowners left their lands idle, and the peasants were starving. Fascist gangs began assassinating well-known republicans. The Workers Defense went into action, perpetrating counterassassinations. A mutiny in the Alcalá de Henares barracks near Madrid had to be suppressed.

On June 17 Gil Robles charged that 251 churches had been burned, 161 rightists killed, 10 rightist newspapers wrecked. He threatened a Fascist putsch.

The churches, said a left spokesman, were burned, not because of anti-Catholicism, but because they were centers of Fascist intrigue and secret arsenals for weaponry.

On July 21 a leading member of the Socialist Youth League was assassinated on orders, it was said, of Calvo Sotelo. Six hours later Calvo Sotelo was gunned down by a civil guard. Two more Fascists were killed during riots at his funeral. The rightists stalked out of parliament. It was the signal for the armed revolt already well planned.

Eight army generals were prepared to strike. Young General Francisco Franco, earlier sent to garrison the Canary Islands, jumped the gun on July 17 and took over in North Africa, where Ceuta and Melilla simultaneously revolted. He was the most audacious of the generals and had strong support from his brother in the air force. He soon assumed the ascendancy in the armed revolt and was recognized as the leader by the other rebellious generals, the Falangists and the Church party.

General Queipo de Llano seized the city of Sevilla. In Barcelona General Domingo Batet moved troops into strategic positions during the night, and had his forces on the streets within a half an hour of receiving the go-ahead signal on July 20. He occupied the chief hotel, the main plaza, and strategic buildings.

The workers threw up barricades, and four hundred regular soldiers joined them. By 4 P.M. the entire Fascist command was captured. Two days later an anti-Fascist committee of workers, militia, civil guards, and police established the "Revolutionary Order."

In Madrid the revolters raised the white flag after four hours of fighting. Several officers were shot by their own men. The uprising never got off the ground.

But 75 percent of the army, though the rank and file could not be counted upon, was in rebellion elsewhere. About half the civil guard and a fourth of the assault militia were led to the rebel side. But the navy and air force stood by the government, and it began arming the workers.

Protected by a German war vessel, Franco again took the initiative. He began moving Moors and Riffs over to the mainland—also the Foreign Legion, largely made up of criminal riffraff. When the dust cleared away, the republican government retained control of half the country and two-thirds of the population. Of the remaining third, the majority were probably anti-Fascist, though the Carlists, who had staged off-and-on insurrections for forty years, appeared in force in red berets and red-cross green armbands.

The republicans were by no means united, but the common danger drew all factions into a common front; republicans, Socialists (three factions), Anarcho-Syndicalists, Communists, and Trotskyites, among others. However, the new resistance government, set up by Azaña was 100 percent republican; not even one Socialist was included. Franco announced to the world that his aim was to save Spain and western Europe from Communism. Gil Robles, curiously enough opposing the civil war, left the country, but remarked on leaving that there were now only two solutions: a military dictatorship or a Communist Spain. For him, of course, anything not overly pro-monarchical, pro-church, pro-land monopoly, was Communism. Anybody and anything not adhering to the extreme right was Red.

Spain was not merely the battlefield of contending factions but the testing ground for forthcoming World War II. Franco moved at once to obtain international aid. Mussolini was offered a base in Africa; Ceuta, across from Gibraltar, as well as Port Mahón in the Balearic Islands. Germany was also to receive a reward of territory in the Balearic Islands. German participation had already been arranged for by the exiled Sanjurjo, and bombing planes and munitions, ordered by him as early as March, were on hand for Franco within weeks of the uprising. German and Italian agents and officers swarmed into Morocco, the Balearic Islands, and Spain itself.

The third great outside force backing Franco was the Catholic church, which had suffered loss of property, subsidies, and suppression of the orders by the republic. It now beat the drums of the Red Menace everywhere, particularly in the United States.

In August the *Deutschland* escorted more Moorish and Riff contingents to the mainland, via Cádiz. Twenty German heavy bombers and five pursuit planes reached the city of Sevilla, besides those sent to Africa, the islands, and various ports of the peninsula. Other war materials were sent in via Africa, Cádiz, and Portugal, for the rebels controlled the frontier. The 55th, 57th, and 58th Italian air squadrons were flown to Morocco. Two planes crashed at Oran. As early as August 5 an Italian plane bombed the Loyal cruiser *Liber-*

tad, which was shelling Tarifa. The Italian destroyer *Antonio de Noli* arrived off Sevilla. Before the republic was overthrown, the Italian planes would destroy Guernica and its people, a massacre of men, women, and children, so vividly portrayed in Picasso's huge mural.

The republicans received some early aid (as did Franco) from France, till Socialist Premier Léon Blum clamped down an embargo. Great Britain and the United States also cut off aid to both sides. A neutrality and nonintervention agreement was worked out, which was meaningless, since Portugal did not even attend the conferences, while Germany and Italy ignored it. Mostly the agreements benefited Franco. Certainly the United States embargo was far from effective. American planes were sent to Franco via Canada; whereas Cordell Hull forced Mexico to stop trans-shipping United States aircraft to the republicans, American oil companies sent in gas and oil to Franco (very little to the republic), and merely sent the State Department a fine of fifteen thousand dollars for each shipment—much as Kansas saloons operated wide open during their prohibition before Carry Nation days. In short, Franco received massive aid throughout the struggle from Germany, Italy, and elsewhere. The failure of the so-called democracies to support the Spanish republic was thus the first Munich—and significant because it gave the Fascist allies a stage on which to try out their weapons.

By September the ineffective republican cabinet, which had failed to take aggressive military measures, gave way to a Popular Front coalition, headed by Francisco Largo Caballero, the left Socialist, who was commander of the powerful UGT (General Union of Labor). It now affiliated with the National Confederation of Labor (CNT), the Syndicalist labor union. The new cabinet included six Socialists, three left republicans, two Communists, one Republican Unionist, one left Catalan nationalist. For some, Largo Caballero, though the most powerful popular figure of the day, did not wholly inspire confidence. He had accepted a high position under Primo de Rivera and thereby had kept the Socialists and labor government quiescent in support of that dictator. Not until the Fascist repressions and assassinations of 1934 had Largo come out strongly in opposition. "We are fighting for the Democratic Republic," the new government announced.

The new setup, since nearly all aid from the West was cut off, made a bid for Soviet support and received it. The aid was too little and too late, but it came—at a price. Soviet agents and military officers or Spanish Communists quickly moved into key positions, controlling much of the army, the secret police, and propaganda. Thereby the unity of the republic and its people was destroyed. Anarcho-Syndicalists, Trotskyites, nationalists, and other nonorthodox leaders were purged by the new commissions, and some went before the firing squad.

Outside volunteers flocked in from all countries to fight the Fascists (who also received quite a few foreign volunteers). From the United States on the side of the republic appeared the Lincoln Brigade and such writers as John Dos Passos and Ernest Hemingway. Tito managed to send in thousands of Yugoslavians, some of whom later became leaders in the Yugoslavian resistance fight against the invading Italians and Germans.

Had it been purely a domestic civil war, there can be little doubt but that the democratic republic would have come out on top, and as a democratic republic, not a Communist state. But it was destroyed by the African Legion, by the Germans and Italian Fascists and Nazis, and by the indifference and even double-dealing of the Western democracies. When Socialist premier, Léon Blum, refused to aid the republic and clamped down an embargo, he stuck a knife into his own back—and into the back of France, it turned out. Finally, in a dark hour the republic was destroyed by its only friends, the Soviet government, who in the name of defending it, struck it down. Spain thus became a testing ground for all the dark forces of European imperialism, of Fascism, Nazism, and Stalinism, and the deluded "capitalist democracies."

The republic had been a struggle of the Spanish people against feudalism, war, imperialism, and Fascism; its downfall marked the further spread of the dark forces that were to engulf the world. The light went out first in Spain. Its republicans and intellectuals fled to France and to Latin America. Alvarez del Veyo joined the staff of the *Nation* in New York. Printing skills, for which Spain had long been famous, were greatly advanced in Mexico and Buenos Aires by émigrés. Argentines became the greatest publishers of Spanish books and, during the Vichy government in France, the greatest publishers of French books in the world, a position the publishers of Argentina held until the United States, fighting Juan Perón, backed Pedro Aramburú's dictatorship. Economic decline set in, which was further accelerated by the Onganía military dictatorship, now in power. Mexico, and Guatemala have been the only governments in the world to abide by the United Nations' decision not to recognize Franco. Today his greatest ally is the United States, whose billions have helped keep him in power long after his normal span.

His end is now in sight, and what will come after, no man can foretell.

CHAPTER 10

THE CELESTIAL EMPIRE

SUN YAT-SEN, LEADER of the Kuomintang party, one-time University of California student and doctor, the revolutionist who declared the republic of China in 1911, had been a member of the Society of Righteous Fists, the Boxers, who staged an anti-foreign uprising in 1899. It was suppressed by the United States and European powers. They laid a fuse that was to explode in the great revolution of 1930 to 1949.

The Boxers were an offshoot of the secret White Lotus Society, founded by a Buddhist monk in the fifth century. Six centuries later they ran the Mongols out of China, founded dynasties, fought the Manchus for hundreds of years. The white lotus is a flower that rises to greet the sun and sinks into the water at night. Though often led by monks or wealthy landlords, the order backed peasant revolts century after century, which fought and sometimes succeeded in overthrowing feudal rulers. A White Lotus revolt broke out in 1760 and was suppressed, but by 1807 the society controlled much of South China.

The Taiping Rebellion, the greatest revolution in China's history before that of Mao Tse-tung, began in the Yangtze Valley in 1850. It was led by a Christian fanatic, who called himself the Prince of Heaven. His regime ruled all of South China for fifteen years. The Taiping guerrillas were forbidden to take food from the peasants by force or to enter any dwelling without an invitation. Women, many of whom fought in the revolutionary armies, were given the same rights as men. All land titles were abolished, and land was tilled in common. "No man shall be without food or warmth," said the Prince of Heaven. He wrote five new gospels—"In all things men

[187]

shall be equal." "Wealth Must Be Shared" was the slogan, an early version of Huey Long's "Every Man a King."

The Taiping empire was finally overthrown in 1865 by the Manchus, aided by the British and Americans. Nanking was captured, and all the defenders slaughtered, as the Manchus had been slaughtered when the Taiping forces entered more than a decade before. In all, some forty million people were killed in these struggles.

The Chinese empress of the restoration rebuilt the feudal system and was adamant against change or new ideas. Nevertheless a period of enlightenment ensued, chiefly due to Yen Fu, a naval cadet who had studied at the Greenwich naval academy. The greatest translator of all time, he put into Chinese Darwin's *The Origin of Species*, Huxley's *Evolution and Ethics*, Adam Smith's *Wealth of Nations*, Herbert Spencer's *Principles of Sociology*, Montesquieu's *L'Esprit des Lois*, John Stuart Mill's *On Liberty*—at least 112 books in all from 5 foreign languages. Several were banned, but most had a wide circulation. They influenced all Chinese thinking. They also laid the ground for further revolution. Scholars began finding historical wisdom in Confucius' neglected *Li Chi* (*Book of Rites*) which brought about both an intellectual and a religious revival. "When the great Tao was practiced, the world was common to all men; men of talents, virtue and ability were selected; sincerity was emphasized and friendship cultivated." There was security for the aged; the able bodied were employed; child care and education were provided. "Everybody had the wherewithal to support themselves. People worked for the common good." This was known as the great Ta Tung—the Great Unity.

As a result of such teachings, young Emperor Kuang Hsü headed a great reform movement—the famous hundred days—and attempted to reorganize all society—army, banks, postal services—on the basis of universal equality. He sought to abolish money and private property. Eventually the state would wither away.

The old dowager empress shook the sleep out of her eyes and the arthritis out of her body, took back the power, and exiled the emperor to an island on one of the lakes within the high purple walls of the Forbidden Palace City. Reform and reformers were strangled.

After the defeat of China by Japan in 1895, revolutionary discontent, particularly among students, merchants, businessmen, and professionals, gathered force and concentrated in the Boxer Rebellion. The surge of nationalism had been channeled into bitter antiforeignism by the Manchu rulers, to save themselves. The targets were foreign capital, which was penetrating China with eager voracity, and the governments that supported the take-over by bayonets and diplomacy. The Boxer Rebellion was quickly suppressed by the European imperialists and by the United States. The dowager empress had to pay a whopping big indemnity, of which the United States returned half its share—$12,500,000—for exchange students.

If this generosity contrasted brightly with the conduct of the other powers, it did not fool the Chinese people. They saw the gift and the American Open Door policy—the United States had previously been kept out of China—as the wedges for economic penetration and participation of American investors in the exploitation of China's resources and her cheap labor. The only hope was that the United States' policy might prove more beneficent.

But the Boxer Rebellion opened the door to political and social upheaval, the vast revolution that eventually swept across the land. Its first leader was Sun Yat-sen, a revolutionist since 1895, who was gradually forging his organized militant group, the Kuomintang nationalists. He was born in 1866, and from 1895 on launched thirteen unsuccessful invasions from Hong Kong and French Indochina.

He knew the history of the earlier Taiping revolt and considered that the Kuomintang had inherited the mantle of that movement. It had sought to overthrow the Manchus, and that was the hope of Sun Yat-sen also. In 1905, faced with growing discontent, the Manchu regime initiated a few moderate reforms and in 1906 announced a seven-year program of constitutional changes. But the empress' death brought to the throne the three-year-old Pu-yi, with his father as regent. The father attempted to halt all reform and dismissed Sheh-Kai, China's ablest administrator. However, the revolutionists and reformers obtained permission to meet in Peking in 1910. This convention disbanded after a promise was made for the election of a parliament in 1913.

But in 1911 there were a number of insurrections and troop revolts, demanding local autonomy or violently denouncing concessions to foreigners. On January 1, 1912, a revolutionary assembly chose Sun Yat-sen president of a provisional republican government. The Manchu government abdicated February 12, after 270 years of rule. Actually Pu-yi was allowed to live on in seclusion as nominal emperor in one of the imperial palaces until 1924.

Sun Yet-sen appealed to the Western powers for help. None responded. Lenin, not yet in power, wrote that the Chinese leader was

a militant sincere spirit of democracy . . . . Without equivocating he presented the problems of the conditions of the masses and of the mass struggle, with warm feelings toward the toilers and exploited. He believes in the justice of their cause and in their strength . . . a really great ideology of a really great people.

He was fighting "age-old oppression."

In 1913, per previous arrangements, Sun Yat-sen handed over the presidency to Yüan Shih-kai, controlled by the north. He soon had trouble with southerners and Sun Yat-sen and the Kuomintang over democratic forms. Ill feeling came to a head when the more conservative dictatorial Yüan negotiated a $25 million loan from a consortium of European, Russian, and Japanese bankers. An effort was made to throw him out—"the second revolution." He ousted all Kuomintang deputies and dissolved parliament entirely, becoming an out-and-out dictator. With his death in June 1916 Vice-President Li Yüan-hung took over and reestablished parliament. Dissension over foreign loans and the granting of concessions continued. From 1909 to 1914 Japan had given about $50 million and from 1914 to 1918, nearly $200 million more.

In June 1917 Li Yüan-hung dissolved parliament again, and an armed effort was made to restore the monarchy. Late that year the Kuomintang plus a majority of parliament set up the separate constitutional government in Canton. By then a dozen military leaders were carving out their own individual spheres. But the only government recognized and receiving outside aid was that of Peking.

Early in 1914, after declaring war on Germany, Japan had invaded China to take over the Kiaochow Bay area leased by Germany in 1898. Asked to withdraw, they pressed with twenty-one demands, practically making all China a protectorate. A Japanese leader called it "the opportunity of a hundred years," to solve the Chinese question—"When a cat eats a rat it assuredly solves the rat problem." The demands were presented on war office stationery, watermarked with machine guns and dreadnoughts. When the demands became known, the United States and other allies protested, but on May 25, 1915, the president of China, who had taken over from Sun Yat-sen, had to bow to Japan's demands, following threats of invasion, for special privileges in Manchuria, control of the railroads, and oil, iron, and coal concessions. The Kuomintang swore never to recognize these arrangements.

World War I gave Japan an even freer hand in China. In February 1917 England, France, and Russia, in return for assistance from the Japanese fleet in the Mediterranean, secretly granted further Japanese claims on China and also permission for China to join the war. The Allied hope was to secure Chinese coolies to work in the factories and fields behind the battle lines in Europe. Five hundred, incidentally, were drowned when a French ship was torpedoed August 14, 1917.

When it became known that the Allies, including the United States, had ignored China and recognized Japanese claims, violent demonstrations occurred. Student unions were particularly active and pro-Japanese officials in the government were hotly denounced as traitors. The merchants and bankers backed the students. Trade with Japan came almost to a halt. As the situation worsened, President Warren G. Harding called an eight-power conference on the Far East (1921–1922). Except for promises for the future, China was given the cold shoulder in favor of Japan. The parley did, with certain conditions, restore Shantung to Chinese control. Japan subsequently sent in troops.

Hostility against Japan and Allied betrayals gave the new Soviet government the chance to forge strong ties with the Canton government, which was almost independent in south China. In 1923 it sent over General Adolph A. Joffe, one of the negotiators with Trotsky at Brest-Litovsk, to Canton. He paved the way for Mikhail Borodin to come over as a political mentor and to take over the military instruction. Chiang Kai-shek was sent to Moscow.

Even in those early days, the Chinese Revolution, which was to gather volume and majesty over the years, was a frightening prospect for the West. At the outset the country was torn asunder. It was to take many years before the warlords in the provinces, plundering the people, could be brought under control or destroyed. But fears of a rejuvenated China still plague the heads of state in Europe and Washington, and by 1969 those of the Soviet Union as well.

Undoubtedly the Chinese Revolution has been and is the most formidable event of our era. If less immediately menacing to Western capitalism than that of Russia, it has far greater significance. The Celestial Empire occupies a continental area greater than all Europe, and its nine hundred million people are known for their industry, ingenuity, patience, wisdom, and courage—a people in whom cruelty and friendliness rub elbows, above all a highly cultured and aesthetic people.

China has a long coast indented by handsome harbors with great cities. Its enormous rivers nourish the richest, most densely populated areas. The Hwang Ho, or Yellow River, rising in the northwest near the Great Wall, passes through the rich "yellow earth," fertile loesses from four to six hundred feet deep, to the China Sea. Further south the Long River, the Yangtze, flows thirty-four hundred miles from high in Tibet's snow mountains through the iron gorges of the Szechwan Mountains, past the great cities of Chengtu and Chungking, crosses great alluvial plains that grow rice and tobacco, cereals and vegetables, cotton and soy beans, and enters the ocean through the rich delta near Shanghai, where the population density reaches more than thirty-one hundred persons per square mile.

From the great harbors to the far-flung frontier are to be found every known mineral resource. There are vast iron and coal deposits, oil and shale, great quantities of tin, tungsten, manganese, lead, copper, zinc, antimony, bauxite. Rapidly industrializing since the Revolution, Chinese production is likely to rival that of all other countries by the end of the century and with its vast resources and population could soon become the most powerful country on earth.

It already has the H-bomb, thanks to its fine scientific university and its scientists, greatly favored and assisted, most of whom were well trained in the Soviet Union or in the United States, principally Dr. H. S. Tsien, so harassed when in this country. For five years, from 1950 on, he was arbitrarily detained in Los Angeles County. China has or will soon have rockets, though perhaps not ICBM ballistic missiles, to deliver bombs.

The revolutionary regime in China, nearing its sixtieth year—twenty-one years under Mao Tse-tung—has actively promoted every type of production. China can be baited and annoyed—with grave consequences for the future—but nothing seems likely to halt its ascending spiral. Under more normal international conditions her development and her contributions to man's knowledge and progress would benefit the world.

We are fifty years ahead of our story. Here we are concerned with the origin and course of China's Revolution. As early as the twenties the United States attempted to win control of the new China and block the revolutionary trends, especially as the Soviets were also on the scene. United States officials believed that the way to block popular upheaval—a forlorn hope at best, scarcely based on reality—was through the military, the most corrupt part of powerful ruling north China—and particularly, through Chiang Kai-shek, later described by Mao Tse-tung as the "imperialist sheep-dog."

Chiang did block the popular forces of China for many years, causing much bloodshed. He was the son of a small merchant, took highest honors at the imperial military academy in Peking, spent three years in Japan with the Takada artillery regiment, then left the army and joined the Kuomintang in 1911, administering various posts, in which he quickly amassed a fortune. In 1923 Sun Yat-sen sent him off to Moscow. He returned with Bolshevist general Vassily Blücher, and they reorganized the Kuomintang army.

After Sun Yat-sen died in 1925, Chiang became generalissimo, or commander-in-chief. He put down the powerful northern warlords in the three summer months of 1926. In 1927 he seized Nanking and married Soong Mai-ling, his second wife. Two members of her family, T. V. Soong and H. H. Kung, already rich, proceeded to loot Chinese and United States aid funds. His marriage caused Chiang to become a Protestant, which more than ever endeared him to the United States, and his rich in-laws had important financial and business ties with the West. Their wealth and his own wealth caused his sympathies with the Soviets and the Communists to fade rapidly. He was ambitious, and the Communists became a serious barrier to his desire to control the army and the state.

Chiang broke openly with Moscow in 1927 and sent Borodin, head of the Kuomintang military academy, and Indian revolutionist M. N. Roy flying back to Russia. He thrust Ho Chi Minh, the Vietnam revolutionist, in jail for a year. Presently he ordered the destruction of all labor and peasant organizations, and he put down a Canton strike, backed by schoolteacher Mao and General Chu Teh, with blood and steel. With Mao, Chu Teh took up guerrilla warfare at Changsha near Mao's birthplace.

Mao was born in 1892 in Hunan Province on a farm near the

great Hsiang River, where he watched the soiled sampan sails drift by. The best soldiers and the best scholars were said to have come from Hunan. If true, Mao certainly lived up to both traditions. He was only seven when his father, something of a stubborn martinet, put him to work in the rice paddies, chiefly to scare away the birds. He went through the 1906 year of famine and its peasant riots and the insurrection of thirty thousand coal miners, peasants, and secret societies. It was put down with beheadings. Still another insurrection of the Big Brother Secret Society, a purely local peasant revolt was also suppressed.

He soon disliked working in the fields and preferred to read. When he was ten he devoured the four great Chinese novels: *The Dream of the Red Chamber, The Journey to the West, All Men Are Brothers,* and the *Three Kingdoms.* He was particularly fascinated by *All Men Are Brothers,* the story of bandits who took to the hills.

He went off to school against the wishes of his father, who refused to help him. He picked up odd jobs, saved his candle drippings to make new candles, half starved and half froze. Ridiculed by his well-to-do classmates, he was not daunted and won the close friendship of a wealthy student. They studied strange doctrines, became nudists, and loved to swim. He studied Confucius, though he hated religion and had abandoned Buddhism when still a boy, to his mother's sorrow. As time went on, he learned Confucius by heart, became enamored, not perhaps of his stuffy maxims for the deference of peasant serfs, but of his interpretation of history and his vision of utopia. All his life Mao has quoted Confucius.

To guerrilla tactics he applied the battle principles of Sun Wu's famous sixth-century-B.C. treatise on war, and he studied the military strategy of previous civil wars and European conflicts.

He went on to preparatory school. Still half starved, he went down the river to attend the University of Peking. There he wandered through the gardens of the imperial palace, where a few years before he would not have been admitted, and thought about human freedom, not foreseeing the day when he would review the troops of his victorious armies from these historic balconies.

His faithful associate in his guerrilla efforts and on the Long March, General Chu Teh—his name means "Red Virtue"—became the military genius of the Revolution. Son of a rich landlord and a graduate of the Yünnan military academy, he became a revolutionary brigadier general, held high posts, became wealthy, had nine concubines and a sumptuous palace, and smoked opium. In 1922 he kicked his opium habit cold turkey, abandoned his wealth, and became a common sailor on a Shanghai-Hankow riverboat. Turned Communist in 1923, he went to Germany and Paris, where he organized Communist cells among the resident Chinese. In Moscow he studied the doctrines of Marx and Lenin. Returning to Peking, he resumed his military career, but broke with Chiang Kai-shek when the latter drove the Communists out of the Kuomintang.

From 1930 to 1934 Chiang sent five great expeditions against the forces of Mao and Chu, armies of hundreds of thousands of men, equipped with the most modern weapons and advised by the German military mission. All but the last were routed.

In October 1934 the rebel army broke through a massive encirclement, and Mao and Chu led ninety thousand men 4,000 miles across China—the Long March—to Yenan. Forty thousand men survived, and most of these had never started on the march. They crossed the great plains, through the great iron gorge near Tibet, over 15,000-foot snow passes, floundering through swamps as big as Texas.

In northwest Shensi Province at Yenan near the Mongolian border, Mao set up headquarters in caves, safe from airplanes, where he wrote poetry about the Long March and the snow passes, in addition to four notable books on politics and society, on the new democracy and the Japanese war—each marvelously prophetic. The Japanese had invaded Manchuria as early as 1931, setting up a puppet state, and by 1933 they forced the Chinese to abandon all territory between the Great Wall and Peking.

Once more Chiang tried to extirpate Mao's forces. This time he moved against them in person, but was taken prisoner by a rebellious young warlord. Mao secured Chiang's release, and after July 7, 1937, when the Japanese invaded north China, a united front was set up. The Red army was reorganized as the Eighth Route Army. Chou En-lai, Mao's minister, was seated in the Central War Council and in the People's Political Council, organs of the Chiang regime. Presently Red guerrillas in central China were reorganized as the Fourth army.

But Chiang was more concerned, as during the previous annihilation campaigns, with fighting the Communists than the Japanese invaders, whom he considered the lesser of the two evils. He told his United States advisers—who were sent in with large quantities of war material and who wanted the Japanese destroyed—that unless national unity, i.e., the supremacy of his own government, was attained, nothing would be gained by throwing out the Japanese. He ringed Communist-held Shensi and Kansu provinces with ten thousand blockhouses and pillboxes, which tied up two hundred thousand troops or more. For a short time the leftists were confined to ninety thousand square miles, but the Japanese overran all northeast and much of central China, the islands, and coast cities. Chiang was pushed back to southwest China. The Communists, however, pushed into central China and even crossed the Yangtze River here and there.

By the time of the collapse of Japan in 1945, the leftist armies controlled four hundred thousand square miles and a hundred million people, an army of nine hundred thousand men and a militia of two million. They had borne the brunt of the fighting in Manchuria and other areas.

General Douglas MacArthur ordered the Japanese not to surrender to the Communists, and the United States rushed Chiang's troops north by plane and sea. Also, Stalin, in Moscow, in return for joint control of Port Arthur, a free port at Dairen, and joint operation of the Manchurian railroads, threw his support to Chiang and not the Communists. Stalin was contemptuous of Mao's brand of communism, was not happy at the idea of erecting a powerful Communist rival, and felt that Russia's national interests could best be served by securing immediate concessions from Chiang, who he felt, given his strong Western backing, would come out on top in any case. He himself could make a quick grab at Mongolia and Manchuria and gain a warm-weather port in the Pacific—something he could not, in any case, obtain from Mao. For similar reasons he had already sold Tito of Yugoslavia down the river.

The Russians took over the industrialized cities of Manchuria and, while obeying Chiang's orders not to surrender them to the Communists who held the western areas, proceeded to strip them of all factories, machinery, railroad ties, even office furniture. The great province, larger than half a dozen European countries, was thoroughly plundered before Chiang could take over. The United States, and hence Chiang, were chiefly concerned over Manchuria, the wealthiest province, and Chiang committed his best United States trained troops there—moving them from warm Burma north to snow country, a violent shift of climate. Thereby he thrust them into a trap, from which they never escaped. The Communists soon cut the rail links with central China.

However, even before the surrender, the anti-Communist General Patrick Hurley, special emissary of President Franklin Delano Roosevelt, tried to set up a coalition government. His failure spawned General George Marshall's attempt to perform the same difficult task. Two and a half weeks after the Japanese surrender on August 10, 1945, Mao Tse-tung took his first air flight in a United States plane to work out an agreement with Chiang. They even appeared before the public on the official balconies. On January 10, 1946, a cease-fire was ordered. But Mao went home not overly optimistic. Chiang had refused to come to any compromise with Mao on military control, though the leftist leader had offered to cut his forces down to one-fifth the total for the entire army. Furthermore, Mao noted that the United States, far from being neutral, was supplying Chiang with vast amounts of war material and planes; Chiang even flew north in Marshall's personal plane.

Soon both sides, particularly the Nationalists, were breaking the armistice. Before long, great battles shaped up in Manchuria. On March 19, 1947, the Kuomintang troops occupied Yenan, but elsewhere they were in bad trouble.

By July, when torrential rains brought northern operations to a halt, Chiang Kai-shek had given up half the territory he had held in Manchuria, had even been forced to abandon two thirds of the railroads and had lost enormous quantities of weapons and supplies, most of it of United States manufacture.

The Communist discipline and morale, commented Colonel Max Chassin, were "incomparably better than [that of] the Nationalists." By October Chiang's forces had withdrawn into the cities, which were quickly surrounded and cut off and eventually captured. With the fall of Mukden the following year, Manchuria was lost.

By the end of 1947 the Reds were in full control of Shensi and Hopei provinces. The Communists moved on into Shantung Province, and the Nationalists threw half a million men against them by sea and land, but met with bitter defeat.

In central China, the Red army, fifty thousand strong, under General Liu Po-Ch'eng, moved toward Hunan and seized fifty thousand rifles from the Nationalist arsenal in Liuan. By August 22, 1947, twenty thousand Red troops had crossed the Yellow River and pushed on toward the Yangtze.

Soon Mao's entire Eighth Route Army crossed the Yellow River. From then on the Communists began taking the offensive in force everywhere—a change that Mao formally announced on December 25. By then the Basic Agrarian Law, confiscating estates and giving land to the peasants, had been issued and was being put into effect, winning the rural people to Mao's cause as never before.

The great cities north, west, and south were captured. Peking was surrounded. The revolutionists entered the city January 31, 1949, and Mao Tse-tung arrived March 25 and took over the one-time royal palace behind the Purple Walls, where he viewed a million fighting men and millions of Chinese carrying banners with his portrait and that of Augusto César Sandino who had fought the United States Marines in Nicaragua twenty years earlier. Many portraits of Marx and Lenin were also displayed. School children, dancers, musicians in flaming costumes, paraded past.

On April 21, Mao Tse-tung and Chu Teh ordered the crossing of the Yangtse in force. More than a million men moved. Mao swam across—he gloried in swimming.

Before the end of the year all the great southern cities had surrendered and Chiang had fled to Formosa (Taiwan). On October 1, in Peking, Mao established the People's Republic.

The end result of United States intervention had been to prolong the civil war perhaps three years, at the cost of millions of lives and vast monetary expenditures. In the end all Marines had to be withdrawn. Only Hong Kong and Macao remain in European hands. Even the rich opium trade has passed into control of the Thais, the Laotians, and the Vietnamese, considerably curtailed these days by the changed China.

It was the beginning of the end of effective military domination of Asia, though the United States would hang on in the Philippines and Japan, and futile military adventures would kill millions in Korea and Vietnam. It was the beginning of what the Japanese had called Asia for Asians. It is a process that cannot be halted, whatever the outlays in men and money and propaganda. The French and British have already folded their tents, except in Hong Kong. The Portuguese have been driven out of Goa; their hold in Macao is tenuous. Neocolonialism is likely to linger on for a long time, for old-style imperialism, if greatly weakened in Europe, is still a powerful force in the United States. But it is also a force, though motives may vary, in the Soviet Union, and perhaps to a lesser degree, in China.

The causes of Mao's victory are very obvious. Communalism is a much more ancient tradition in China than the relatively new system of capitalist democracy. Mao inherited the great Taiping revolutionary traditions. He was well grounded in the social doctrines of Confucius and Taoism. He knew the Chinese classics by heart and those of the West that had been translated.

The way was paved by the collapse of the Manchu dynasty and the prior revolution of Sun Yat-sen. The Manchu corruption soon crept into the Kuomintang republican regime, and Chiang Kai-shek and his clique outdistanced all previous regimes in corruption, with all its erosion of public services and efficiency, the ostentatious display of wealth and waste in the face of poverty and deepening misery of the people in prolonged war. The countryside was looted, only the landlords (and not all of them) escaped; peasants went hungry; and millions starved to death. War, anarchy, and famine made violence the only avenue of escape. Chiang had little to offer the people, except oppression, exploitation, and war—not even a mythical democracy or freedom.

Mao, in his *The Chinese Revolution and the Communist Party* and in his *New Democracy*, saw the whole on-course of the Revolution as a historic process.

China has gone through thousands of years of primitive communist society: Afterward there was a collapse . . . and the era of class distinctions began . . . a society based on serfdom from which feudalism arose . . . [a] process that has lasted five thousand years . . .

China is no longer a feudal society. Since the 1840 Opium War, Chinese society has gradually become semi-colonial . . . The invasion of foreign capital broke up Chinese economy by destroying the self-sufficient natural economy of town and rural handicrafts, substituting a commodity economy, a destruction . . . that created markets for capitalist commodities . . . . [The resultant] bankruptcy of the peasants and handicraftsmen enabled the capitalists to exploit cheap labor . . . . The chief enemies of the Chinese revolution are still the imperialists and semi-feudal forces . . . the dagger of the revolution should not be directed against . . . the private property of the capitalists but against imperialist and feudal monopolies. [The aim should be] a New Democratic Revolution [essentially bourgeois], but helping middle and small private industries, and creating a precedent for socialism.

The Revolution had first to succeed in the rural areas, independent of the strongholds of imperialism, the cities. The four determining characteristics of revolutionary war in China, he wrote in the caves of Yenan, were "A vast colonial country unevenly developed politically and economically that has gone through a great revolution [Taiping?], a powerful enemy; a weak and small Red army; and the agrarian revolution." The Red army would not be able to defeat the enemy quickly and it might even fail.

There should be no adventurism and no campaigns seeking quick decisions, no fixed positions, but fluid operational fronts and mobile war. The Red army was not the Revolution; it had to be "propagandist and an organizer of the Chinese revolution." The aim in the army, he maintained, should be a democratic way of life within the limits of necessary military discipline, in order to win over all possible allies among the people.

There was no democracy in Chiang's armies. The soldier was dirt, abused and starved by his officers, despised by the peasants for his brutalities and thievery. His morale was almost nonexistent.

But the Mao cause was a crusade, the forces well organized, well fed, but not permitted to prey on the peasants. His forces were soon respected; morale was of the best, sustained by study and training. Mao instituted a general campaign called, "Officer love soldier; soldier love officer." The lesson was clear, as it is clear in Vietnam today, that even in this era of materialism, mechanization, and electronics, the spirit remains predominant, that morale—not merely manpower and superior material—is necessary to win battles. The Mao soldiers were instinctively heroes, for they had a faith, a belief for which they were glad to give their lives. Part of that belief and faith was an extreme nationalism and patriotism, a pride in China, for the moment defiled by foreign imperialism.

Mao saw direct benefits brought into being: the confiscation of landlord estates, the abolition of serfdom and sharecropping, the lowering of taxes, land distribution, the end of crop speculation, the setting up of democratic village institutions and self-government, an army that plowed and planted and harvested for the peasants yet did not steal their crops and animals. Add to this the goal of a powerful free China respected among nations. A moving force was built up, which could not be resisted. Victory in the long run is won by those who know how to gain the support of the people. Neither Chiang nor the Japanese nor the United States had the means to win such support. The bombs that fell on civilians were all labeled "Made in the U.S.A." Mao, by the time of Japanese defeat, had grown very strong, though still not equal to the American-equipped and trained Chiang forces. But he had more than armed forces. His crusade and his propaganda spread out in widening circles. His land policy pulled the peasants in by the millions.

In contrast, well before the 1945 peace with Japan, the Kuomintang stank with rottenness. Nor could Chiang afford to discipline the provincial warlords, who continued to despoil the people. General Barr, chief United States military adviser of Chiang from 1947 to 1948, during the height of the civil war, understood, aside from Chiang's stubbornness and greed, the reasons for failure.

The government armies, he noted, were scattered along thousands of miles of railroads necessary to supply them. To hold the railroads it was necessary to hold the cities. The forces were pinned down. Inactive, they degenerated. As garrison and lines-of-communication troops, they lost offensive spirit and capacity. The enemy's military strength, popular support, and tactical skill were "seriously underestimated." The communication lines were always vulnerable. The Communists steadily grew in numbers, ability, and confidence.

The Nationalist leaders were chosen for family, financial, or political reasons, not for ability or efficiency. "No man, no matter how efficient, can hope for a position of authority on account of being the man best qualified . . . he simply must have other backing." The Generalissimo, i.e., Chiang, favored his old army cronies, however incompetent they might be. The air force, with more than five thousand United States pilots, accomplished little, other than lifting troops and operating for personal gain. It was doubly resented for killing Chinese civilians and soldiers who had no air protection. The navy, instead of suppressing smuggling, participated in it at the cost of millions in customs revenue. The Communist leaders, Barr concluded, were "Men of great ability who invariably out-generaled the Nationalist commanders." Morale and fighting spirit was very high because they were winning. The Nationalist soldier rarely stood up under heavy fire, but the capacities of the well-equipped, well-trained Chinese soldier, the competence of his officers, their knowledge of supplies and logistics, need never be questioned after MacArthur's terrible defeat in North Korea. They were as invincible as the armies of the French Revolution. Until the Revolution was destroyed, they could not be defeated.

Today, the 1967 to 1969 Young China, or Red Guard, movement reveals that the Chinese revolutionary spirit is stronger than when Mao took power in 1949. Far from weakening China as the Western press hoped, it means that China, if necessary, is ready to march.

CHAPTER 11

MAU MAU

WHEN TWENTY-SIX-YEAR-OLD Karari Njama of Kenya abandoned the school where he was headmaster and set out to join the Mau Mau guerrillas in the great Aberdare Forest Reserve north of Nairobi, the capital, his eyes were fixed on high Karari Hill which had once belonged to his grandfather. There, among other things, his grandfather had raised bees, and it was still famous for wild honey.

His grandfather had lavishly entertained the first white men ever to venture into Kenya. Soon many whites came, with fire weapons that could kill at a distance greater than a man could throw a spear. The newcomers stole the land, the richest soil in Kenya, which had always belonged to the Kikuyu people, who had lived so well they could even bathe in milk.

The forest was high country, often icy. Beyond Karari Hill, well to the east, rose snow-clad Mount Kenya, toward which the Mau Mau turned when they said their morning and evening prayers to Ngai, the all-powerful God of the Kikuyu. Since many missionaries had come into Kenya, his image had become confused with that of the white-bearded Christian God, and Christ was accepted as a great prophet. The first National Independence Parliament in 1954 was composed of twelve members—the number of Jesus' disciples, "sufficient to carry the true faith around the world." So would the justice of the Mau Mau fight for "land and freedom" be made known to liberty-loving men everywhere. But the Kenyans, Njama declared, could not compete with the British, who had wines and whiskies and press and movies and radio to send their lies around the world. The Mau Mau had no access to such instruments; they were isolated.

[203]

Afterward, in January 1966, a Kenya delegate to the Tri-continental Congress in Havana, John Mbiyo Njonjo, told the assemblage, "We began the struggle with only hatchets, lances and crude home-made weapons . . . ten years of bloody war . . . and our final victory . . . proved . . . that modern armament and bombs will never be an obstacle for oppressed peoples determined to recover their independence and social justice."

But to the outside world the black Kenyans, from 1952 on, were painted as bloodthirsty savages and bandits. There was plenty of savagery—on both sides. The revolt against the apartheid colonial regime was finally suppressed by methods as brutal as any in human history. Even so the colony was forever lost to England.

After four years of struggle the great Mau Mau leader, Dedan Kimathi, was captured in October 1956, quickly tried, and hung. Armed revolt flickered out. But the British victory left smoldering hate in the hearts of the people. The British realized they had won nothing and never could win anything. Never again could they restore the white feudal system. Without full freedom for the blacks, no white man's life could be safe. On December 12, 1963, the Union Jack came down, and the founder of the Mau Mau, the massive, ever-smiling Jomo Kenyatta, held in jail with eighty-three other leaders during the whole of the Aberdare struggle, became president. Sixty years of ugly colonial apartheid came to an end. The Kikuyu took back their lands.

The story of this struggle that led to this victory goes back to the end of the previous century. The British had incorporated Kenya into the empire in 1890. The 1915 Crown Lands Ordinance made all Africans "tenants at the will of the Crown." Some were placed in the reservations. Others flooded into Nairobi, the capital. By 1934 six and a half million acres were seized in the central highlands without compensation, of which the British cultivated only about half a million, but excluded the Africans from the rest. They kicked the Kikuyus out of six thousand square miles of the Aberdare Forest Reserve, forcing the Africans thereafter to buy firewood.

Njama's father, after losing his land in the White Highlands when it was incorporated into the forest reserve went to the Great Rift Valley where he became a sharecropper and put up a shack. He soon improved his lot by becoming a cook, a big handsome one, on a Boer plantation. He came to own six hundred cattle and many sheep and goats. But presently the government forbade all Africans to own more than one cow and more than fifteen goats and sheep. He had to dispose of his cattle for almost nothing. Kikuyu people were forced into servitude or into "reserves," where they were restricted to one-acre plots and forbidden to grow coffee and other commercial crops. Such small holdings ended traditional crop rotation, causing rapid soil exhaustion and starvation.

A heavy poll tax was imposed on all Africans. They were obliged to carry identification cards bearing their fingerprints—*kipande*—and could not travel from the plantations, in or out of the reservations or the cities, without special permission from their employers or the police. Population was heavy, from an average of 283 per square mile in three Kikuyu districts up to more than 500 in some areas.

Those who found employment in factories earned only seventy-two dollars a year or less, which sum included estimated housing and food, if provided; peasants far less. Many were sold into virtual slavery in adjacent colonies.

Education, in the hands of the missionaries, was limited and not free. The people were hungry for education, and made every sacrifice to put their children in school. The head of the East African Protestant missions drew up the Blucher plan, which excluded most African children from more than four years of schooling. Less than a carefully selected 10 percent could enjoy high school—just enough to provide needed government employees. "Between a missionary and a settler, there is no difference" became a typical Kikuyu saying. Ardent supporters of colonial rule, the missionaries were active against the guerrillas. Thus, except for the sixty thousand whites, the nearly nine million people in that vast lofty country of 245,000 square miles were reduced to a slavery rarely paralleled. Every day there were more landless, more unemployed, more starving families.

The 120,000 Asians enjoyed a small representation in the national council, which had only one dutiful African, appointed by the governor. Not until 1948 was African membership increased to four appointed members as compared to eleven elected whites and sixteen appointed white settlers.

The achievement of Kenya freedom thereafter was a forty-year struggle. Native organizations arose to denounce the Crown Lands Ordinance. Labor organizations appeared. In June 1920 the Kikuyu Association of Chiefs and Headmen denounced abuses, and the

Young Kikuyu Association held mass meetings. In February 1922 Harry Thuku, a telephone operator, organized the East African Association and told his followers to throw away their *kipande* cards and not work for Europeans. He was arrested. A thousand protestors surrounded the Nairobi jail. The police mowed them down, leaving twenty-one dead, many wounded. Thuku was deported without trial.

His outlawed organization was revived two years later as the Central Kikuyu Association (KCA). Parallel organizations were started among three other tribal groups. In their newspaper *Mwiguithania* (*The Unifier*) they demanded the return of Thuku, restoration of stolen lands and the right to grow commercial crops. They demanded farm training, high schools, freedom of movement, the abolition of the *kipande* system and of forced labor, exemption of women from the head tax, elective representation in the legislative council, eventual Kenyan independence. They denounced the missionaries for outlawing female circumcision, polygamy, and "pagan" songs. Since only religious schools were allowed, independent black church organizations were started and some three hundred Kikuyu schools were founded and an independent teachers' college.

When the KCA backed a dock strike in 1938, the organization was declared illegal, soldiers occupied their headquarters and shut down their newspapers. Twenty leaders were arrested and held for four years. The movement went underground as the Kenyan African Union (KAU) and created the secret Mau Mau with its stern brotherhood oaths.

"Mau Mau," a white designation, may have been derived from a pig-Latin version of *Uma Uma* ("Out! Out! "), an early version of the "Go home, Yankee" slogan. It was started in 1948, following arrests. By May 1950 many Africans from three tribal groups were being put on trial for having taken or administered the secret Mau Mau oath.

Njama was converted to the cause in July 1952 at a big gathering where he listened to Jomo Kenyatta and saw the flag of independence: black, with the red blood of blacks running down into rich green below. A crowd of thirty thousand cheered the speech. Jomo reminded Njama of a thundering Jove or Moses, though his beard was rather sparse. His arms and shoulders were powerful, a mighty man. He demanded land; he demanded freedom in an independent Kenya under its red, black, and green flag. He recited the abuses of

[*206*]

Africans, unable to find decent employment or to till the land, no justice in the courts, no access to the forest. Animals grew fat and multiplied, while black men starved.

Not so long ago Njama had been defrauded by a plantation owner. He had spent three months in jail merely for visiting a European farm near Nanyuki on business. He knew the truth about the schools. Money from the tax on Africans went mostly to white schools, which received eight times that spent on African schools. The whites were a handful, the black children numbered millions.

The audience roared out a song.

> The White community are foreigners
> The land they must quit . . .
> The House of Mumi (Mau Mau) we are many
> We are everywhere . . .
> The land they must quit . . .

In his autobiography, Njama described his subsequent initiation. Forty persons were guarded in a black hut by three men with *simis*, the local double-edged sword. All had to remove their shoes and any coins, watches, or metal objects. A guard announced: "Anyone who refuses to join in the struggle to get back stolen lands will be killed and buried right here in this hut." One man refused and was immediately struck in the face.

The initiation was conducted under an arch of banana leaves, adorned with sugarcane, cornstalks, and greenery, from which hung a *ngata*, the head and spinal column of a dead goat, and a chunk of meat. A fifteen-inch banana stalk, adorned with a goat's eyes, pinned on by "sodom apple" thorns from a prickly shrub with yellow tomatolike fruit, was filled with goat's blood, soil, and crushed grains. Njama was required to wrap a strip of twisted goatskin about his neck and hold a damp clay ball against his stomach—symbols of dedication to the association. He walked seven steps from the banana stalk, took seven small bites of the goat meat, pricked the goat eyes seven times with a reed, and thrust a reed into each of the seven holes in the *ngata*, the neck bone of the goat. (In later special-status rituals he had to insert his penis into the holes, i.e., life itself). Cold water was poured over his feet; and a cross was made on his forehead and his body joints, with the goat-blood-grain concoction.

[*207*]

"May this blood mark the unity of the faithful and brave members of Gikuyu and Mumbi [founder of the Kikuyu tribe and his wife]. May this blood warn you that if you ever betray our secrets or violate your oath, our members will . . . cut you to pieces at the joints marked by this blood." Blood was drawn from his middle fingers, which he licked, saying, "If I reveal this secret of Gikuyu and Mumbi to a non-member, may this blood kill me." Spectators pulled at the goatskin around his neck, counting up to seven—a symbol of future punishment if the oath were violated. He was obliged to pay a large initiation fee and donate a ram. This ritual, considered "obscene and disgusting" by Westerners, was "pure and inspiring" to Africans. To them, many white customs, in essence quite as primitive, seemed both obscene and disgusting.

The oath was a serious affair. It was illegal to belong to a secret organization, and anyone who did was liable to possible execution if the police discovered he was a Mau Mau. The oath consisted of twenty-one clauses; each followed by the chanted refrain: "If I reveal this, may the oath kill me."

It covered secrecy, help to fellow members, obeying calls to work day or night, obedience to the leaders. He was to hide any arms or ammunition, sell no land to any European or Asian, never steal any member's property. No racial intermarriage was permitted. He must never touch a prostitute, never make a girl pregnant and abandon her, never seek divorce, never let a daughter go uncircumcised. He must never give information to the government, never help missionaries overthrow Kikuyu customs. "I shall always follow the leadership of Jomo Kenyatta [then in prison] and Peter Mbiyu Koinage." The latter had taken the Kenya land question to the British Parliament and later carried protests to the United Nations. Both had been educated in England, where Jomo had lived for seventeen years.

The military service oath and the leader's oath were even more binding. Not all the people in Kenya were Kikuyu. Two fifths of the 245,060 square miles is poorly watered semidesert in the north near the Tanganyika border and in the east between the highlands and a coastal strip. It is inhabited by pastoral peoples belonging to half a dozen tribes. The major population is on the mountain plateau from 3,000 to 9,000 feet above sea level, particularly in the Great Rift Valley with three beautiful large lakes and in the Kenya portion of Lake Victoria Basin to the west. Six major groups lived in this area;

in the east the Kikuyu and closely related Embu, Meru, and Kamba, who at times joined with the Kikuyu in their organization and protests. The Kamba fought alongside them in the final battle for the forest reserve and the Great Rift Valley. The Kikuyu, the most numerous, totaled 30 percent of the population of these four groups, or about 3,000,000. The Europeans in this area were about 30,000. There were also 120,000 Indians, Arabs, and Goans. Few of these people, since all were underprivileged and abused, had any love for the small wedge of Britishers.

Some Mau Mau began engaging in all sorts of sabotage. By 1952 four hundred were in jail. Most had broken no laws, but membership in itself was an automatic ticket for incarceration. Actually 75 to 90 percent of all Kikuyu people had taken the oath, also a small percentage of adjacent peoples.

The government moved in on the Mau Mau with sterner punishment. This merely increased resistance and reprisals. In granting no rights and using terroristic methods, the government provoked the war it hoped to prevent. The soldiers burned the homes of suspects. In reprisal in October 1952 the Kiambu chief, Waruhiu, a government backer, was killed, and in March Mau Mau warriors organized the Naivasha raid to free prisoners. The raiders captured forty-seven precision weapons, including eighteen Bren and Sten machine guns, and 3,750 rounds of ammunition. Another raid killed Chief Luka of Lari, another government helpmate, and his wives, and their homes were burned. The government troops then killed most of the villagers, burned their houses, and declared a state of emergency. Arrest without warrants was instituted. Two hundred native leaders were seized.

The harshness brought everybody strongly behind the movement —native church and school officials, union leaders, journalists, students, farmers, shopkeepers. Terrorism in the reservations drove still more people into the forest to fight. More troops were rushed in: three battalions of King's African Rifles, a battalion of Lancaster Fusiliers, the Kenya regiment, and outside police—some fifty thousand in all.

Heavy levies were placed on peasants to pay British costs, and villagers were made to build barracks and heavy duty roads without pay. Rift Valley peasants, sharecroppers, or laborers on plantations, south and east, were driven from their homes into the reservations beyond the forest. Schools were closed down, some three hundred teachers and sixty thousand children were thrown out. No more than five people could assemble. There was a dark-to-daylight curfew.

The Europeans declared open season on all Africans; beatings, stabbings, shootings, and raping of women (Njama's wife was raped and made pregnant) took place. Livestock was stolen, food and clothing looted. More and more people fled to the forests of Mount Kenya and Aberdare to survive. War was on in earnest.

In spite of all repressions the Mau Mau had members everywhere, even in government offices. Some government home guards were almost 100 percent Mau Mau. Chief Nderi, pro-British, pushed into a banana grove to stop a Mau Mau ceremony and was cut to mincemeat. This was only five miles from Njama's school. Everywhere Mau Mau raids grew more frequent and successful. More troops had to be rushed in from the Middle East, also thousands of Somali and Turkestan mercenaries.

An arrested African had to confess to being a Mau Mau and disclose his associations, or he would be killed. If he did confess, he might also be killed; at best, he was likely to receive a fifteen-year sentence. A common police stunt, in questioning an African, was to drop a cartridge into his pocket, accuse him of being armed, and send him to prison for ten or twenty years.

By 1952 the Mau Mau were operating from strong forest camps, under two leaders who had escaped arrest, Stanley Mathenge and Dedan Kimathi. Heavy prices had been put on their heads.

Mau Mau raids were made on police stations and homeguard barracks. Guns and ammunition were captured. Mathenge's headquarters were known to be on Othaya Ridge, but a government expedition was hurled back with great loss. The Mau Mau seized Othaya home guard posts. Eighteen guards were killed, more arms and supplies taken. At Gatumbiro, the home guard post was overrun and thousands of head of cattle were captured or destroyed. Hundreds of European settlers began fleeing to safety.

By the time Njama had taken the Mau Mau oath in September 1952, most leaders were already in prison. His school was not yet suspect, and he concealed and outfitted recruits going to the forest and transmitted messages and supplies. However, he was ordered by Chief Mathenge to leave his school and join the rebels in the forest. "You cannot keep on serving two masters" i.e., be a Mau Mau and act as a government-paid schoolteacher.

The Aberdare Black Forest, around the 11,000-foot level, extends for 6,000 square miles, 120 miles by 50 miles, between the rich Great Rift Valley of white plantations and the Kikuyu reservation. In lower hill reaches there were a few villages and clearings, and some lower valleys were open enough to be farmed, but the forest was so dense there was rarely any sunlight and no underbrush. It was full of wild animals: rhinos, elephants, buffalo, deer, bush bucks, gazelles, wild hogs, sykes, colobuses, monkeys, baboons, leopards, cheetahs, hyenas, lions. The Mau Mau made friends with all the animals except the rhinos, who always charged them. The other animals came to accept them as fellow forest denizens, and when they smelled the soap, cigarettes, and laundered clothes of the government forces, they always set up alarm. The monkey bands made a terrific uproar. "They are our best sentinels," said one fighter. "We take it for granted that all the animals, except the rhinos and rats, have taken the Mau Mau oath."

Above the forest was the bamboo belt, some fifteen miles wide, almost impenetrable except by known animal trails, for the bamboo grew thirty feet high. No daylight penetrated; the sun and stars gave no guidance. Sharp leaves cut clothes to shreds and lacerated the skin. Pointed shoots pierced through even thick-soled shoes.

Still higher under the twin peaks of Nyandarua were the cold desolate grasslands, a treeless area that stretched for seventy-five miles, full of ponds and swamps. The dew froze every night, and for long periods the ground was a sheet of ice. It grew good wheat, and there was much honey, but few permanent rebel camps were set up here, though the enemy could easily be seen far below.

Njama traveled toward Mathenge's big cluster of camps in the forest during cold days of thunderstorms and heavy downpour. By then at least twenty thousand freedom fighters were in the forest under various leaders. Ngai—God would aid them, they believed, but they had brought their *pangas* or machetes and their double-edged *simi* swords. They slavishly followed the advice, not always sound, of their *Mundo Mugo* religious seers.

Njama and his companions climbed up the Kiandongoro Ridge and by sunrise were a mile inside the forest, still in the fringe. They moved on through empty maize fields—all crops had been destroyed by government troops so the forest fighters would lack food. It was fertile land, topped by black humus from six inches to more than a foot in depth.

After they finally crossed the River Gura in Kigumo Valley, six Mau Mau guards challenged them and Njama's *muirigo*, guide, gave the password *"Hiti"* ("Hyena"). The guards were armed with one Sten gun, one two-barreled .44 gun, two .303 rifles, one shotgun, two grenades, and a *simi*.

The camp, some four hundred yards ahead, had thirty 9 by 12 open rain shelters, under slanting split-bamboo roofs. It was very clean. Long split bamboos brought water to two central kitchens; two girls, a woman, and three men were boiling meat in two tins and a big saucepan. Much care was taken that no smoke could be seen by airplanes. "We were given a cow's cold tongue and hot soup which had a half-bitter taste of wild herbs supposed to increase health and remedy some diseases," Njama said later in telling his story.

All the people, about three hundred, gathered for evening prayers, facing Mount Kenya. All held soil in their hands. They chanted:

Oh God, the most powerful! We praise thee for guarding us throughout the day. We have raised our hands to show you that the soil you gave our forefathers is now being used by strangers who . . . are killing us for our lands. God, mercifully look upon the spilled blood of our brothers and hear our call and cry. We have no weapons to fight against these people, but we believe that thy sword will defeat our enemies for we are your sons and daughters; we believe that you did not create us to become servants of other people in the lands you blessed for our Father Gikuyu and Mumbi . . . . We praise Thee, O God.

Njama learned the signals. A green branch planted in the middle of a path meant, Do not pass, danger ahead. Two green branches dropped on either side of a path or bent meant that the camp and the guards were near: give the proper signal; a whistle like the night bird, *"Kuri hono-i ndirara ku?,"* meaning, "It is cold. Where shall I sleep?"

The password was changed daily; it might be a number or the name of a tree, animal, or mountain. The guards would shout, "Number," in English. If the stranger replied, "Seven," he was an enemy because the reply should be *mugwanja*, seven in Kikuyu.

Camp rules were explicit: Everyone must wake up before dawn, when birds begin their morning songs, and all together say morning prayers. Everyone must hide his belongings—clothes, blankets, cup, plate, spoon, and the like. Nobody is allowed to go out of the camp without a written pass to be shown to the guards when leaving or entering. All fires must be completely covered if an airplane has roared overhead during the night. A guard found asleep will be put to death. (Actually caning was the only penalty imposed.)

After morning prayers four armed warriors and a porter were ordered to escort Njama to the main headquarters. En route he could see places where bombs had been dropped, grinding the bamboo into thin threads. At the River Thuti the path became as big and wide as a road. Thousands of cattle and people had been using it for many months. Beyond a steep hill was a small flat grassland patch. His *muirigo* whistled the proper signal, and he was allowed to cross open grassland. Suddenly twenty well-armed guards appeared with five automatic weapons.

Guard huts—several hundred of them, a hundred yards from the main camp—were open to wind and cold, though each had a fireplace. A cold clear stream ran beside three big kitchens with gabled roofs down to the River Thuti. The main camp was located half a mile beyond in the bamboo zone at the bottom of a steep thousand-foot hill. A hospital was nearby.

Two thousand people gathered for evening prayer. About eight hundred wore various government uniforms seized from security forces. A few men had long shaggy hair and beards; some had braided their hair like women, with wool strips. Nearly half were armed with swords or *pangas*, while the rest had European guns and more than six hundred homemade guns. They had some good gunsmiths in the forest. Most fighters were between twenty-five and thirty; a few were more than sixty. The leaders wore turbans, shoes, or boots, owned either a wristwatch or pocket watch, and carried a hidden pistol and a walking stick.

Nearly a thousand youths, armed with only a *panga*, were ready to fight against the government tanks and cannon of the Royal Field Artillery Forces, the machine guns and the bombers. "This was exactly what was prophesied ten years ago," noted Njama, when he was sixteen and had danced the *Muthuu*. This was a war dance in which the participants offered to fight. In 1942 such dancers had called themselves Italians, or Germans, because of their hatred of the British. Since those youthful days more than a hundred thousand people, including Jomo Kenyatta, had served an average of seven years in prison. "All the prophecies had come true."

Njama pondered. "Our victory will be a miracle, but the Kenya Highland is our inheritance from Heavenly Father Ngai. God did not create us to provide the white men with cheap labor and starving servants." There were sixty thousand Europeans against six million rebelling Africans. Each European had to fight against a hundred Africans. Even if he killed half, he would finally be killed himself. The Mau Mau would win, overthrow colonial rule, and form an African government.

After dinner the whole camp sang praise to the country and warrior leaders.

> God created Gikuyu and Mumbi
> And kept them in Kikuyuland,
> They were deceived by Europeans
> And their land was stolen.

> *Chorus:* I'll never leave JOMO
> I'll never leave him.
> I've been solemnly promised
> The return of our lands.

> The children of Gikuyu live in the forests,
> Under the pouring rains;
> With much hunger and cold
> Because we want land.

> *Chorus:* Woeee! Woeee! Woeee, Ayahee!
> Will you face death, troubles and imprisonment
> Because you want your lands?

Stanley Mathenge arrived with three other leaders and a girl. He was six feet tall, of medium build, black moustache, but with little beard on his chin. He wore a woolen gray beret, a red-spotted scarf, a khaki raincoat with leather buttons, long black trousers and black shoes, a wristwatch, a walking staff, and carried an automatic pistol in his belt. He thanked Njama for coming to the forest. He was illiterate, but now with Njama as his secretary, he would be able to speak to the government and the world.

He had Njama send out a letter to the British, saying that the successful Mau Mau raid into the valley that day, was an example of our series of planned attacks . . . . our next all-out attack will make you flee the country or commit suicide. The more you punish the civilians in the reserves, the more they hate you and the more they join our forces. We are glad that you are spending thousands of pounds daily paying pilots' wages [for] oil and bombs which kill hundreds of buffaloes, elephants, deer, etc. [which] . . . supply us with plenty of meat right here in the forest. Whatever worst you do against us, God changes it to be our best help.

The hospital where Mathenge had his headquarters was ringed with bamboo and under big trees alongside a swamp of long *ithanji* reeds. It was too cold for mosquitoes, and for warmth the hospital had enclosing walls to protect the patients.

They discussed tactics. Government forces that followed stolen livestock, hoping to surprise the Africans slaughtering the animals, were invariably ambushed, and the Mau Mau gained arms and ammunition. Arms were also obtained by ambushing individual soldiers in the reserves and towns, by raiding government camps and posts, by raiding European homes. Other guns were bought from the police, military, home guards, and from Europeans and Indian traders. Many government servicemen were Mau Mau, who often supplied weapons and ammunition free. Bullets had become payment to prostitutes, who later sent them to the forest warriors.

It was difficult to track the guerrillas. Mathenge instructed warriors how to hide footprints by moving on toes and heels, straightening any weeds behind, stepping on dry leaves or hard soil, always moving backward when crossing paths or roads. "Pray hard and obey the instructions of the seers, the Mundo Mugo."

Torture in government camps grew worse. Men were castrated, beaten, and had their legs and arms broken. On testicles or in women's vaginas were placed leaves of the *thabu* or *hatha*—a poisonous stinging nettle that caused great pain and swelling. Breasts or testicles were pinched and twisted with pliers. Hundreds of such tortured can still be seen in the country or in towns as crippled beggars having lost one or both legs or arms or suffering other deformities. Njama came across six castrated men. One survivor was nicknamed *Mapengo* (toothless) due to having had his front teeth knocked out while a prisoner. Some Mau Mau were scarcely more gentle.

During the first half of 1953 various attacks against Mau Mau headquarters were ambushed with the loss of enemy arms and supplies. British punitive actions against the peaceful population were intensified. Taxes were raised, and more forced labor was imposed. Restrictions on movements of all Africans were tightened. The entire Kikuyu reservation was made a special police area, where any person failing to halt could be shot. The forest of Mount Kenya and Nyandarua were proclaimed prohibited areas, where any African was to be shot on sight. A zone one hundred miles long and three miles wide between the reservation and the forest was laid waste. All homes, crops, granaries, were wiped out, animals driven off or killed, peasants ejected on a six-hour notice. They were told, according to Njama, "Forget your gardens as you have forgotten your houses. This area is our battlefield with Mau Mau. It will be called a SPECIAL AREA. You have now lost both house and garden for helping Mau Mau . . . . You will lose more if you continue."

Government forces prodded them into camps without shelter and took whatever pleased them—furniture, clothing, utensils, money— and set all the houses on fire. Whatever livestock was not stolen or killed was put in one guarded herd so the Mau Mau could get no more food.

In attacks against the guerrillas, whenever the government forces found themselves outnumbered, they signaled for airplanes to drop bombs a few hundred yards in front of them. Once the air force— twelve airplanes—dropped their bombs on their own people, killing forty-two of them, a larger number than the Mau Mau lost to planes during the entire revolt. The British said the victims had been killed by the Mau Mau. Presently Lincoln heavy bombers flew over daily, dropping thousand-pound bombs—apparently mostly at random.

In late July, just before harvest, a British order was issued to cut down all native maize plants, banana trees, sugarcane, etc. The condition of the homeless peasants in the freezing nights, at an altitude of more than six thousand feet, during the heavy long winter rains became almost hopeless.

On their side the Mau Mau warriors were getting foodstuffs from the gardens and driving livestock into the forest. The peasants there, also mostly Kikuyus, ate any such edible growth as sweet potato leaves to survive. Disease swept the unsanitary concentration villages. The destruction of wealth and health reached catastrophic proportions. Children were thrown homeless into the forests. After thousands of children and aged persons died, the International Red Cross came to aid survivors. Aged persons, taken from one village to the chief's center, to be fed by the Red Cross, failed to survive.

After driving off one raid of white settlers and capturing guns, the Mau Mau phoned British headquarters that if the prisoners they had captured were to be kept alive, planes must drop food for them at a designated point. The government dropped bombs instead, and artillery was fired constantly, penetrating from three to twenty-five miles into the forests. Even so, a Mau Mau daylight raid netted 130 head of cattle.

But large forest camp clusters had to be dispersed, and many fighters shifted over to the Rift Valley side of the mountains, resulting in more attacks on the European settlers. The number of lawless bandit groups increased beyond the areas controlled by Mathenge and Kimathi. These *komeraras* respected neither white nor black farmers.

In August Dedan Kimathi, who headed the forces north of the Mathenge area, sent out a call for a central meeting on the banks of the Mwathe River to try to establish unity of command for all fighters in the Aberdare Forest.

Njama read the call to Mathenge. The general was chewing native tobacco and spitting. He believed that any such call should have come from him and refused to go, but sent Njama.

He was allotted a luggage bearer and an escort of twenty-eight warriors, with safari food, roasted meat, and pancakes, to be supplemented en route with wild honey. The going was foul, amid heavy mists, wet vegetation, mud, and icy streams swollen by two months of steady rain. They had to cross a new heavy-duty road constantly patrolled by British Land Rovers. Once they were charged by a furious rhino. They came upon a dead elephant. The flesh had been eaten by hyenas, but they carried off the three-foot ivory tusks. They forded two large streams and crossed three miles of moorland burned over from a fire caused by a fallen airplane.

One afternoon a hailstone storm froze their feet, and they had to make camp beside a small stream. The mist was so thick that they risked lighting a big fire and prepared hot coffee. They smeared their bodies with fat for warmth and used leaves and grass thawed out by the fire for mattresses. The frozen dew did not melt until 10 A.M. the next day. Reaching Mwathe River, Njama caught sixteen fish in less than an hour with safety-pin hooks.

They checked in at the officers' camp, and their supplies were taken to an underground storehouse. Since the temperature was below freezing, their meat was hung on trees. Special rites were carried out because their ivory tusks were from a single-hoofed animal, hence unclean and taboo. The witch doctor smeared a little fat on their hands, feet, and face, and with a cow's tail flicked them with a thick liquid made of the rumen of a hyrax, wild herbs, and the sap of the *mwembaiguri* (a creeping plant), the sweet roots of which were used in soup.

They were assigned to grass huts across a cold river under a big tree. The officers' mess was 25 by 12 at two long rough tables covered with cedar bark. Kimathi and three other top leaders sat at small separate tables. At Kimathi's hut, warmed by a big fire, they drank a mug of honey water. A whistle was blown. "Prayers! Prayers! Prayers!" was the cry. The big throng outside looked toward Mount Kenya.

Kimathi was put out that Mathenge did not come. "Whatever good we do here," he said, "will be supported by all the people, even the unborn." Njama delivered Mathenge's excuses, but added that all he had been doing for more than a month was sitting under a big camphor tree.

"He should be here to meet the leaders," replied Kimathi, "I hope he is not suffering from megalomania . . . . His vacant chair will be in front of all the leaders during the sessions." Kimathi was an educated man, but more likely he intended to say "a swelled head."

The leader ordered his evening meal served in his hut. Two girls brought in pancakes in a thick meat gravy with potatoes, from the enemy zone.

About this time a raid made by six hundred *itungati* (warriors) on Kagunduini Center, where Njama had lived, proved successful. The home guards ran away, and the raiders filled up sacks and blankets with clothes, medicine, sugar and salt, beans and flour, then blew the whole place to pieces with an airplane bomb that had not detonated when dropped. From the school they had taken a radio and blank books for keeping guerrilla records.

"How many warriors have been killed by bombs?" Njama asked. "Few of us," Kimathi replied, but early in March, squatters, taking a large herd of livestock through the Nguthiru moorland, were spotted by a police air wing plane. The herdsmen hid in a small cluster of bamboo, but all were killed. "We drove off the surviving animals. The hyenas and leopards ate those killed."

Toward the end of March, he added, planes sighted a camp with more than three hundred warriors. Grenades killed nine. After that the guerrillas learned to hide the smoke of their fires in the daytime and the flames at night. Since then bombs had been dropped aimlessly, and no one had been killed.

There were 4,600 people in camp for the Kimathi reunion. Morning prayers were held before daybreak. The stars were still shining brightly, and the birds were beginning their own prayers—so Njama described the scene. A little beer was poured on the door frames "to cleanse the dwellings," and all fires were extinguished with ritual beer. "As the fire goes out so may all the evils go out of us; as these charcoals turn cold, so may our enemies; let peace reign."

Kimathi poured beer on the ground and made offerings of honey, domestic animal fat, and cereals.

That is yours, Father Gikuyu, and that is yours, Father Waciuri. God, we beg you to defeat our enemies and to defend us from them; close their eyes so that they will not see us . . . our homes have become ruins and the dwelling places of foxes . . . . Please, O God . . . Bless all our warriors wherever they may be.

The worshippers threw a bit of food and a handful of wet soil into the fire and faced Mount Kenya with raised hands.

Njama was made secretary of the Kenya Defense Council and keeper of the records. He was to go from camp to camp gathering data and advise the separate groups on plans and organization.

At a camp near the edge of the forest he typed out eviction notices to European settlers near the forest, giving them seven days to pack their belongings and quit the country. Unless the settlers changed their selfish superior manners, racial discrimination and monopoly, there would be "no room for them in Kenya or anywhere in Africa." In World War I the African people had died to defend them by fighting the Germans in Tanganyika and the Italians in Somali. White Kenya soldiers had been given land as a reward for their services; black people were given only *kipande* identification cards and forced to dig ditches. "A Kenya African

[219]

government must prevail at all cost . . . . If you are against us, pack up and quit. We shall not need your help after achieving freedom." These messages were left in bamboo tubes in front of each door.

The guerrillas systematically destroyed bridges, wire fences, and telegraph lines. They ruined the wells and carried off pipe to make guns; once, enough to make ten thousand guns. But gradually the British scorched-earth policy along the forest edge began to pinch. One Mau Mau force, unable to make a raid for a month, was reduced to eating potatoes and arrowroot.

After visiting many camps, Njama returned to Mathenge's headquarters and later related what happened. The big chief leaned on a five-foot man-head carved walking stick, regarding him fixedly, "How are you, Njama?"

"Very well."

Mathenge remarked dourly that Kimathi had taken control of everything.

"You did not attend, I warned you. Kimathi has been made head of all the warriors, but people have you in mind as his chief deputy."

"What rank will I have?"

"That will be decided by the Defense Council, on the basis of your personal activities and capabilities."

"Then Kimathi does not dictate whatever he wishes?"

"No. You can confirm that by going with me to another leaders' meeting in Murang'a September 9, where reports on the various armies will be presented." Mathenge, unable to carry out raids, did not have enough food for the journey, and Njama had to remain with him until October.

A widespread air raid occurred on November 17 in Nyandurua. Everybody was inside the camps, warming up after a bad rainstorm. A heavy bomber dropped eight bombs fifteen miles away. The plane roamed north and south along the edge of the Abendare Forest and the bamboo region dropping thousand-pound bombs at two-hundred-yard intervals along the Guria Valley west of the camp. Everybody was knocked down, and almost every tree in a radius of three hundred yards was damaged.

The planes, Lincolns, which the Mau Mau nicknamed Protruding Navel Bearers, bombed four other valleys, the mountain fringe of the Great Rift Valley, and Mount Kenya. The roar could be heard for fifty miles. One dud bomb was opened to get the powder. It exploded, injuring six men. One lost his eyesight. Kimathi held a ceremony and had the blind man pull down the British flag and raise Kenya's national flag—the first time in history.

Toward the end of 1953 eight hundred youthful volunteers of the Kenya Young Star Association showed up for the Aberdare Christmas celebration to feast on sweet maize and *hatha*, the edible nettle, and to dance and sing. Kimathi dragged a spotless all-black ram to a big fig tree where it was slain and roasted. "Heavenly Father," he intoned, "we beseech you to accept our roasted sacrifice; we know no other God but you, Almighty Father."

In February 1954 Kimathi and Njama held a reunion of major guerrilla units under big trees in a grassy open area. Forty leaders and 750 warriors attended, but not Mathenge. The Kenya Council was supplanted by a national parliament of twelve members, chosen not from geographical units but for personal qualifications, with Kimathi as president.

Should they pick educated men over illiterate? Educated men, too steeped in the history of British wars, armament, and capabilities, were often not good fighters; whereas ignorant peasants, not knowing the enemy's power, found in their ignorance a source of strength and courage. Should they elect from those present or from those in other places? Should they stress their ancestral ways or the new European ways?

A big sheet was laid out with ballots, which tellers dropped into the hats of the leaders nominated. Everybody faced Mount Kenya and prayed God to bless and guide the new parliament. After dinner they sang and danced and practiced military drills.

All Mau Mau in and out of the forest were advised to concentrate on destroying enemy property; they were to cut down coffee, tea, and fruit trees; burn all the fields of corn, all wheat and barley, stores and houses; they were to spray the grass with cattle-dip to poison cattle.

Wanjiru, a girl accused of being an informer, was put on trial. She had slept promiscuously in a police post. For six weeks now she had been the companion of rebel leader General Rui.

She testified as to what she and seventeen companions had been instructed to do by the police: they were to report where fighters were hiding and trick guerrillas into the hands of the police. They were given poisoned tablets with which to kill top leaders. Each girl swore to kill at least five. The Mau Mau court thanked her for her frankness and let her off with a warning.

A report of the Colonial Office Parliamentary Delegation to Kenya brought out that Mau Mau courts functioned right in Nairobi, the capital. Money was collected for bribery and the purchase of supplies. A passive resistance movement boycotted European-owned buses and businesses. The report urged the adoption of a new constitution and the forming of a multiracial government. The forest leaders were exultant. They had achieved more in fifteen months of fighting than politicians had won in more than thirty years of talk.

Nevertheless, the two-pronged British Operation Anvil was started April 24, 1954, with twenty-five thousand soldiers and police to isolate the Mau Mau from sources of food in Nairobi and the reserve. The entire African population of Nairobi, a hundred thousand persons, were rounded up into a huge field for screening. Fifty thousand were sent to concentration camps, their wives and children to the concentration reserves. Farmers and serfs and their families were thrust into barbed-wire communities, mostly to starve. By the end of 1954 more than a million people had been uprooted. These prison villages were hit by terrible epidemics and hunger.

At the same time, to separate Aberdare and Mount Kenya from the Kikuyu Reserve, a wide trench, planted with vines, fenced with barbed wire, and protected by many military posts, was dug by forced labor along fifty miles of the forest fringe. Any settler would be paid five shillings bonus for any Kikuyu he killed. Leaflets were showered down from planes. The Mau Mau were called on. "Come out with a green branch and surrender." One important general did surrender.

But two thousand new armed recruits reached the well-disciplined force of six hundred Mau Mau in Murang'a and attacked the strong government Kandara outpost. The soldiers there fled, and the post and all the houses were set on fire. But on their return a ninety-two-man force was forced to surrender at the Kayahwe River. They were ordered to take off all their clothes, then were shot down.

The guerrillas sang a grieving hymn about it.

> Kayahwe is a very bad river,
> Kayahwe is a very bad river,

Kayahwe is a very bad river,
This is where our heroes were exterminated.

General Ihura gets no sleep,
General Kago gets no sleep,
Our warriors get no sleep,
They sleep not when remembering Kayahwe.

Kimathi issued a denunciation of British robbery and raping and burning of homes, the destruction of wealth, the closing of schools and trade centers, the creation of concentration areas and unsanitary prison villages, the seizure of parents and consequent starvation of homeless children. Copies were sent to British members of Parliament, who had favored Kenya's cause, to Russia, India, Egypt, and the United Nations.

Njama was given the title of Knight Commander of East Africa. With his *itungati*, he proceeded on a difficult trek across swollen rivers. Food in this area had to be brought from the Great Rift Valley or the reservation twenty miles away and was scarce. One night they ate meat—five bushbucks from traps, and a buffalo they had shot. At eight-thirty in the morning the enemy started shooting up their camp.

He grabbed his satchel, which contained his records, and his blanket and fled barefoot. He reached a camp in the bamboo, but again they were attacked and had to flee. Eighteen of them camped at the headwaters of a small river. They found only poisonous plants, and their only food was a single corncob. The following night they tried to get to the reserve, but the enemy was shelling the forest—two more foodless nights.

Looking through binoculars, Njama saw a small spiral of smoke above a tall tree, where rebel fighters were smoking the bees out of trees for honey. He and his companions followed their faint track and reached friendly IDa 4/1 camp. The refugees were fed all the elephant meat they could eat. It was taboo, but the near-starved wanderers ate ravenously. Njama found the meat tender as pork, the fried fat no different from cattle fat.

A general meeting was held after one of the medicine men counted stones and seeds and said to do so was safe, no danger of attack. Njama read from Ecclesiastes 3: 1–8. "To every thing there is a season, and a time to every purpose under the heaven: A time to be born, and a time to die; a time to plant, and a time to pluck up that which is planted; a time to kill, and a time to heal . . . a time of war, and a time of peace." With peace all would receive happiness equal to the sufferings endured. Their enemies, now happy, would be very miserable.

By the end of 1954 the twelve-man Mau Mau parliament, headed by Kimathi as president, a thirteenth member, had pretty much established its authority over all Aberdare forces, except those of Mathenge and two other strong leaders, but operations in the smaller forests had been broken up, the warriors dispersed, and many bands were running short of food, arms, and ammunition. In parliament Njama favored the distribution of land among the landless as soon as the fight was won. Others wanted to renounce all outside religion and castigate the missionaries. Some still resented it that the Mau Mau parliament was made up of educated men.

Wambararia, Kimathi's brother, was brought before parliament for wounding a warrior who, he claimed, had stolen his girl friend. He was obliged to pay a fine of a billy goat and a tin of honey and to take care of the victim until he recovered. This decision created resentment. Some claimed that Kimathi had "picked out stooges to hear the case," and that the accused should have been more severely punished.

A successful raid was made at Rurthaithi by girls who, on instructions of their witch doctor, had made an eleven-year-old boy their general. Kimathi said bitterly all the witch doctors should be killed.

Hardly had Njama left camp at 7 A.M. when it was attacked by the enemy. He retaliated that night by raiding Major Owen Jeoffrey's house in the reservation with twenty-eight *itungati,* armed with a dozen homemade guns and six manufactured ones. That was at the end of August 1954.

The major had left an hour earlier, but his servants welcomed them with food and skimmed milk. The *itungati* ransacked the house and took all his clothes, army uniforms, bedding, radio, hand sewing machine, new camera, medicine, tin food, utensils, etc. In the nearby store they found two bags of cornmeal, but no guns or ammunition. The store was burned, and the flames lighted their way in the dark.

According to his book, *Mau Mau from Within,* written in collaboration with Donald L. Barnett, Njama wrote the major:

[224]

All we want is freedom to form an African Government and to ban all discriminatory bars. We do not hate the white man's color, but we cannot tolerate seeing a foreign ruler with 50,000 acres . . . most of which only the wild game enjoy while thousands of Africans are starving . . . . Your only alternative is to cooperate with the Africans as equal human beings by creating friendship and good relationship which your bombs and guns will never achieve . . . . The more you fight Africans, the more you endanger your future in Kenya. You cannot kill ideas by killing people . . . . Six million Africans standing for right will definitely beat sixty thousand Europeans standing for might.

On October 1 Njama met Mathenge again to try to persuade him to attend the forthcoming November 11, 1954, meeting in Mihuro to elect new members to parliament. Unless he came, he would be dismissed as head of the Ituma Ndemi army. Why did he not cooperate with Kimathi?

Mathenge showed up with four section captains friendly to him. At a midnight meeting the two leaders pledged never to harm or undermine each other. But their differences struck down into the roots of changing tribal traditions, and it was also the illiterate, such as Mathenge, versus the educated nationalist, such as Kimathi, "tainted" with a European outlook.

Parliament met in a 120-by-20-foot room with a platform and three rows of seats. Guards were posted for three miles. Njama opened with a prayer: "Courage and unity" were their greatest weapon.

A general meeting started at 2 P.M.: first, parliament members, then other leaders. Only seven hundred warriors could get inside to sit down; the rest stood against the wall or outside. A *Mundo Mugo* was stationed at the door with Kimathi, each with gourds of fermented millet flour and water, and of honey. The entrances were properly sprinkled and blessed, with a fly whisk. The hall was dedicated to the memory of all their miseries since the Europeans came: the evictions and deportations; the harsh drumhead trials, in which thousands had been sentenced to death; dread Lokitaung Prison, where their leader Jomo Kenyatta and his five colleagues were serving sentences.

Kimathi called for two minutes of silence for the dead. Njama told of his peace negotiations as a result of recent governmental offers of concessions and amnesty. Messages had been exchanged, but

[225]

he warned them to beware of informers within the camps. He told them of the propaganda he had conducted. After two years of fighting, both the white settlers and the authorities were split into quarreling factions—from white-supremacy independents to those advocating white African neocollaboration. The colonial government had had to borrow almost thirty million pounds from Her Majesty's government. European migration out of Kenya had been so great the British government no longer let whites leave.

However, there had been a decrease in revolutionary manpower, and government forces had increased to one hundred thousand soldiers heavily equipped with lorries, Land Rovers, planes—the police air wing, Harvard reconnaissance planes, jets, and Lincoln bombers. But eight planes had been brought down, and bombs had failed to crush the Mau Mau.

There were plenty of animals in the forest itself to supply food and clothing. The guerrillas could live there for years. The Mau Mau rule against killing animals was changed to forbid anyone to kill an animal he was not going to eat. "*Ucio uri ho!*" ("That is right!") the warriors shouted. The secretary recorded the interchange.

"What animals would you eat?" Kimathi asked.

"Anything I catch in my trap that God has sent me."

"A monkey or a leopard?"

"Yes, many of us have eaten them."

Kimathi said he, too, would eat anything caught. "No!" cried one. "Would you eat a hyena?"

Njama explained that all animals known are eaten by one or another people: small birds, tortoises, locusts, flying ants. The French ate frogs' legs; the Turkestans ate monkeys; the Luo and Byluhya ate porcupines. In any case, the guerrillas had enough vegetables, fruit, and honey to keep them alive for years.

"We have bravely fought the battle, and we have scored more victories than our opponents. . . .. The Kenya white settlers are in a worse situation than we are," Njama concluded.

"*Ei! Ei!*" ("Yes! Yes!") the audience roared and sang:

> The children of Gikuyu live in the forest
> Under the pouring rains
> With much hunger and cold
> In quest of their land . . .

At 9:30 P.M. Mathenge spoke eloquently, warning against jealousy and false pride. He told the story of a single warrior left alive, who hid out, using different weapons, fire and poison. He fought in many places, ambushed many soldiers. The enemy believed the forest was full of fighters and released the people from prisons and detention camps to form the first free government. They called on the forest fighters to march out to be honored. Only one warrior appeared, carrying many kinds of weapons, beating his big drum, "He who perseveres wins," concluded Mathenge.

More prayers, more singing, more speakers. They broke up at 3 A.M. Many were already asleep.

December 1954 marked the strongest assault yet: Operation Hammer, in which more than a division participated. Many bands were dispersed, but it was far from being a success. A plane dropped thousands of leaflets, urging guerrillas to leave the forest and return to peaceful life. No previous crimes would be punished. They would be detained, but would be given food, medical treatment, and clothing. It was signed by General Sir George Erskine, His Excellency the governor of Kenya, commander in chief of East Africa. Such an appeal for surrender, Njama argued, showed how desperate the British government was.

The Mau Mau parliament, which had been expanded to twenty-eight members, was henceforth to total thirty-three—one from each Kenya district—so that all the tribes would be represented. Strong forces of Kambas, south and east of Kikuyu had joined the struggle. The Independence parliament reconvened on December 31, 1954, at Mihuro. Many military leaders did not appear. Only fifteen Kenya parliament members attended. Total attendance, including warriors, was only 500, of which 350 had to stand guard. But that night everybody sang and shouted and prayed for the New Year. They were nearly surrounded.

Njama and others went to a camp in the forest above the reservation. The camp already had two bomb craters. Even so, every morning and evening the camp fighters managed to go down into the valley near the enemy and gather corn. On January 15 the enemy withdrew, and Njama went fishing. He caught nine trout. From the heights overlooking his home, he looked down on the enemy's strongest military base, with more than seven hundred Devons, a home guard camp, and a police camp. He could see his own garden a mile and a half away, his fruit trees, and the remains of his unroofed house.

February 5 with three other leaders and fifteen *itungati*, he started out for another parliament reunion at Mihuro. The enemy had burned the memorial hall there and all the huts. What most grieved Njama was that their bookstore had been burned. Kimathi had left a note on a bamboo post, "You will find us at Chieni."

They found only Kimathi, Mathenge, and a few section leaders. Only 8 parliament members and 420 warriors arrived. Plans for a meeting had to be abandoned. Fighters everywhere had been badly mauled. Letters were sent out to all leaders to attend a general meeting March 6 to elect leaders. There Kimathi was named prime minister. He was still president of parliament, but henceforth he would conduct no military operations. Njama was elected marshal in charge of all armies.

During all of February the government sent in no forces, quit guarding the villages, and sent wives and mothers into the forest with food and clothing to persuade the fighters to surrender. The few who accepted the amnesty were allowed to move freely in the villages to persuade other relatives to get their men to give up. Women used their blandishments on the guerrillas and delivered some over to the authorities at gun point. The fighters were now referred to as "spies, thugs, ruffians, gangsters, thieves, murderers and outlaws, terrorists, bandits, greedy enemies of peace." Government forces were always "Security Forces, Defenders of Peace, Restorers of Peace, Home Guards, Loyalists."

The missionaries constantly accused the rebels of being atavistic barbarians, betrayers of the Holy Trinity. It came in over the radio. God had given Christians the power and the forces to punish the rebels. If the fight against God persisted, the people would perish. Kenya African leader Jomo Kenyatta, incommunicado since April 8, 1953, was constantly reviled as the "evil leader of darkness and death." The anti-Mau Mau propaganda became incessant, and the government had given radios to all the villagers so the people could listen to it.

Njama wept tears at having no way to communicate his side of the story. "In spite of how hard I shouted, my voice could only be heard a few yards from me in that dense forest."

For the Chieni conference, March 2, 1955, 150 fighters showed up and 12 parliament members. On March 5, four other important leaders arrived with 130 more fighters. Neither Mathenge nor any-one from his army appeared.

Njama estimated that 35 percent of the guerrillas were still oper-ating. More than twenty-two thousand Kenya guerrillas had been killed, eight hundred captured, seven hundred surrendered. All told at least fifty thousand persons had perished, including those dying from starvation and disease in the unsanitary prison villages and the reserves.

Kenyatta had promised he would hold the lion's jaws so it could not bite us if we could bear its claws, Kimathi said. The clawing had been worse than expected. "The Government has increased the brutality, strength and methods of defeating our people." The peo-ple in the reserves were being killed like unwanted game. There were a lot of rumors that the Communists, among others, would help them, said Njama, but this was the third year of the struggle, and no one had come to help them, no one at all.

The ceremonies for installation of officers this year were more traditional and elaborate. The ceremony started at nine o'clock, March 6.

Njama smeared his body with castor oil and dressed as an elder, putting on a sheepskin cloak and feathered beret, rattles on his legs, and rubber sandals. He tied on a red-sheathed sword and carried a leather satchel, a black walking stick, an elder's leaf handkerchief, a fly whisk, and a three-legged stool. Every fighter who entered was purified with a mixture of sheep fat, blood, and dung. Kimathi and his second wife were duly sprinkled with beer.

His first wife and daughter were held in Nairobi. Waicanguru, a pretty brown girl, had been living with him for six months now. She was duly awarded the highest woman's military rank, colonel and knight commander of the Gikuyu and Mumbi empire. In the reserves, or concentration areas, Kimathi had organized the way for the fighters in the forest to be supplied. The first three years he had organized eight armies, had planned attacks, and had sent letters to the government and abroad. He had become known all over the world.

All were surprised when Mathenge entered, bearing a jar of honey, a fly whisk, and a cane, and sat quietly in the audience. He was asked to speak to the assemblage for five minutes. Afterward he flicked honey water on all the warriors. A big feast was spread in Kimathi's hut. Singing and dancing lasted far into the night.

But Mathenge was behind unauthorized peace overtures to the British, and within two months the split between the two leaders again grew ugly. Various independent bands demanded Kimathi begin "official" peace negotiations.

A new memorial hall, 150 by 30 feet, was opened with all members of parliament present. Visitors from the reservation brought food. Soon after, on March 25, Mathenge rededicated the same hall on his own. He told those present he had been neglected because he was illiterate. "Does a fire burn any brighter when it is lighted by an educated man?" He set up the Kenya Riigi (Sacred Doors Council) as a rival to the Mau Mau national parliament—an open break.

The Mau Mau national council ordered that the Mathenge and the Kenya Riigi members be disciplined. They were brought in as prisoners. Three junior officers were released on promising to obey the Mau Mau national parliament. On March 30, cases were heard. All the accused were released after paying fines of twenty-five shillings each.

The following day all remaining prisoners except one escaped, and two guards deserted. Kimathi visited the prison camp and ordered the guards to strangle the only prisoner. Other dissident leaders were caught and sentenced to severe canings. One was executed, and one *komerera*, bandit leader, was shot by Kimathi before he could be tried.

Infuriated, Njama called parliament together and urged that it impose restrictions on the powers and actions of its president. He must not be allowed to become a dictator. Kimathi stalked out angrily. Njama was named minister of war. But parliament was split down the middle, and it never met again.

Njama went with eighty-two men to try to bring Mathenge back into the fold. Enemy forces came within a mile of his camp, and he moved out with his men west, then south, then east. Lacking food, they had to split into smaller groups. With ten men Njama slipped into a dry bamboo area, from which they could see a great distance. A heavy rain began pouring down. At daybreak they were surprised by the enemy. Njama lost his tent, blanket, and shoes, and ran east toward the Kariani Garden Reserve. He and his companions found enough wild vegetables for three bites each. Moving north they crossed the Thuri River and passed within 150 feet of a government force. They could easily have ambushed them, but they had only two rifles and ten rounds of ammunition. They lay low all that day, less than a mile from the forest boundary. A fourth night was passed without food, and the next night they ate *marerema*, a wild vegetable. Njama decided to escape into Ethiopia where he hoped to get help.

But on June 5 they were surprised. Shot twice in the ankle, Njama fell after running eighty yards. Crawling through a berry bush, he ran north through the forest. At a stream he tore up his vest to bandage his ankle. A small artery had been severed, and he had lost much blood. Enemy scouts were all about, but he lay in the bushes unseen. A large enemy force began making camp nearby.

He climbed up the ridge, planning to sneak into the reserve at night and reenter the forest further up. But he ran into two African home guards. They knew him and took him to Gitugi village, so he would not be shot by the British. He was held prisoner, but eventually he was released and later wrote his brilliant book about the war and his experiences.

The *itungati* were now surrendering in droves. The Mau Mau national parliament ceased to function. Kimathi, almost isolated, left for the Fort Hill area to join a strong North Tetu force.

There were now only about fifteen hundred fighters left in the entire Aberdare Range, split into numerous small groups, recognizing no outside authority except their local *mundo mugo*. The peasants had abandoned the struggle, and nearly all non-Kikuyu tribes now sided with the government. The fighters had no hope any more except in Ngai, their god. They prayed constantly against the whites, who "rejoiced" when their people died, and who were killing innocent women and children, starving them, and working them to death. "The whole of Kenya is full of tears . . . . When will freedom come?"

By mid-1956 the Mau Mau revolt came to an end, except for a few small groups that continued to harass government forces. In October 1956 Kimathi was captured, swiftly tried, and hanged.

The state of emergency was lifted in January 1960. The British, to the fury of the resident white settlers, agreed to an African majority in the governing council and independence under native rule. The British flag was pulled down on December 12, 1963. Long imprisoned and reviled, the majestic Jomo Kenyatta became the head of the new independent nation. Big, wily, and jovial, he proved to be an able, reasonable, and constructive leader. Whites were treated with fairness and justice, and settlers were paid for all land taken from them. Two antiforeign laws have required noncitizens to get work permits and special licenses to trade. Those chiefly affected were Asians, and a big exodus began. Those holding British passports headed for Great Britain. But the British didn't want them either, and all such refugees are now excluded from the British Isles.

The Mau Mau struggle for independence, though the black Kenyans little realized it, was a continental struggle which brought to life more than a score of new independent governments, and which continues in the Portuguese colonies of Guinea, Angola, and Mozambique, and against Rhodesia and South Africa. A small number of white settlers struggle to retain their control over millions of blacks in the southern end of the continent. The costly and bloody process of revolution seems destined to continue, perhaps for decades.

CHAPTER 12

THE NEW CUBA

DURING THE CUBAN TEN YEARS WAR for independence (1868–1878) patriot General Calixto García Iñiguez, defeated on the battlefield and about to be captured, put a pistol in his mouth. The bullet came out his forehead. He plugged up the hole with a piece of cotton and lived to fight many a battle. When the leader of the insurgents, Máximo Gómez y Báez, an exiled Dominican, celebrated the Peace of Zanjón in 1878 with Spanish Captain General Arsenio Martínez de Campos, he promised never to fight again and exchanged Cuban freedom for an amnesty, liberation of the slaves in the rebel army, and a few civil rights. García refused to accept it. Along with the mulatto General Antonio Maceo, who was to become Cuba's greatest military genius, he fought on for nearly two years.

The liberation movement had really begun, after the turn of the previous century, when the rest of Spanish America was liberated. But the United States government had frowned on Cuban independence, warned Mexico and Colombia not to intervene, and offered Spain military aid in crushing the island revolt.

Thirty years of brutal repression had followed, until Carlos Manuel de Céspedes, a wealthy plantation and slave owner, started a revolt near Yara in Oriente province in 1868. Slaves, free Negroes, indentured Chinese, and many whites flocked to his banner, and he swept into Bayamo with fifteen hundred men. The slaves were declared emancipated, and a provisional government was set up, with Céspedes as the first president. His attempts to protect the large landholdings and a bid for annexation by the United States cut away his following, and Máximo Gómez y Báez took over the leadership. Revolutionary ideas were emerging. The patriots wanted not merely independence but also democratic freedom and economic and social change.

The struggle became bitter, and both sides pursued a scorched-earth policy that laid waste much of the island. At last, Gómez' followers divided into bitter factions. His people starving, his resources almost exhausted, Gómez made the best settlement he could with the Spaniards and went into exile. Several leaders kept up an unequal struggle, but by 1880 Cuba became relatively peaceful, except for a few insurgents here and there, for ten years.

Some ardent patriots had not fought during the previous uprising because they were in exile or in jail. In 1870 José Martí, a student of sixteen at the Havana Institute, was condemned to six years in prison for allegedly insulting Spanish soldiers and probable disloyalty. He was held for three months in Havana, La Cabaña, and the Isle of Pines prisons, and then was deported to Spain.

He studied at the universities of Madrid and Zaragoza, from which he was graduated in 1874. He published a pamphlet in behalf of Cuban independence, traveled in Europe, then went to Mexico, where he worked for the *Revista Universal* and had a play, *Love Is Paid with Love,* produced. He visited Guatemala briefly. A general amnesty in Cuba led him to return, but in 1879 he was again deported to Spain.

On January 3, 1880, he reached New York, where he wrote a barrage of brilliant articles, many of them advocating Cuban independence. As a thinker and revolutionist he was in most ways superior to Giuseppe Mazzini, the great intellectual of the Italian Risorgimento. Even if people won political independence, he wrote, it would soon be lost unless they also won economic freedom.

He began organizing Cuban exiles, particularly in Miami and Tampa, where there were many tobacco workers. He collected money and bought vessels for an invasion. They were seized by the United States government.

Undaunted, he persuaded Máximo Gómez y Báez and Maceo to resume the struggle. Maceo came over with twenty men. Martí and Gómez landed with four men in Oriente. Martí was soon killed in battle.

Within a very short time the two remaining leaders had recruited about four thousand men and seized Matanzas, near Havana. Maceo then marched with fifteen hundred men 500 kilometers to

Pinar Del Río. Spain sent over two hundred thousand soldiers, who succeeded in driving the rebels back beyond the *trocha,* or armed trench, across the island. The Spaniards rounded up tens of thousands of peasants, including women and children, and placed them in concentration camps where many were starved to death or killed. But the insurgents were getting large shipments of arms and money from the United States. Spain's power began to crumble; there was little doubt by 1898 that the patriots would take over the island in the near future.

The United States battleship *Maine* was blown up in Havana Harbor with the loss of nearly all its crew, except the officers who were on shore. The cause of the disaster is not known for certain, but it is thought to have been an internal explosion. It was not to the interests of the Spaniards to blow it up, and at once they offered to facilitate a United States investigation, and acceded to every demand in the ultimatum sent to Madrid from Washington. But feelings in the United States, already so inflamed by tales of Spanish atrocities, became uncontrollable.

The belief, long held by United States radicals, that the Spanish-American War of 1898 was promoted by American sugar interests has little foundation in fact. The big American plantation owners and refiners moved heaven and earth to the very end to try to prevent war—they were pro-Spanish and opposed to Cuban emancipation. A small group of bankers, who had aided the insurgents, undoubtedly tried to provoke the break—the only way they could get their money back—but the war was mainly the product of Hearst's sensational journalism and his exposés of Spanish atrocities, many of which were true. It was a war presold to the Midwestern farmers, middlemen, and industrialists. Teddy Roosevelt began organizing his Rough Riders. The seriocomic aspects of that war have been related poignantly and devastatingly by Walter Millis, in his *Martial Spirit,* one of the finest war chronicles ever written.

The war, considered by the American people as a righteous and altruistic crusade and so characterized in most school textbooks ever since, had a number of unforeseen results, some of them unfortunate. It created the myth that Teddy Roosevelt had stormed up San Juan Hill, when actually he scrambled up Kettledrum Hill on the heels of a New York Negro regiment. The fiction helped launch a spectacular political career, and in due time the Bull Moose movement.

The most serious misfortune was the abortion of the Cuban independence movement. Spanish rule over Cuba was ended, but the war fell far short of creating a free Cuba for the Cubans or an independent government. From the first the Cubans were shunted to one side. It is doubtful whether Santiago could have been captured had it not been for the Cuban insurgents, led by General García. They were on the eve of capturing it before United States troops were landed.

The American forces, under obese General William R. Shaffer, accepted the surrender without allowing any Cuban officers or troops to be present. They were actually denied admittance to the captured city. It was a bitter disappointment and a slap at the face of veterans, some of whom had fought for years for a free Cuba. Instead, American soldiers, who had fought only hours or days, received all the laurels of victory. Many a Cuban heart, from that day on, was eaten by the acid of hatred for the Yankees.

As in Santiago, all over the island the Americans not only ignored or disarmed the independence fighters but for the most part restored the hated Spanish officials to their positions. Nor did any Cuban sit in at the Paris peace conferences, which decided the fate of the island. A United States military regime ruled the island for three years.

A United States-made constitution was imposed, which the Cubans were obliged to accept without the alteration of a word or comma, and the Platt Amendment provided United States control of Cuban finances, restricted her diplomatic rights, provided for American military intervention at the will of the United States and for American military bases—in short, a full-fledged protectorate, a colony status remote indeed from the wartime promises of independence. Puerto Rico was annexed outright. So were the Philippines. An attempt to seize the Isle of Pines was finally abandoned after stubborn Cuban opposition. United States business interests began taking over the country by army concessions, buying out Spanish plantations, refineries, public utilities, and other enterprises at bargain-counter rates. An educational system, based on that of Massachusetts, was set up, but it would take half a century to restructure it for Cuban needs and traditions.

Not until May 20, 1902, did General Leonard Wood and his forces withdraw from the island, leaving a trussed-up *Cuba Libre*. A reciprocity treaty, denounced by Miguel Sanguilly as "colonial vassalage," was imposed in 1903. However, the Cubans were able to whittle down United States demands for bases in Guantánamo, Cienfuegos, Nipe, and Bahía Honda, by limiting occupation to the single Guantánamo base with enlarged boundaries—a thorn in Cuban flesh ever since.

The believers in complete independence were harassed, jailed, and exiled by the military occupation forces of the United States. But by 1904 Carlos Baliño founded the Cuban Workers party and the following year the Cuban Socialist Workers party. At the end of the four-year term of President Estrada Palma, armed uprisings occurred, and William Howard Taft, on a special mission, called in troops and imposed the lawyer and politician Charles Edward Magoon, ex-governor of the Canal Zone, as interventor.

Of course, before and after, there were repeated military and other interventions by financial, military, and other advisers, usually having carte blanche for whatever they chose to do. No Cuban president drew a breath without first getting permission from the United States Embassy, yet the country was touted to the world as a free republic.

Magoon "the Magnificent," a massive man with a massive abdomen and "a round face like a California apple," ruled as provisional governor from 1906 to 1909, four years of plunder, looting, and immorality beyond anything ever known before in Cuba. Magoon was personally honest, though he made some fortuitous local investments and decreed many well-intentioned laws, but he handed out too many high-salaried jobs and concessions. By the end of his so-called administration, American investments totaled four hundred million dollars.

He left the country in the hands of José Miguel Gómez, governor of Las Villas Province, and known as the *Tiburón* ("Shark"). Gómez tried to outmatch Magoon's spending talents. He outlawed all political organizations of Negroes and mulattoes and put down the resultant uprising with armed forces.

The students were rebellious from 1917 on, and their efforts came to a head during the "Dance of the Millions," especially after the collapse of sugar prices from 22½ to 3¾ cents a pound, which brought a wave of unemployment and unrest. Sugar cane workers' wages sank as low as 10 cents a day for dawn-to-dark toil. Families living packed together, clad only in dirty rags, were to be found under all the arcades of Havana and other centers. Such was the

[237]

situation when Liberal party candidate Gerardo Machado y Morales, head of an electric company taken over by the Electric Bond and Share Company, assumed the presidency after a campaign financed by American corporations.

He managed to hold the lid on until he set aside the constitution, determined to remain in power beyond his elected term. The students went on permanent strike. All opposition to his illegal rule was ruthlessly suppressed. Students, workers, teachers, and political oppositionists were murdered in the streets. A wave of counterterror made life in the cities unsafe. Julio Antonio Mella, the student leader, was arrested, but escaped to Mexico, where he was assassinated January 10, 1929, by killers sent over from Havana. A general strike paralyzed the island. It grew worse in 1933, when the great depression was piled on top of thirteen years of economic agony. The only answer by the corrupt Machado government was more brutality and terrorism.

The counterterrorism of the ABC secret organization, started largely by intellectuals, students, and professors, soon honeycombed the land. Organized in separate seven-man cells, with only the leader of each cell knowing the names of a single person in the parent cell, or in any subordinate cell, it was almost impenetrable by the police, yet suggestions or orders could be flashed up or down with great rapidity and independent or joint action carried out quickly and efficiently. Soon it penetrated the army, and Sergeant Fulgencio Batista y Zaldívar became the chief military ABC director.

Caught in the web of the great depression, President Herbert Hoover set a timetable for ending the long-time military interventions in Nicaragua, Haiti, and the Dominican Republic, which had aroused hostility and loud criticisms throughout Latin America, and had stirred to life a continentwide boycott of American goods. A year later President Franklin Delano Roosevelt dramatized the withdrawals as the new Good Neighbor policy and sent Sumner Welles as ambassador to Cuba to try to straighten out the scandalous situation on the island, torn by terrorism and assassinations.

After briefly attempting to consolidate Machado's shaky position, Welles arranged for a take-over by the army and amenable politicians, and gave the dictator his walking papers. Before taking a plane to fly to the United States, Machado phoned the manager of the Electric Bond and Share Company's subsidiary, "I am going now. Look after your properties."

Exuberant crowds surged into the streets. They looted the palatial homes of the Machado grafters. Everybody from top to bottom rejoiced: the upper classes, the middle class, the workers, the students, the *guajiros* or peasants.

Welles set up the Carlos Manuel de Céspedes provisional government. Céspedes was a Machado associate and close to powerful United States business interests. The people felt defrauded, and his government lasted only weeks. Batista staged his famous shower-bath revolt, establishing a student-professor junta headed by Dr. Ramón Grau San Martín, who became provisional president. Welles was furious, and the United States withheld recognition, sending thirty "goodwill" naval vessels to ring the island. The big guns of one pointed up the main street of Havana.

Welles stubbornly combatted Grau's mild reforms, perhaps not because of the reforms but because Grau was an "illegal usurper"—also, and more likely, because of the turbulent land seizures by the peasants. An American sugar manager was held prisoner in his home by strikers. Grau's agrarian minister, Antonio Guiteras, was promoting a revolutionary land program, which threatened the enormous landholdings of American corporations. Grau set up a minimum wage of one dollar for an eight-hour day; he permitted liberty of the press and political freedom, recognized the right to strike, reduced electric light rates, the highest in the world, which Welles insisted was a treaty violation, since they had been established during the military occupation of General Wood, all of whose acts had been ratified by the first Cuban authorities in 1900.

Under the protection of Sumner Welles, the Machado army officers turned the National Hotel into a fortress. Batista blasted them out with artillery, further winning the enmity of the ambassador, who began plotting for the government's overthrow by a leader of Machado's party and with the ABC terrorists, most of whom had broken with Batista and the Grau government—the period known in Cuba as "garage diplomacy."

Jefferson Caffery, sent down to replace Welles, continued the process, but more realistically, for he realized that Batista was the real power. He and the sergeant, now a colonel, the highest rank left in the army, formed a mutual admiration club. Before long Batista betrayed Grau. His planes bombed the national palace, and the police stations were stormed.

Carlos Mendieta, head of a wing of Machado's Liberal party, a dull dutiful man, was put in as president, in a coalition including the ABC, which had issued a Fascist-type manifesto.

New terrorism filled the land. Workers, students, peasants, were jailed. Violence grew in Havana. When asked why he did not end the bombings, Mendieta said, "How can I when I can't even prevent bombs under my own chair?" (One had been discovered under his seat at a banquet.)

A series of puppets was installed by Batista. In 1940 he himself ran for president. He enjoyed the support of the Communists—and was elected.

The Second World War brought the island great prosperity, but in the 1944 elections, Grau San Martín was chosen by a landslide. Batista ran a poor third. He refused to recognize Grau's success, but the United States pressured him to leave the island, an almost ludicrous reversal of its position ten years earlier.

But the State Department knew its Grau. His moderate reforms were now acceptable; the danger of an agrarian revolution was over. Guiteras had been assassinated years before.

Grau's chief accomplishment was to follow the Magoon tradition and steal the country blind. He was followed in office by Carlos Prío Socarrás. By then the Cuban Confederation of Labor had become powerful. At the behest of the United States government, Prío kicked out the Communists and installed at its head his own stooge, Eusebeo Mujal.

In 1952 Batista came back to run for president. When he realized he did not have a chance, he walked into Camp Colombia, threw out Prío, and took over the power, preventing elections. Batista won Mujal over to his side, and as a reward, Mujal was able to utilize union retirement funds and to become many times a millionaire and owner of a $4 million plantation. He also raked in such concessions as luxury hotels, radio stations, newspapers, and gambling casinos.

Cuba was prosperous at this time, at least for the privileged. Members of the American Mafia and the Las Vegas gamblers' syndicate descended on Havana, and a casino was set up in every major hotel in the land. Tourists flocked in, and Havana prostitutes swarmed in the streets and were reputed to be the most proficient in the world.

The prosperity did not reach far down. Most *guajiros* still went barefoot in rags. They could afford meat only once a week, if at all. They enjoyed work only three or four months a year at $1.50 a day or less; the rest of the year they piled up starving in the cities; their daughters, if good-looking enough, were lucky to become harlots; their children went uneducated and often hungry.

Cuba was a sugar sweatshop, an industry controlled from top to bottom by United States corporations. Probably less than a million people in the island were consumers of modern civilized goods. Those luxuries were paid for by the speculation in sugar and molasses and, to some extent, by tobacco and citrus fruit exports. There were some ten million head of cattle, and American corporations had begun refining nickel, cobalt, manganese, and copper. Mostly untouched, held as reserves, owned largely by the Bethlehem Steel Company, were vast iron-ore deposits, among the largest in the world. Batista catered to all these interests, which owned or controlled Cuba's economic life and took out a hundred million dollars a year in absentee profits, but left little in the way of taxes or wages. Trade was buttressed by loans and handouts from the United States. Both the American taxpayer and the Cuban citizens paid the piper.

Two years after his coup Batista celebrated a one-party, one-man election. He had the support of labor, the Communists, the army, and the United States government.

His coup nipped a political career in the bud. Fidel Castro, a student leader, lawyer, university graduate, son of a well-to-do plantation farmer, had been running for congress in the Orthodox party, which had opposed Batista. After the coup its founder, Eduardo Chibas, committed suicide.

Castro, cheated out of his seat in congress, began preparing for revolution, and on July 26, 1953, staged an armed attack on the Santiago Moncada barracks and fortress. Taken prisoner, along with other survivors, including his brother, Raul, he was tried. He delivered a long defense speech, in which he attacked the dictatorship and United States imperialism, narrated the crime of enormous landholdings by United Fruit and other American corporations, and set forth the miseries and hunger of the Cuban peoples. "History will absolve

[*241*]

me," he declaimed. He and Raul were incarcerated on the Isle of Pines—fourteen-year sentences. On May 15, 1955, following a general amnesty, Fidel was released. He escaped to Mexico, where he trained and equipped an expeditionary force on a hacienda near Mexico City.

They sailed for Cuba on the little *Granma* in November 1956, eighty-two men with guns, uniforms, and supplies. Delayed by weather, a poor engine, and serious leaks, which kept them bailing frantically, they followed the southern coast of Oriente Province and, several days behind schedule, put in toward shore at dawn December 2 off Playa de las Coloradas, more a mangrove swamp than a beach. The vessel stuck on a sandbar. It was quickly detected by Batista's planes, and the rebels had to wade ashore, holding their guns aloft, abandoning all their ammunition and equipment.

They struggled through the tangled roots and needle-sharp thorny branches of the mangroves. It took about four hours to advance a hundred yards before they found firm clumps of grass. By then a naval vessel had begun firing on the deserted *Granma;* planes dropped bombs on it, then began raking the swamp with machine guns and automatic cannon fire.

Soon the army was hunting them down. They split into small groups. The planes strafed the thatched peasant *bohíos* on the edge of the swamp, evidently believing the expeditionaries had taken refuge in them. Fidel and his men hid in thickets; further on, in cane fields. Once Castro and his immediate companions had to dash out of a cane field that had been set on fire on three sides by enemy bullets.

At one point Fernando Sánchez Amaya found himself alone with cane crackling all about him. Ahead he saw rebel uniforms and crept forward, his finger on the trigger of his gun. They dragged or carried their wounded into another cane field. Sánchez tore his shirt into strips to bandage the wounds.

With six men, after a week of travel, the fugitives found themselves back at the coast. Three took off alone, were captured by Lieutenant Julio Laurentz, chief of naval intelligence, and were gunned down as soon as they handed over their weapons. Fourteen other men, completely lost, surrendered and were shot on the spot.

Sánchez hid out for weeks alone in the jungle, drinking water from vines and spitting out the bugs. He came upon a *guajiro* who seemed friendly, and he sent him in to Niquero to buy civilian clothes. He picked up a ride in a farmer's truck and reached Bayamo, where he calmly took a bus for Havana.

The Negro Juan Almeida, later minister of war, was joined by wounded men. They came upon Che Guevara alone, blood gushing from a wound in his neck. They dragged him to a place where he could be bandaged. Traveling only at night, they, too, found themselves back at the shore east of Cabo Cruz. There in a hut they found big bearded Camilo Cienfuegos and two of his men.

Fidel had only two companions left—Universo Sánchez and Dr. Faustino Pérez. They lived on sugarcane, and finally met up with Raul Castro and several survivors. On December 19 Almeida and Che and their little group located Fidel.

They finally came on a friendly landowner who provided them a guide for the Sierra Maestra. Only twelve of them were left. They had only their badly torn uniforms, their wounds, and their guns, no ammunition. But they struggled deep into the Sierra Maestra, determined to carry on.

Batista, informed of the abandoned *Granma*, the bodies in the swamp and the fields, felt confident telling the world that the invaders had been wiped out. But in spite of his powerful army, the will of the twelve men prevailed over his large, lavishly equipped army, and today the dictator lives in exile in the far-off Azores, while Fidel sits—though mostly he is a perpetual motion machine—in the National Palace.

"Pizarro began with twelve men and conquered an empire," Fidel announced—not exactly an accurate statement and scarcely a happy parallel.

The story of his success against Batista's American-trained and -advised army—fifty thousand men provided with planes, tanks, rifles, ammunition, bombs, and napalm—is the old story of dauntless men fighting for a cause versus sullen, ill-paid conscripts who have only their bellies at stake and are likely to be drilled full of holes.

The Sierra Maestra was a friendly place for the guerrillas. It is a vast, rugged, heavily forested area surrounding high peak Turquino, which became a symbol of freedom and independence.

The rebels roamed widely through the wilderness and the deep canyons. Here and there were little clearings and peasant huts. Fidel won their friendship and from them obtained food for survival and refuge for his men when they fell ill. His men in turn helped the peasants with farm tasks and Pérez and Che treated them when they were sick. Later, in more open country, Castro freed peasants on larger plantations and handed out land to them.

The first attacks on small government outposts were carefully planned and easily successful. Guns and ammunition were gathered. The word spread, and volunteers trickled in. Reliable messengers were found who could pass through the lines and bring back supplies and food, particularly oilcloth and medicines. Ammunition was sometimes brought in. Women concealed it under their skirts.

Already there were secret revolutionary groups in the towns and cities, and little by little their efforts were coordinated with those of the guerrillas. The students were strong in Castro's behalf, and many were killed. Urban terrorists answered each volley in the hills by killing police and soldiers, dynamiting factories and buses and even barracks.

Several armed revolts were staged. The most ambitious of these was the naval uprising at Cienfuegos in September 1956. The sailors at the island naval base and local insurrectionists took over the city. Batista hit back quickly by land and air. His air force is said to have killed at least five hundred persons on the city streets. The rebels were driven out of the municipal buildings and schools. All those who surrendered or were captured were savagely tortured and most of them killed. But though the revolt was crushed, it revealed the shaky position of Batista, and all Cuba was aroused.

An attack was made on March 15, 1957, on the National Palace in Havana by the Revolutionary Directorate, headed by José Antonio Echevarría, president of the University Students Federation. (Castro had been active in that body when a law student.) Over Radio Reloj, seized by the attackers, came the news at 3:25 that armed civilians had entered the palace and that Batista had been killed. The announcers then fled, but Echevarría was shot down in the gutter outside.

At the palace the attackers shot some of the guards, and a score or so of them managed to get inside. They blew out the telephone switchboard with a hand grenade and raced up the marble stairs to the second floor where Batista had his offices. They blew open a locked door with a machine gun and dashed through a kitchen and dining room, shot two guards at the doors of the presidential suite, but found that Batista had escaped—to the floor above by secret stairs, it was said. The alarm had been spread, and they were unable to reach the heavily guarded third floor. By then the palace it-self, the square in front, and the gardens in the rear were swarming with soldiers.

Of those who got as far as Batista's office only Luis Goicochea survived and was able later to give a vivid account. He had lain down under the stone rim of the garden pool, then had escaped across the plaza.

The names of those who fell are now inscribed on a large bronze plaque at the palace entrance, where most of them died.

For weeks the police searched for supposed conspirators and par-ticipants; they are said to have gunned down more than seventy-five persons. The body of the prominent Dr. Pelayo Cuervo Na-varro, a persistent critic of Batista, was found by the country club lake a few hours after he was taken by the police. The killing, it was later ascertained, had been ordered by Batista himself. Dr. Vidal Morales, a prominent attorney, was held incommunicado for four days. He was forced to drink out of a dirty toilet bowl.

Another terrifying event occurred in Havana in midsummer 1957 when the main underground light and power cables were destroyed at a point near the plant, leaving the entire city in darkness for three or four nights. Several buildings on one side of the street where the blast occurred were practically demolished. The disaster brought life to a standstill: no refrigeration, no electric lights, no streetcars, no elevators, no newspapers, no cabarets, no theaters or movies.

The dynamiting was done as an act of reprisal by striking electri-cal workers who had been threatened by the army and badly abused. The head of the union had escaped to the United States. Later he came back with an armed expedition and was killed. The army rounded up workers, including women office workers, and tried them by emergency courts, sentencing them to long prison terms.

Those who perpetrated the dynamiting were not apprehended, but several suspects were shot, and their bodies lashed to small crosses, with a noose about their necks, were displayed in the pub-lic streets for passersby to look at in horror. The union official who had planned and executed the sabotage reemerged only after the Revolution. He was actually anti-Castro.

It was charged by Castro that the Batista regime murdered some twenty thousand civilians—men, women, and children—a genocide that failed to arouse the American public or its press. If true, all these persons had families, many relatives, and friends, so that his brutality probably alienated at least half a million Cuban people.

All over the country by this time, Masses for peace were being held. People attending, especially women, were badly roughed up by the police. So were women in Santiago who demonstrated and brought a petition to the city hall protesting against the murder of their sons. They were dispersed with firehoses and clubs.

One American was wounded in a Havana café when the police rushed in with whips, driving the patrons out. The American Embassy hushed this up and got him out of the country.

Batista was now bombing intensively with napalm, burning villages and citizens, but few rebels. He ordered thousands of peasants out of their mountain homes, announcing that everyone who remained in the rebel zone would be shot on sight. They collected together on the fringe of the towns, hungry, destitute, sick.

In the mountains Castro's forces were growing. Volunteers came in from all parts of the island. Some came armed, if only with bird guns. Others had to be armed.

Raul invaded Ubero, a town on the south coast, and overran the garrison, making off with trucks, a sally that blew to shreds the government's story that the rebels had been wiped out. Batista's credibility was now gone.

Against his better judgment, Castro was prevailed upon to call for a general strike. It had some brief success in Santiago, but elsewhere it fizzled out because of the opposition of the confederation leader, Mujal, the opposition of the Communists, and the bullets of the police, who shot down any suspected persons on the streets. The Castro sympathizers in Havana failed to put in an appearance at the crucial hour. It was a bad setback.

But he had won the support of much of the Catholic hierarchy, the middle-class sports clubs, the Lions and the Rotary clubs, the medical, dental, and legal societies. Prío Soccarás, in exile in Havana, was sending in his own fighters and guns and ammunition to the tune of five million dollars. He was led in handcuffs through the streets of Miami on a charge of violating the neutrality act— unnecessary humiliation to a leader who had long been considered a friend to the United States.

Meanwhile Castro lay in his hammock in the Sierra Maestra, his telescopic rifle by his side, reading Montesquieu, pondering the future, and planning immediate strikes.

Batista redoubled his efforts at repression. More people were as-sassinated. In that effort Cuban security, order, and social life were disrupted. One rural guard officer, Jesús Sosa, later executed by Castro, rode about the countryside, killing peasants. All members of the family were tied to the beds, the *bohío* was burned, and a sign on a stake was left behind the blackened ruins: SOSA HAS BEEN HERE. The situation, as during the period of Machado, became an interna-tional scandal.

The Batista horrors were read into the *Congressional Record* by Representative Adam Clayton Powell on March 28, 1958. He was calling for an arms embargo against Batista. The week before he had presented a list of United States arms—which the State Depart-ment had refused to disclose—that had been delivered to Batista during the previous two years or were in process of being deliv-ered, including machine guns, automatic rifles, hand and mortar grenades, armor-piercing cartridges, one thousand rocket launchers, four thousand rockets, howitzer bombs, armored cars, tanks with 76-millimeter guns, etc., etc. The assistant secretary of state for Latin America, Roy R. Rubottom, Jr., testified before the House Foreign Affairs Committee that the military equipment was being used to beat back armed insurrection rather than for national de-fense: this according to Charles O. Porter, Oregon representative in the House of Representatives, March 26.

The United States was persuaded to place an embargo on further arms to Batista. But many surreptitious violations occurred—arms sent to other Latin American countries, then sent on directly to Cuba, sometimes without transshipment. Dictator Rafael Trujillo of the Dominican Republic filled the gap by sending in munitions and napalm.

In the Sierra Maestra, raiding parties by the army were am-bushed and wiped out. Some went over to Castro's side with their arms. As he became more secure in a widening area, hospitals were set up, arms-repair and munitions shops were established, land dis-tribution extended. Strong radio receivers and transmitter stations were set up. An airplane landing strip was built. Soon Castro was ranging along the lower foothills with armored cars, jeeps, and trucks. Bayamo, a large center, was entered, and supplies and medi-cine were carted off.

He split his forces into smaller commands under Raul, Cienfue-gos, Almeida, taking over the mining and ore-refining areas, the Guantánamo Bay area, and elsewhere. A second front had been opened up by Fauré Chaumont, head of the Revolutionary Directorate, in Escambray, not far from Havana. Rebels were now operating in Pinar del Río province, just west of the capital.

All eastern Oriente province fell into rebel hands. The railroad line had been permanently cut, bridges blown up. Bus travel between Havana and nearby Matanzas became dangerous. Several planes were hijacked.

Late in November 1958 Che Guevara set out with a small force on a fabulous march through Camagüey province to Las Villas province. He established radio contact with Fidel on December 2 and began systematically cutting highways, taking smaller towns, and steadily converging on Santa Clara, the provincial capital and the island's chief sugar center. On Christmas Eve he captured Espíritu Santos, a battle concerted with armed insurrectionists inside the town.

Back in Santiago, on Christmas day, after two days' battle from house to house, Fidel entered Palma Soriano close to Santiago, where the best of Batista's troops were bottled up. There Commander Eulogio Cantillo, behind Batista's back, made a deal for surrendering Santiago to the rebels. He was plotting a two-edged double cross by which he would seize power from Batista and fool the rebels also.

But the real menace to Batista was the attack on Santa Clara. Its capture would cut the island in two. To save it, the dictator sent out a million-dollar armored train, with troops, supplies, ammunition, for a two months' campaign. He dug to the bottom of his barrel to equip it.

Che tore up the tracks; the train was dynamited; and all its supplies captured. Guevara acquired more guns than his men could use, but he found volunteer hands eager to use them against the Santa Clara police and troops. The battle raged through the streets under strafing airplanes and bombers. His men and the volunteers attacked and overturned and burned military vehicles. The Gran Hotel, heavily fortified, was stormed, and while the police chief and the military commander quarreled over who was in charge, the police station fell, and by the night of December 31 Santa Clara had been "liberated." The news was flashed to Batista after he was already prepared to flee. A few days earlier he had sent two of his young sons to New York. By New Year's Eve, i.e., early on the morning of the first of January 1959, Batista flew off with his entourage to the Dominican Republic to enjoy the protection of Dictator Rafael Trujillo. In his *Respuesto,* written after his downfall, Batista claimed to have been betrayed by his generals and by the United States ambassador, who offered him, he said, if he would get out, asylum in the United States, where the dictator owned millions of dollars' worth of property—a promise never honored. Later he took refuge in the Azores, under the Portuguese dictatorship of Antonio Salazar.

A few days later Castro rode into Havana, his arm around his little son, in a Batista tank, and delivered his "Speech of Peace" at Camp Colombia.

Castro was not yet a Communist; at least he denied vociferously being one. He was, however, definitely an anti-imperialist. As early as 1948, at the Pan American Congress in Bogotá, to which he came as a student observer and protester, he showered handbills on the delegates, demanding, among other things, the end of United States ownership of the Panama Canal.

After the take-over in Cuba, he hastened to visit the United States, but was pretty much rebuffed officially. He flew on to the Inter-American Congress in Montevideo where he outraged the United States delegates by demanding $20 billion of United States aid to Latin America.

This demand was finally met, in a double-talk fashion, by promising that much over a ten-year period to the new Alliance for Progress set up by President John F. Kennedy. It was not a bona fide offer. Much of this sum was to be derived from United States private investment and bank loans; actual aid was not increased. Startlingly enough, a good share of it was to be provided by Japanese and German investment, if and when, though the United States had been very exercised over such investments prior to World War II. Actually, in retrospect, it may be noted that the Alliance for Progress never got off the ground, despite all the whoopla. As for Castro, he continued to assert that he was not a Communist and plastered the walls of Havana with big posters and banners, reading, "The Revolution is not Communist; it is a humanitarian revolution."

Ah, but his associates and advisers were Communists! critics exclaimed. The *bêtes noirs* are Che Guevara and Raul Castro. American magazines and newspapers have stated that Che was already a Communist during his student days in Buenos Aires. He was an excellent student, completing a four-year medical course in three years. He went out for sports. His later asthma was not yet in evidence. He had little time for university politics, but the alleged campus group he joined was nationalist and antigovernment. It was not a Communist group at all.

He was a nonconformist and was adventurous. Not wishing to be conscripted into the Argentine army, he went on a bicycle trip through Latin America. He had little money. In Bolivia he hobnobbed, not with Communists, as alleged, but with Trotskyites, who are bitter anti-Communists. In Peru he went around with Apristas, a very vocal anti-Communist group.

There he fell in love with Hilda Gadea, an Aprista, who had to go into exile. He followed her to Guatemala, where Jacobo Arbenz Guzmán was president—also improperly charged with being a Communist. Che was never employed by the Arbenz government, as has been alleged. He almost starved to death in Guatemala and tried to make a living selling books. He did offer to enlist when the CIA-powered rebel putsch moved to oust Arbenz. When the government fell, he went with Hilda to Mexico, where he met Castro and joined the *Granma* expedition. Later on, when he was head of the Cuban Nationalist Bank and was asked whether he was a Communist, he denied it. Asked whether he was a Marxist, he gave the evasive answer that he did not know enough to be a Marxist. He became one *after* the Bay of Pigs invasion.

Nor did Raul Castro admit to being a Communist. Apparently he did attend a student congress behind the iron curtain. Many who attended it were not Communists, and the American students there were actually subsidized by the CIA. After becoming head of the Cuban army, he issued an extensive manual for the troops. This was denounced as being a Communist document. But it contained no mention of Communism or Marxism. It did quote extensively from José Martí. In the section on strategy and tactics it devotes long passages to British, French, and American operations in World War II. The manual does not mention the Soviet army, except in a single sentence lauding the defense of Stalingrad as a notable example of able patriotic defense.

The latter part is devoted to an extensive exposition on the program of the Cuban Revolution—what it proposed to do for the Cuban people, particularly land reform. Except for land reform, the treatise has little that has not been proposed by American advocates of the welfare state. Naturally this was quite revolutionary for Cuba.

In a speech at the University of Havana in 1959 he was incensed by the United States embargo on Cuban sugar and said, "For every step of aggression they take, we shall take two steps forward." He added, "They call us Communists. We are Cuban patriots. If we were Communist we would shout it from the housetops."

Of course, disclaimers by political leaders are usually not outstanding for their truthfulness. Such statements can be wool over the eyes, but at the particular stage that Raul made the statement, the Cuban leaders had practically written off all possibility of United States cooperation.

One of Castro's first acts was to cut house rents and utility rates 50 percent. He threw out the American military mission, which had consorted with Batista to the end. Just before they had to get out, they attended a big banquet together and drank toasts. "They have nothing to teach us," Castro said sarcastically at Camp Colombia, the day he arrived in Havana after the take-over. The entire Cuban army was furloughed, sent home with five dollars a head. Most of the police were also kicked out, though many were rehired individually after their records had been checked.

The bureaucracy was also dismissed. Batista judges were fired. Senators and congressmen were turned out of the big white parliament building, which was converted into an exposition hall. No elections have ever been held.

By mid-January the new agrarian law was ready. It confiscated all estates over thirty-three acres. The biggest landholders, some of them owning hundreds of thousands of acres, were the American corporations. The large estates were kept intact and administered by the government. Smaller farms were run by cooperatives. About two hundred thousand small owners remained in possession. A vigorous program of new land-use, diversification, irrigation, and road building was inaugurated. The island was divided into fifteen zones, each controlled by an agronomist, and soil tests were made to determine the best crops to be planted.

The pressures by the United States became more punitive. The purchase of Cuban sugar was ended, presently all trade was cut off, all travel prohibited. Cuban government assets in the United States were frozen. The loss of tourist trade, about fifty million dollars a year it was claimed, would soon bring Castro to his knees. Actually he gained far more than that by stopping the drain of a hundred million dollars in annual United States absentee profits from the island. Soon he proceeded to expropriate the light and telephone companies. When petroleum from American companies was cut off, and the United States companies refused to refine Cuban oil—a very small share of the total—or Soviet oil, the country's very existence was threatened, and the refineries and gas stations were confiscated. Efforts were later made to sabotage or bomb the refineries. At least one new refinery has been built.

When the United States State Department refused to permit the Cuban Embassy to increase its eight-man personnel by two more members, Castro cut the American Embassy down to the same number. The embassy burned papers on the roof all night. President Eisenhower broke off relations, and more than a hundred Americans came home.

The following year Castro's forces crushed the Bay of Pigs invasion, after heavy aerial bombardment of supposed Cuban airfields, including Camp Colombia, already converted into an educational center. After that experience Castro declared himself to be a Communist and turned definitely to the Soviet Union.

About the only elections permitted—and these are closely controlled—have been in the labor unions. Candidates must be accepted by a control board, and no undesired individual can attain office. Since there have been no general elections, the old-style political parties, which admittedly were pretty much of a disgrace, have withered on the vine. This includes the old-line Communist party, quite a few of whose leaders are in exile, in jail, or on the shelf. The members had to seek admission to Castro's new Communist party as individuals. That party has no electoral activities, but has large influence in the selecting of government employees.

In short, Cuba technically is a one-man, one-party dictatorship. Things have run fairly smoothly so far, because Castro is greatly adored by the mass of the people, as is apparent from the fact that 90 percent are now armed—an impossible situation did he lack popular support.

Castro is interested in revolution in Latin America and elsewhere in the world. His agents were active in the Communist coup in Tanganyika; Cubans make up the palace guard in the former French Congo. The first bag of cement from the big new factory was sent to North Vietnam, and he is ready to send soldiers, as well as free sugar, to the Viet Cong if they call for them. He has close relations with North Vietnam.

The first three "rowboat" expeditions, which set out shortly after the Revolution for the Dominican Republic, Haiti, and Panama, did not have his sanction, nor did the attempt to seize one of the British Keys not far from Cuba's northern coast. The Panama expedition was promoted by a son of a Panama supreme court justice, who had presidential aspirations. The air strike from Venezuela against Dictator Rafael Trujillo was actually promoted by a provocateur, who was received at the Dominican National Palace, decorated, and raised in rank after he was captured and his dupes shot down.

It is doubtful if special camps and training have been provided for foreign expeditionaries. Some arms shipments may have been acquired from Cuba, but some supposed shipments have been hoaxes by hard-pressed dictators. Shipments to Guatemala, Nicaragua, and Venezuela, the Cubans claimed, were planted on the beaches by the governments in question, apparently with CIA cooperation.

But Castro has made his influence felt on the Guatemalan and Venezuelan guerrilla leaders, sharply criticizing the Guatemalan effort for harboring Trotskyites, and breaking with the Communist party of Venezuela and most of Latin America for their efforts to halt or control guerrilla activities.

There is little doubt that he gave his sanction to the Che Guevara efforts, though again how much actual aid—if any—was given is not known. It would seem odd that Che would first go off to the Congo to attempt to support the guerrillas there, then end up in Bolivia with inadequate preparation and supplies.

Castro considers Cuba an integral cultural part of Latin America. But all diplomatic ties have been broken except with Mexico, and these have at moments been touchy, as when the Cuban government in mid-1969 asked for the recall of a Mexican Embassy official, caught red-handed sending and receiving coded messages from the CIA. Mexico hotly denied this, but Cuba published a truly massive documentation. Foreign Minister Raul Róa flew to Mexico and talked personally with the Mexican president and straightened the matter out. The offending attaché was recalled but not punished.

Cuba was kicked out of the Organization of American States early in the game. Castro declares that Cuba has not been isolated, but that the dictatorships have isolated their countries from Cuba and progress, that this is true also of the United States. He refuses to beg for recognition, but looks forward to a new intercontinental organization completely free of American imperialism and overlordship. He has praised the new military dictator of Peru for his confiscation of oil and mining properties, and his revolutionary land program. He will support any bona fide revolutionary effort anywhere in Latin America, and is somewhat sarcastic about the Peruvian dictator's refusal to seek Cuban recognition. He recognizes the difficulties that any true revolutionary government will have with the United States—cutting off of aid, trade boycotts, and other punitive measures. Cuba knows that story by heart.

At the same time, he has repeatedly stated that no revolution to the south can be a slavish imitation of Cuba's effort. It must spring from its own soil and needs, be led by its own leaders, and carry out its own program, in accordance with its own culture, economy, and popular desires.

The émigrés, some of whom have suffered greatly, are naturally bitter and unreconciled, as is true in the history of all revolutions. Habeas corpus, rarely honored in Cuba's past, has ceased to exist. Some political prisoners—there are probably at least twenty thousand—have been incarcerated ten years without trial. Few civilians have been executed, unless caught with arms in hand or working for the CIA. Most of those tried and executed immediately after the Revolution were Batista officers and secret police, known for their cruelties and assassinations. Just why an officer who had been seizing, torturing, and stringing up scores of youths in the public plaza should arouse no horror, while his subsequent trial and execution by the Castro government should bring the roof down, with almost universal denunciation, must remain one of the mysteries of the human biped.

Cuba has accomplished remarkable advances in agriculture and industry. At the same time it has witnessed an almost feverish expansion in art, literature, music, painting, film making, the dance, and the theater, largely nonexistent before the Revolution— activities that have not been curbed or controlled thus far.

The price for all this has been the loss of a fraudulent electoral and political system; the end of economic exploitation by outside corporations; the loss of American tourist trade, due to United States State Department prohibition; the loss of gambling and wholesale prostitution. It has acquired a somewhat amiable totalitarian system, largely directed by a single outstanding leader who has shown more interest in the welfare of his subjects than any previous ruler. It is a system not without its own peculiar brand of democracy; despite the general regimentation, there are notable pockets of freedom. Cuba has been given a proud sense of national destiny. What that destiny will eventually be, history alone will tell.

For the present there is widespread euphoria from having been able to face up to the most powerful nation on earth and overcome, to a considerable degree, the formidable obstacles it has placed in the path of the Revolution. Most Cubans feel they are rapidly outdistancing the rest of Latin America, doomed under present feudal regimes to unemployment, much hunger and misery, vast illiteracy, declining education, terrible exploitation, and unenlightened military rule. If they are right, the continent one of these days is going to quake.

REVOLUTION AND THE
POWER STRUCTURE

Is REVOLUTION UPON US in the United States? Or are the high-level snipings merely the strong smell of cordite that will drift away into the smog of police-style law and order? Can the hippies, the university and high school students, the peace marchers, the draft-card burners, the black militants, yes, even the grape pickers, be persuaded or coerced back into the conformity of Suburbia and the squares? Of course the protesters have no suburbia; mostly they hold the rotting cores of partly abandoned cities.

All the protesters have valid reasons, often lost sight of in the righteous cry of law and order but rarely of justice. The disorders are the product of a society that has lost its glue, except for sniffing. We are a society of restless seminomads. A certain income permits moving to the country, not so much to enjoy it as to have status and make it as nearly like the city as possible—but an undefiled city, free of "furriners," "niggers," and poor people. Also about seven million whites, and even more blacks, have shifted from the South to the North, adding to the burden of slums and ghettos. Trailer camps, slums on wheels, multiply. All this jostling and shoving, accompanied by a population explosion, has helped break up family, community, and institutional and political ties, and has created terrible, perhaps insoluble, problems for the cities. The mores change; the old laws do not apply; violence erupts, becomes contagious—like wind-borne disease. Slum houses burst at the seams with uprooted peoples; normal communications break down. Language, hallways, toilets, sewers, get clogged. In part these people are the

[257]

discarded and often radiated particles and waste of the atomic and electronic revolution that has spun us into swirling confusion.

There is the age-old revolt of youth against parents, and today the swift economic changes make mutual comprehension more difficult; a revolt caused by the new pampered idleness and leisure, the conformity to social climbing and mental vapidity, the meaninglessness of career and consumer enslavement, the falsity of keeping up with the Joneses, the conviction that the adults have messed up the world, a disillusionment with the standards of parents which the young consider either hypocritical or inadequate. They sense the credibility gap of life without moral or spiritual unity. They ask whether the rat race of status is worth true and lifelong endeavor. The revolt began a decade ago with skepticism and has shifted to independent dogma, both irrational. And so the sons and daughters, often of the best families, seek escape and sniff the tainted winds of violence and the excitement of danger, or they resort to drugs, an artificial and dangerous soul-lift—and to open sexual experimentation, not a new activity, but at the present juncture defying the false front of Puritanical respectability. They feel the need for meaningful action and turn to revolt against society, from which they are increasingly alienated. It is a revolutionary stance, a war against hierarchy and institutionalized power, against war and imperialism. They test the authority of the state, and their very testing converts it increasingly into a police state.

All this is an oversimplification. A century ago Henry George laid down the dictum that as land monopoly took over and property values rose—a reward not for increased production but as a free increment provided by society—real wages would go down. He saw a powerful [steel] wedge cutting horizontally across society, making the fortunate richer, the underprivileged poorer. It was a post-Marxian concept uttered by one who had not read Marx. Unlike Marx, he did not take into account corporate monopoly, the moderating power of the Industrial Revolution, which, by substituting machines for muscles and back-toting, provided a larger national product of higher wages, though not always a higher percentage of total production, and an improved standard of living for millions. This has led to much academic refutation of both Marx and Henry George, mostly based on too short-term observations, disregard of war, of labor organization, our Point IV program the cold war, or the revolutionary effects of our present electronic earthquake. The reasoning has left out the collapse of the farmers' revolt, various lags in the productive process, the lost corners untouched by economic growth. How much these ugly pockets may be due to progress itself is an open question, but they do exist, and many have widened. The new prosperity has left millions stranded. Even Alexis de Tocqueville, a century ago, laid down the dictum that modern society inevitably creates a large sector of underprivileged misery, which the modern state must mitigate—or else perish.

The underprivileged look at TV, and inevitably it is more than an opiate: It arouses resentments at the plush leisure life it exalts. It stimulates desires among blacks and poor whites and the drudges of routine employment—but society blocks their fulfillment. The impoverished, the slaves of routine, the frustrated, see no hope of enjoying the fine gadgets, and they are psychologically prepared for violence, for breaking into stores and looting, as in New York City, and this in turn inspires similar violence in Chicago, Cleveland, and Philadelphia. The Negroes, the poor whites, the sharecroppers, the subsistence farmers, were always on the underside of the moving wedge. The driblets, dropped down the perforations in the steel ceiling, were not enough and still are not enough, nor do they represent a reasonable or decent manner in which to handle the problem. Welfare is a sad substitute, which precipitates indignity. Thus the electronic revolution, by further increasing the national product, seems likely to refute, not only part of Marx, but the critics of Marx as well.

Norbert Wiener, the father of cybernetics, said in the forties that unless precautions were taken, within a quarter of a century it would bring about catastrophic displacement of human beings. He foresaw the social bone-breaks and the tragedy ahead. His timetable was not far off, even though as yet only a few bands of the vast radiation spectrum have been studied or tapped, and only a few crumbs fall from the electronic banquet upon the tables of either the hungry or the gorged. Mostly the efforts have been directed at making war and delving into space, types of escapism. But more and more the computers march into every factory, office, and shop, and every government bureau, to become superhuman operatives. The individual becomes a statistic, a number out of a hat. Only a relatively few persons are technically prepared for the cybernetic

[259]

world. What is worse, few scientists, well paid by business enterprises doing war work and the military, have shown concern for the evil uses made of their findings.

Meanwhile the steel wedge moves on inexorably, pushing the underdeveloped countries, despite the little sops of aid and Alliances for Progress, deeper into poverty, misery, and hunger; pushing our own underprivileged, despite welfare and antipoverty programs, into a helpless role.

Rebellion grows in the semidarkness of the underside of the steel wedge, and not all of those who toss Molotov cocktails and dynamite skyscrapers call themselves revolutionaries or are even dimly aware of what is happening to them or to society, let alone what to do about it. Nor are those who run the show, trying to maintain the status quo at home and abroad—which cannot possibly survive.

The creeping arthritis of American society—the superduper world of technocracy—is apparent on every hand. Out of the cracks come the bugs of crime, not merely the powerful Mafia and its political tie-ups, but a terrible army of criminals, whose ages reflect the generation gap. The increasing crime rate is already higher than that of any country in history—this in a time of apparent prosperity and the expensive J. Edgar Hoover regime, in itself a sad commentary on the failure of our era. No sane person ventures into a public park anymore at night.

Not all the criminals come out of alleys or bars or poverty holes. They are entrenched at all levels in the national and local bureaucracies, administering waste and graft and corruption. A few of the dirty little rogues are caught up and punished; but rarely those who have stolen billions in Vietnam or elsewhere—some say, as *The New York Times*, that 25 to 40 percent of all our arms and supplies for East Asia go down the black market drain.

An increase in crime has always been symptomatic of a revolutionary situation. Criminals, a symptom of malaise, blaze the trail of disrespect for law and order. No police action can cure it; only a healthy society insures healthy citizen corpuscles.

The refuse mounts up not merely on our streets. Smog has become a menace to millions. Our streams and lakes and bathing beaches are polluted beyond prompt cleaning, and such sources of poison as insecticides and chemical fertilizers even then will keep them unsafe. The insecticides have ripped apart our ecology, nature's balance—one does not even need to read Rachel Carson's

Silent Spring to know that our vegetables, our meat, our water, and our bodies are often poisoned, even when without atomic radiation.

Nor has the antipoverty program provided more than a trickle of new jobs; it has not raised living standards, except to provide a few heads-above-water flotations and a large number of twenty-to-forty-thousand-dollar-a-year jobs. It has, in short, rehabilitated the habilitated and enabled rapacious fangs to prey on the taxpayers' money. At best it's a thrice-removed way of solving a national problem.

Public services falter. The postal service limps badly. Trains have become filthy and uncomfortable. Inadequate airports—controls years behind the times—have become dangerous and overcrowded. Concrete highways wrap strangle loops about city and country, and the death toll rises. Red tape and endless filling out of forms entangle government, business, and personal transactions. People are stupefied by frustrations. It may be an affluent society, but it is not a wholly liked or likable affluent society.

A revolution consists of those below taking the power and position from existing ruling groups through a rising of the people. It means a restructuring of society, its institutions and government.

How far has any such change been effected? The rioters, protesters, and self-styled revolutionists have made little dent on the American power structure or its economic system. Negroes have obtained a few more jobs, a few better jobs. A few black candidates have been elected in several northern cities and in a few small southern towns. A number of school districts in New York have been partly taken over by their black communities.

Participatory democracy has made minimal progress in our universities, so badly torn with violence; a few new committees, here and there, occasional banishment of Dow Chemical and military recruiters, the phasing out of ROTC training. The last is financially serious, for it automatically cuts off federal funds. A few university presidents have resigned, and one died of a heart attack. But appointed trustees, largely corporation men, knowing little of education or school administration, still run them, still eliminate unwanted professors, and make messes worse when they meddle. In many institutions the faculty has only nominal autonomy. Harvard, for instance, is pretty much an exception. In many universities a great many black cultural courses have been added, and books on black history and culture have now become a profitable business for publishers. The percentage of admissible Negroes and faculty members has tended to increase, not wholly a good thing, for it has seriously drained all Negro colleges of their best teachers and students.

To obtain meager crumbs, students have occupied buildings, been beaten bloody by the police, have gone to jail. All that has been gained, from a revolutionary standpoint, has been the creation of hard-core militancy, knowledge of the strategy and tactics most effective for confrontations. It has created a new atmosphere of uncertainty in all the institutions and has led some of them to reassess their subservience to the CIA and the Pentagon, which has warped academic independence to further the aims of government and the military at home and abroad. Traditional university tranquility and isolation have been shattered.

Some of the student revolts at Yale right after the Revolutionary War were more violent than any of those today at that institution. Harvard and William and Mary both suffered serious early revolts. The first thoroughgoing student revolt of our times began not in the United States, where students were rolling along like ball bearings, but in the Argentine University of Córdoba in 1918. The students there soon learned that they were fighting not merely backwardness in the university, a medieval curricula, and incompetent politician professors; they were face-to-face with all society and more particularly the military state. As the movement spread, they began carrying guns and using them throughout all Latin America. Their spirit of revolt infected the armies. Presently the continent had its series of sergeants' and colonels' revolts. It is almost axiomatic that in such countries, when students rebel, revolution is waiting in the wings; as in Primo de Rivera's Spain. But Spain still has Franco.

Are overturns such as these possible in the United States? It seems less likely, but not wholly unlikely.

The Latin American upheavals did not bring freedom or any substantial modification of the feudal structure; their fruits were, if anything, more tyranny and iron-handed rule. But one important gain was made: Universities emerged everywhere as autonomous institutions, governed by students and faculty, without overt political intervention. Police and soldiery were outlawed from campuses, a freedom more extensive than that enjoyed in most American universities, then or since. On the whole the movement led to greatly improved academic standards. Only lately has this freedom been pushed aside, most grievously in Mexico, where the army has been parachuted into every institution in the country. Autonomy has been set aside at the cost of considerable loss of life and the prospect of instability and revolutionary disorders.

The peace marchers have faced even worse dilemmas. Mostly they come from the heretofore malleable conformist middle class. Until the Vietnam war, most peace marchers were pacifists in peacetime, war mongers in wartime. Never have they been so militantly pacifist as during the Johnson and Nixon administrations and the Vietnam war. To their ranks have flocked housewives, Negroes, students, professors, hippies, youth organizations, draft-card burners, nonviolent Ghandiists, even business and professional men.

However, their militancy has been blunted, the movement splintered by various peace maneuvers, featured ironically, even in Nixon's day, by war escalation. Though Johnson was forced to abdicate, the politicians did not bring the Vietnam issue squarely into the final election campaign. Humphrey hemmed and hawed. Nixon said he had a program for bringing peace. After a year in office it has not been revealed to the American people, and the bombing of South Vietnam is heavier than before. By December 1969 there were still nearly five hundred thousand Americans in Vietnam, plus added Vietnamese forces more adequately armed.

But our so-called revolutionists have made little dent on the military-industrial complex, against which President Dwight Eisenhower warned, yet did so much to promote while in office. Safer automobiles are being built, for which the aroused consumers will pay higher prices. Corporation profits continue to grow, while inflation eats away the increased wages obtained by costly strikes. The government handouts to the Leviathan combinations continue; general lack of competitive bidding, and government supervision over contracts is not always adequate or effective.

The Truman defense budget of $40 billion dollars, out of which Eisenhower promised to squeeze $20 billion waste, has more than doubled, and is expected soon to reach $100 billion, though Nixon has done a little pruning in some directions. But even greater expenditures are planned in other directions, so even if the Vietnam war ends, the Pentagon will still be the favored customer at the Treasury counter.

The United States has the greatest police establishment in the history of the world, and probably the most efficient, in spite of its inability to check the growth of crime. During 1968 hundreds of millions of dollars were spent in buying antiriot equipment, new types of tanks, electronic devices, and chemicals.

It is difficult to tell whether increased efficiency has led demonstrators to attempt to avoid confrontations or whether this results from a realization that there are more effective means of protest than fighting well-armed forces with bottles, rocks, and tin cans and suffering bloody pates. At the prolonged student-faculty strike at San Francisco State College, the participants agreed not to seize buildings and to avoid fights with the police. The professors set up radio transmitters and receivers, advising demonstrators of the approach of law-and-order forces and providing instructions to move on to new concentration points. Nevertheless the police invaded the campus, broke up small groups, and took severe punitive action, using clubs, etc. After picket lines, joined by students from numerous other state institutions, and by labor union members, were set up outside the gates, sharper melees occurred. By mid-January 1969 some fifteen hundred were arrested on charges ranging from disorderly conduct to felonies. One-third of these, according to defense attorneys, naturally painting as bad a picture as possible, were so severely beaten as to need medical attention. There, as elsewhere, the police are known as "pigs" by the dissidents, an unfair derogation of a fine animal. One commentator has prophesied that within less than ten years the larger American cities will have to be patrolled by units of the regular army. That is unlikely to produce anything but real revolution.

The unrest in American life has been cooled here and there by some reforms, mostly inadequate, but with reluctance and indifference on the part of lawmakers. These gains were hardly won by orderly appeals, but chiefly by militant violence. The chief official reaction, however, has been emphasis upon law and order and the escalation of armed forces and police power. This, of course, provides no long-term solution or security and leads to secret conspiracies, terrorism, and eventual revolution.

Certainly the various New Left revolts in the United States have not as yet appreciably altered the far-from-democratic structure of the two major monolithic political parties, which alternate in handing out little goodies to the great electorate. The parties were described even a century ago as two wings of the same vulture. Many states have such restrictive laws that it is well-nigh impossible for a third party to get on the ballot. In both 1968 conventions the machine elements, the bosses, performed their assigned tasks unblinkingly—just as though Washington had not begun burning within a few blocks of the White House. Chicago had become a place where they could not have met at all, or so they thought, but they carried on behind barbed wire and tiers of helmeted, gas-throwing, club-wielding police, National Guardsmen, and United States federal troops, the sending in of which only a few years ago would have been inconceivable.

The McCarthy movement chiefly managed to restore some hopes in the New Left that elections still had some validity. Thereby he divided the restless revolters. Even so, some additional millions of disillusioned voters stayed away from the polls, but since only 60 percent customarily vote, this may not be such a significant alienation from the traditional political life as it has been painted. After all, the Humphrey-versus-Nixon contest, with soft-pedaling of the major issues shaking the United States, offered the intelligent citizens little choice—only saliva versus moldy crusts. That ex-Governor Wallace of Alabama could poll 14 percent of the national vote —a far larger percentage than the alarming neo-Nazi vote in West Germany—is open to many interpretations, few of them pleasant, even for conservatives and traditionalists. Obviously there has been considerable erosion of traditional American political methods, a considerable loss of faith, apt to increase rather than diminish.

The students, unlike those in France, have found little or no co-operation from organized labor. Even in France they were sold down the river by the Communists. In San Francisco the central labor council came out in support not of the students but of the faculty strikers who had joined them, for the large share of the professors there were members of the AFL. The student-faculty strike was also joined by AFL university service workers and secretarial personnel.

Sidney Lens, himself a labor leader in Chicago, in an article in *Liberation*, "The Road to Power and Beyond," halfway abandons the Marxist concept of a revolution by the proletariat as not being effective or possible in the United States. The working class, he declares, apparently will not play the leading role in transforming society. Given the present stance of organized labor, this verdict seems likely. Organized labor represents the more privileged elements of the American workers and is part of the present Establishment—if only in a coattail role. The AFL, largely boss-ridden, is itself monopolistic, authoritarian, and largely racist, little given to democratic practices. Its president, George Meany, is an out-and-out backer of imperialist policies. By comparison Dean Rusk was a cherubic Pinko. Labor has been well tied in with defense spending and the CIA. Members of the Longshoreman's Union, who have held up United States shipping for so long, have emphasized their patriotism and courage by beating up draft objectors in Boston and New York and refusing to load vessels bound for Egypt, Algeria, and other supposedly pro-Communist lands. In short the AFL-CIO is accepted as a part of the ruling hierarchy of America. The new winds across American life have scarcely ruffled its surface. Labor's position has been and is conservative, even reactionary.

There is little indication, moreover, that, except for a handful, the New Left has any studied revolutionary program. This, of course, has been true of most incipient revolutions. It was some years before the Mexican revolutionists hit upon the slogan of land, water, and schools. The Russian prerevolutionary period was inchoate, nihilist, and terroristic. When Lenin and Trotsky took charge, long revolutionary disorders and misgovernment had already undermined Russian institutions. Attempted reforms during the general World War I collapse became glaringly inadequate and meaningless. Even Mao Tse-tung did not fully know what he wanted at the outset, and he wavered during his long guerrilla struggle regarding both aims and tactics.

The New Left in the United States, for the most part, is disillusioned with both capitalism and Communism, Soviet style. A number, perhaps, are better disposed to Communism, Chinese style, though agrarianism as practiced there seems remote from the more or less urban-oriented revolt in the United States. Certainly most here are sufficiently disillusioned with the all-powerful state, its blundering and corruption, not to wish industry to be put into such hands.

Quite a few New Leftists talk of "democratic socialism." The major revolt seems to be chiefly against the dull intellectual atmosphere of American life since World War II and the distortion of ideas due to the cold war and the anti-Communist hangup. Our disorderly demonstrations are, first of all, a revolt against American culture, against middle-class conformity, against education that produces more regimentation than free inquiry, against the racism built into American institutions, conduct, and thinking—a racism so far-reaching and deeply permeating and inescapable that it is scarcely recognized even by those who disclaim such prejudices. Harangues against status are status-seeking in a new manner.

A few seek economic gains, yet manifest dissatisfaction with American commercialism, the barren type of existence that puts a dollar price-tag on everything from potatoes to higher learning, the imbalance that gives hundreds of thousands of dollars and much applause to movie stars and baseball players, but permits so many poets, painters, and musicians to starve in oblivion.

Of late the dissidents have been reading some of the classic revolutionary literature of Marx, Engels, Lenin, Mao, and Kwame Nkrumah of Ghana, Ho Chi Minh and Che Guevara. The brilliant books of Professor Herbert Marcuse, *The One Dimensional Man, Negations*, etc., have aroused controversy and considerable enthusiasm. Strangely enough, little attention has been paid to the revolutionary thinkers of America: Thomas Paine, Samuel Adams, Henry George, Brooks Adams, Daniel De Leon, Eugene V. Debs. Even less attention has been paid to the great revolutionary thinkers of France, whose words have much bearing on the present events in the United States. The current American rebels likely would have no inkling of the meaning of the charge of Blanquism (seizure of the state by the elite among the dissenters) leveled against Lenin. But the rapidly spreading underground press in the United States reveals much knowledge of the thinking of revolutionary Russia, China, Cuba, Vietnam.

Above all, the American dissidents are aware that in many directions American society is crumbling, that there is a growing sense of insecurity, that fear has become the diet of every man ever since the atomic bomb blasted Hiroshima, that a hidden guilt complex gnaws at even the most comfortable and secure, a growing awareness that for every social injustice, crime, and international misdeed committed by others abroad, the United States has committed the same abuses at home. How can one condemn Iraq's spy hangings after the execution of the Rosenbergs? How can one condemn Israel's bombing of Lebanon or the bombing of Biafra, when the terroristic and murderous bombing of Vietnam has surpassed any ever known in the history of man?

The malaise of the New Left has spread to millions of citizens. The ripples spread out in widening circles. There is no assurance at present that the massive urban and racial problems will be satisfactorily resolved, that our resources will be properly conserved, that the pollution of air, land, and water will be reversed. Here and there a few small fry have been imprisoned for graft, waste, and corruption, but corruption is so widespread in our government, our military establishment, our bureaucracy, that it is not likely to be cured, short of a top-to-bottom housecleaning. Is the solution revolution? Is revolution inevitable? Or is the solution law-and-order by force, the police state? Either way the prospect is terrible. Is it possible that the necessary and fundamental social reforms will be carried out, and soon enough to prevent a violent revolution, left or right? At present there seems to be little inclination to make any such serious effort.

Is there any timetable for revolution, of which at present we have only symptoms? To base such a timetable on the experiences of other countries, with different institutions and problems, is to tread shaky ground. Nor does any man know the resilience of American society. How measure successfully all the contributing factors of stability and change? The rhythm of change and of crises has been greatly stepped up over the last few decades. The knowledge of revolutionary methods and of counterrevolutionary controls is also far greater—though whether that knowledge will produce wisdom or effectiveness in the preservation of the status quo or its intelligent alteration seems doubtful.

We have examined eleven world-shaking revolutions, not merely their causes—social injustice, economic exploitation, and dictatorship—but also their techniques, so to speak, and the mistaken countermeasures including statism, police and judicial repression. Participatory democracy is a demand of students in the United States, as it was in other revolutionary situations, and in every instance a narrow elite power group has progressively narrowed popular access to government and the possibility of influencing decisions.These symptoms have invariably been evident as a result of social decay, usually also of war-disintegration and even disaster. They spring from hunger, discontent, growing impatience, the upsurge of violence, and finally—sometimes after many years, sometimes quickly—the overturn of the state, the restructuring of the state, the broom sweeping out the accumulated debris of the centuries, but never all of it.

All the revolutions told about here were inevitable—as most revolutions are—which is merely to say that there was not enough wisdom in those who wielded power to stave off catastrophe, the cataclysm that engulfed them and their lands. We in the United States can perhaps learn something from such failures by plotting the slow sure rise of revolutionary forces and thus gain an inkling of the process now developing in this country so we can find out how much time we still have.

In general, in the United States, there has until recently been a greater spirit of give and take, despite violent confrontations, than in most countries in similar situations. There is a great sense of justice, though daily becoming more blunted, in the United States. There has always been a willingness to make concessions. But as positions harden, as bitterness rises, as it is bound to rise, can those virtues be preserved? Can they operate?

Social decay is very advanced already. Free expression is being strangled in so many directions. It need not be strangled by censorship or overt suppression, though that will doubtless be the end step. It is strangled by boss-controlled politics, which entrenches itself behind complex and almost impenetrable regulations; by conventions that have little meaning, except as television spectaculars; by the complicated committee controls in Congress; by the secrecy with which government is conducted, and a growing contempt for public opinion; by the failure to recognize the falsity of such silly phrases as "the silent majority"; by the flouting of militant minorities and the attempts to suppress them by all the machinery of the state, the police, the courts, the false slogan of law and order, the jailing of leaders, under flimsy pretexts; by the utilization of massive propaganda by government and other wealthy and powerful agencies. The entrenching of special privileges in government, in business, in the Pentagon, in labor unions and the growing rigidity of all bureaucratic institutions, private and public, promote alienation and frustration. The voice of revolution murmurs, speaks out, roars, and begins its preliminary violence.

To reverse this, Columbia University has set up a university senate, with student, faculty, and trustee representation. A graduate student, quoted in the *Columbia Forum* for the fall of 1969, said

The new Senate is a procedural change. It does not address itself to some of the basic questions—what is the function of a university, and what is its relationship to society, and its responsibility to the community.

There is no question in my mind that the university is geared to preserve American capitalism, to preserve the rich and the super rich. There is fantastic waste in the United States. Not only the waste of material, but waste of human life. I'm not just talking about the waste of lives in the Vietnam war; I'm talking about people's lives being wasted when all their talent, their time and energy, is devoured by American capitalism to produce products which supposedly fill people's needs, but obviously don't. Who trains people to do this? . . .

The university is an agent of oppression. Any talk about a university senate and committees is irrelevant and stupid. It is a form of social control, of pacification, of co-optation. It diverts energy into institutions that are not open to change.

The university should be destroyed and re-created to serve only the needs of the people. The university should be democratically run, restoring human procedures in the classroom and debunking professors as authority figures and students as passive recipients. . . .

. . . Columbia, in its expansion policies, has oppressed blacks and members of the Puerto Rican community by evicting them from their homes and forcing them to move back to the ghetto. In its function as a tool of the corporations, it exploits people in the third world, serves imperialism, and perpetuates colossal and inhuman callousness to people's desperate needs.

Revolutions, we now know, are many decades, even centuries, in the making in any given society. When the wave will crest is less easy to determine. The black revolt began on the first vessels that brought slaves chained under hatches to the New World. Our Civil War may be said to have been incubated when the founding fathers failed to face up to the issue of slavery and created a new nation part slave, part free.

The existing official and police determination to wipe out the Black Panthers, by destroying their leaders, jailing them, and giving them solitary confinement and cruel treatment has merely tended to spread the organization over the land and to create more solidarity. Our present Black Panther militancy finds its roots well in the past. It may be said to have originated when no satisfactory economic or political measures were set in motion to implement the sudden emancipation of slaves. Without that, it was neither bona fide emancipation nor kindness. The Black Panthers were born in spirit in the South after the Civil War, when that area reverted to

Ku Klux Klanism and terror to intimidate the freed slaves. In our day it has spread to Oakland, California, answering the need for self-protection against a brutal and racist police department. Now the organization is nationwide. It can no longer be crushed.

Juan José Arévalo, former president of Guatemala, tells of the tragic police murder of a labor leader. But such leaders, he notes, were expendable. There was always another and another and another, willing to suffer and to die—until at last revolution came.

In Russia Dostoyevsky was sent to Siberia in 1849, an aftermath of the 1848 disturbances in Europe, for belonging to a free discussion literary group. Czar Alexander was assassinated in 1880. The peasants were mowed down in St. Petersburg in 1905. A representative Duma was set up soon after. The czar, however, was not thrown out until early in 1917. These were all symptoms of impending revolution. But Russian society had really crumbled before the revolution took place in 1917. War, famine, riots, land seizures, lashed the realm.

The Cuban Revolution, the independence struggle, began in 1820, with interludes of subsequent violence setting in in earnest in 1868, nearly a hundred years before Castro, and it took thirty years to drive out the Spaniards. Most of the fruits of that revolutionary victory were seized not by the Cubans but by the United States, which set Cuba up as a protectorate, then a camouflaged colony, until Batista flew off to the Dominican Republic on New Year's Eve 1959.

The Mexican Revolution of 1910 burst forth quickly after thirty years of Díaz's iron-handed despotism, but it had been in the making ever since the struggles against Spain, against Emperor Iturbide, against Maximilian and the French. Díaz kept a superficial sort of order with his Rurales, who shot first and inquired afterward, but this did not mean that the struggle for human liberty had ceased to exist or would fail to emerge—as it did shortly.

In 1770, at the time of the Boston Massacre, Reverend Ezra Stiles, the great scholar, then pastor of the Second Congregational Church in Newport, Rhode Island, prophesied that within two generations revolution against England would break out. But in 1774 the Continental Congress was called, and the actual struggle began the following year—after fewer, less bloody manifestations of popular discontent than have occurred in the United States these last few years. In five years, not fifty years, the blowup occurred.

[271]

Naturally the military force against revolutions today is far more massive, and the answer could be, rather, a counterrevolution, that would bring some type of fascism and military suppression, or even World War III, which, of course, would be the end of the so-called capitalist society it would be supposed to protect, and even the end of all society. But Mussolini, Hitler, Franco in Spain, have merely aggravated events, and solved none of the social problems of their countries.

We still sniff for a possible timetable. Dostoyevsky was no revolutionary; rather a pious and somewhat sniveling reactionary. But in the United States the warm-hearted Eugene V. Debs was a revolutionary. He stated, when the conscription laws were passed during World War I,

I am not a capitalist soldier; I am a proletarian revolutionist . . . . I am opposed to every war but one; I am for that war with heart and soul, and that is the world-wide war of the world revolution. In that war I am prepared to fight in any way the ruling class may make necessary, even in the barricades. That is where I stand.

He went to jail. But does this event help us with a timetable any more than Dostoyevsky's jailing did? It was thirty years later that Czar Alexander was done in. It was thirty years after Debs that Franklin Delano Roosevelt died and Hiroshima was destroyed; another ten years or so before John F. Kennedy was murdered. Then came the assassinations of Martin Luther King and Robert Kennedy. Are these any more culminating points than the murder of scores of peace marchers and freedom riders that preceded them?

We do not know how fast the electronic revolution will push ahead or how greatly it will break down American society or in what directions. Technologically, militarily, in space exploration, and otherwise, the United States is moving ahead at a dizzy speed. But this may merely portend the more rapid breakdown of political and economic life, when ideas fail to match other changes in American life. There is danger that the appearance of schisms and dislocations in American society will make revolution inevitable.

Is the United States gaining new moral strength in new directions? Will the present revolutionary trends be understood and rechanneled or merely be suppressed? Can our electoral processes be revitalized enough so that our representatives can become more representative of the people, rather than of corporations, of the military, and of the specially privileged? Can the global and power ambitions of the Pentagon be curbed? Can the CIA be stopped from meddling in the affairs of other nations to the detriment of the peoples and the best interests of the United States? Does "global responsibility" have to remain aggressive and require armed intervention everywhere the smoke of freedom rises? Must decency in international relations be equated with isolationism? More questions than answers. Only a fool is a prophet. Metternich of Austria became so intent on thwarting revolutions around the world that presently he went flying out of the palace into exile, and the students and peasants moved in.

We repeat, there are no easy answers. All we can say is that a revolutionist is a dedicated man; he is a brave man willing to risk his life for what he believes. He is too valuable an individual to be clubbed, jailed, and killed. He is too valuable to be a revolutionist, too valuable to be shot down from an armored tank, or held behind bars.

Juan José Arévalo of Guatemala, in his fine book, *Anti-Kommunism in Latin America,* chided the military club-swingers for their stupidity in not making use of such agitators, who could have made fine contributions to good government—as though military upstarts are very often interested in good government more than in loot or power.

It is not merely that there are ten million half-hungry people in these prosperous United States, that at least thirty million are in poverty, against which the antipoverty program is all but meaningless. How will you teach an elephant that he cannot step on fleas? Or a donkey that a bray does not bring the carrot closer? A vital change in the power structure of America will certainly be resisted by those who wield wealth and power, which brings us right back to the dread specter of revolution. All we can say with any assurance is that the present power structure in the United States has grown foolish and pompous, lacking in judgment and justice. It will be shattered in one way or another, sooner or later, by wise men, by fools, or by violent men—and more likely, by all three. The perfume has become too rank now for social peace.

Perhaps we can figure out how our system, seemingly so efficient, has become so close to being unworkable, our future so uncertain, our way of life so menaced—and in so short a number of years. The reasons are not far to seek: five wars in my lifetime—imperialism, neocolonialism; trying to run the world; millions of underprivileged people in the wealthiest land on earth; social injustice; the desecration of our habitat and the reckless destruction of animal and plant life—the fouling of our own nest so to speak; the too rapid exhaustion of our natural resources; our top-heavy military and police establishment; the narrowing by government of the duties and rights of citizens; the improper exploitation of the Third World.

This, as Dalton Trumbo put it, is "The Time of the Toad," in which the American elite are attempting "to destroy any heretical minority which asserts . . . toad-meat not to be the delicacy which governmental edict declares it."

Unless these trends can be reversed, which is a herculean task, we shall march down the road to revolution—and perhaps sooner than we imagine. A dinosaur with big scales and a peanut brain could not survive on this planet. Brains will have to catch up with the computer and the overwhelming technological advance, thus far used chiefly for war and aggression rather than for the benefit of human beings and their society.

BOOKS FOR PARALLEL READING

Don Quixote Rides Again

Beer, Max. *Social Struggles and Thought.* New York: International Publishers Co., Inc., 1929.

Carter, John F. *Man Is War.* Indianapolis: The Bobbs-Merrill Co., Inc., 1926.

Cook, Fred J. *The Warfare State.* New York: The Macmillan Company, 1962.

Dennis, Lawrence. *Dynamics of War and Revolution,* Weekly Foreign Letter, 1940.

Horowitz, David. *The Free World Colossus.* New York: Hill & Wang, Inc., 1965.

Lenin, V. I. *Collected Works,* Vol. XXI; *Toward the Seizure of Power,* Book II. New York: International Publishers Co., Inc., 1932.

——. *State and Revolution.* New York: International Publishers Co., Inc., 1932.

Lens, Sidney. *A World in Revolution.* New York: Frederick A. Praeger, Inc., 1956.

Nelson, Truman. *The Right of Revolution.* Boston: Beacon Press, 1968.

Ortega y Gasset, José. *The Revolt of the Masses.* New York: W. W. Norton & Company, Inc., 1932, 1957.

Schmalhausen, Samuel D., ed. *Recovery Through Revolution.* New York: Covici Friede, Inc., 1933.

Strachey, John. *The Coming Struggle for Power.* New York: Covici Friede, Inc., 1933.

The Revolution of 1776

Aptheker, Herbert. *The American Revolution,* 1763–1783. New York: International Publishers Co., Inc., 1960.

Beard, Charles. *American Government and Politics.* New York: The Macmillan Company, 1924.

Hardy, Jack. *The First American Revolution.* New York: International Publishers Co., Inc., 1937.

Osgood, Herbert. *The American Colonies in the Eighteenth Century.* 2 vols. New York: Columbia University Press, 1924.

Paine, Thomas. *Basic Writings*. New York: John Wiley & Sons, Inc., 1942.

Parrington, Vernon Louis. *Main Currents in American Thought*. Vol I. New York: Harcourt, Brace and Company, Inc., 1927.

Stiles, Ezra. *Literary Diary*, edited by Frank B. Dexter. 3 vols. New York: Charles Scribner's Sons, 1901.

Van Doren, Carl. *Secret History of the American Revolution*. New York: Viking Press, 1941.

Wood, Gordon S. *The Creation of the American Republic*. Chapel Hill, N.C.: University of North Carolina Press, 1969.

The French Revolution

Brinton, Crane. *A Decade of Revolution*. New York: Harper & Brothers, 1934.

——. *Ideas and Men*. New York: Prentice-Hall, 1950.

Bruun, Geoffrey. *Europe and the French Imperium, 1799–1814*. New York: Harper & Brothers, 1938.

Cassirer, Ernst. *The Philosophy of the Enlightenment*. Boston: Beacon Press, 1955.

Diderot, Denis. *Writings*, edited by Jonathan Kemp. New York: International Publishers Co., Inc., 1936, 1963.

Gershoy, Leo. *From Despotism to Revolution, 1763–1789*. New York: Harper & Brothers, 1944.

Lichtheim, George. *The Origins of Socialism*. New York: Frederick A. Praeger, Inc., 1969.

Salvemini, G. *The French Revolution, 1788–1792*. New York: Henry Holt and Company, Inc., 1954.

Tocqueville, Alexis de. *The Old Régime and the French Revolution*. Garden City, N.Y.: Doubleday & Company, Inc., 1955.

Warwick, Charles F. *Danton and the French Revolution*. Philadelphia: G. W. Jacobs & Company, 1908.

——. *Mirabeau and the French Revolution*. Philadelphia: G. W. Jacobs & Company, 1907.

The Revolution of Latin America

Arciniegas, Germán, ed. *The Green Continent*. New York: Alfred A. Knopf, Inc., 1944.

Beals, Carleton. *Eagles of the Andes*. Philadelphia: Chilton Book Company, 1965.

Cunninghame Graham, Robert Bontine. *José Antonio Páez*. London: William Heinemann, Ltd., 1929.

——. *Portrait of a Dictator, Francisco Solano Lopez*. London: William Heinemann, Ltd., 1933.

Herring, Hubert. *A History of Latin America*. New York: Alfred A. Knopf, Inc., 1955.

Plenn, Abel. *Southern Americas*. New York: Creative Age Press, Inc., 1948.

Robertson, William S. *Life of Miranda*. New York: Oxford University Press, Inc., 1930.

Vaucaire, Michel. *Bolívar the Liberator*. London: Constable & Co., Ltd., 1929.

The Paris Commune

Beer, Max. *Social Struggles and Thought*. New York: International Publishers Co., Inc., 1929.

Marx, Karl, and Lenin, Vladimir Ilich. *The Civil War in France: The Paris Commune*. New York: International Publishers Co., Inc., 1940, 1968.

Marx, Karl. *The Civil War in France*. Introduction by Frederick Engels. New York: International Publishers Co., Inc., 1940.

Morton, A. L. *The Life and Ideas of Robert Owen*. New York: International Publishers Co., Inc., 1969.

Seton-Watson, Hugh. *The Pattern of Communist Revolution*. London: Methuen & Co., Ltd., 1961.

Taylor, A. J. *From Napoleon to Stalin*. London: Hamish Hamilton, Ltd., 1950.

Williams, Roger L. *The French Revolution of 1870–1871*. New York: W. W. Norton & Company, Inc., 1969.

The Mexican Revolution

Beals, Carleton. *Porfirio Díaz: Dictator of Mexico*. Philadelphia: J. B. Lippincott Co., 1932.

——. *The Stones Awake*. Philadelphia: J. B. Lippincott Co., 1936.

Bell, Edward I. *The Political Shame of Mexico*. New York: McBride, Nast & Company, 1914.

Cockcroft, James D. *Intellectual Precursors of the Mexican Revolution*. Austin: University of Texas Press, 1969.

Gibbon, Thomas Edward. *Mexico Under Carranza*. Garden City, N.Y. Doubleday, Page & Company, 1919.

Gruening, Ernest. *Mexico and Its Heritage.* New York: Century Company, 1928.

Guzmán, Martin Luis. *The Eagle and the Serpent.* New York: Alfred A. Knopf, Inc., 1930.

Lansford, William Douglas. *Pancho Villa.* Los Angeles: Sherbourne Press, 1965.

Millon, Robert Paul. *Zapata.* New York: International Publishers Co., Inc., 1969.

O'Shaughnessy, Edith. *Diplomatic Days.* New York: Harper & Brothers, 1917.

Plenn, Jaime H. *Mexico Marches.* Indianapolis: The Bobbs-Merrill Co., Inc., 1939.

Priestley, Herbert Ingram. *The Mexican Nation.* New York: The Macmillan Company, 1923.

Reed, John. *Insurgent Mexico.* New York: D. Appleton & Company, Inc., 1914.

Simpson, Lesley Byrd. *Many Mexicos.* New York: G. P. Putnam's Sons, 1941; and Berkeley, Calif.: Univ. of Calif. Press, 1965.

Stevens, Lewis. *Here Comes Pancho Villa.* Philadelphia: Frederick A. Stokes Company, 1930.

Tannenbaum, Frank. *Mexican Agrarian Revolution.* New York: Institute of Economics of the Brookings Institution; The Macmillan Company, 1929.

Turner, John Kenneth. *Barbarous Mexico.* Chicago: Charles H. Kerr & Co., 1910.

Wilson, Henry Lane. *Diplomatic Episodes in Mexico, Belgium and Chile.* Garden City, N.Y.: Doubleday, Page & Company, 1929.

The October Revolution: An Empire in Convulsion

Bergamini, John. *The Tragic Dynasty: A History of the Romanovs.* New York: G. P. Putnam's Sons, 1969.

Bukharin, Nicolas. *Historical Materialism.* Ann Arbor: Univ. of Michigan Press, 1969.

Carr, E. H. *The October Revolution: Before and After.* New York: Alfred A. Knopf, Inc., 1969.

——. *Dostoevsky (1821–1881).* London: George Allen & Unwin, 1931.

Kirchner, Walther. *History of Russia.* New York: Barnes & Noble, Inc., 1958.

Lenin, Nikolai, and Trotsky, Leon. *The Proletarian Revolution in Russia.* New York: Communist Party, 1918.

Lenin, Vladimir Ilich. *Imperialism: The Highlight of Capitalism*. New York: International Publishers Co., Inc., 1939.

——. *Collected Works*. 21 vols. New York: International Publishers Co., Inc., 1929–1932.

Reed, John. *Ten Days That Shook the World*. New York: Boni & Liveright, 1919; and New York: Modern Library, Inc., 1935.

Seton-Watson, Hugh. *The Pattern of Communist Revolution*. London: Methuen & Co., Ltd., 1961.

Schuman, Frederick L. *Russia Since 1917*. New York: Alfred A. Knopf, Inc., 1957.

Trotsky, Leon. *The Essential Trotsky*. London: George Allen & Unwin, 1963.

Valentinov, Nikolai. *The Early Years of Lenin*. Ann Arbor: Univ. of Michigan Press, 1969.

Williams, Albert Rhys. *Journey into Revolution: Petrograd, 1917–1918*. Chicago: Quadrangle Books, Inc., 1969.

The March on Rome: The Black Shirt Revolution

Beals, Carleton. *Rome or Death: The Story of Fascism*. New York: Century Company, 1923.

Dante Alighieri. *The Divine Comedy*. New York: E. P. Dutton & Co., Inc., 1928.

Malaparte, Curzio. *Coup d'Etat: The Technique of Revolution*. New York: E. P. Dutton & Co., Inc., 1932.

Moravia, Alberto. *Roman Tales*. New York: Farrar, Straus & Cudahy, Inc., 1959.

Schneider, Herbert W. *Making the Fascist State*. New York: Oxford University Press, Inc., 1928.

Wiskemann, Elizabeth. *Fascism in Italy: Its Development and Influence*. New York: St. Martin's Press, Inc., 1969.

Woolf, S. J., ed. *The Nature of Fascism*. London: George Weidenfeld & Nicolson, Ltd., 1967.

The Spanish Republic

Beals, Carleton. *The Great Circle*. Philadelphia: J. B. Lippincott Co., 1940.

Eby, Cecil. *Between the Bullet and the Lie, American Volunteers in the Spanish Civil War*. New York: Holt, Rinehart & Winston, Inc., 1969.

Conze, Edward. *Spain Today: Revolution and Counter-Revolution*. New York: Greenberg: Publisher, Inc., 1936.

Gannes, Harry, and Repard, Theodore. *Spain in Revolt*. New York: Alfred A. Knopf, Inc., 1936.

Hemingway, Ernest. *For Whom the Bell Tolls*. New York: Charles Scribner's Sons, 1940.

Langsam, Walter Consuelo. *The World Since 1914*. New York: The Macmillan Company, 1935.

The Celestial Empire

Brandt, Conrad; Schwarz, Benjamin; and Fairbanks, John R., eds. *A Documentary History of Chinese Communism*. Cambridge: Harvard University Press, 1952.

Chang, John K. *Industrial Development in Pre-Communist China*. Chicago: Aldine Publishing Company, 1969.

Chassin, Lionel Max. *The Communist Conquest of China*. Cambridge: Harvard University Press, 1965.

Chen, Nai-Ruenn, and Galenson, Walter. *The Chinese Economy Under Communism*. Chicago: Aldine Publishing Company, 1969.

China Yearbook, The. New York: The Macmillan Company, 1937–1945.

Echstein, Alexander; Galenson, Walter; and Liu, Ta-chung; eds. *Economic Trends in Communist China*. Chicago: Aldine Publishing Company, 1968.

Fitzgerald, Charles P. *Son of Heaven: A Biography of Li Shih-Min, Founder of the T'ang Dynasty*. London: Cambridge University Press, 1933.

Liu, Chih-pu. *A Military History of Modern China, 1924–1949*. Princeton, N. J.: Princeton University Press, 1956.

Mao Tse-tung. *Selected Works*. 5 vols. New York: International Publishers Co., Inc., 1954–1956.

Moore, Charles A., ed. *The Chinese Mind*. Honolulu: East-West Center Press, 1969.

Payne, Robert. *Portrait of a Revolutionary: Mao Tse Tung*. New York: Abelard-Schuman Limited, 1962.

Stilwell, Joseph Warren. *Stilwell Papers*, arr. and ed. by Theodore H. White. New York: William Sloane Associates, 1948.

Suyin, Han. *Asia Today*. Montreal: McGill-Queen's University Press, 1969.

Wright, Mary Clabaugh, ed. *China in Revolution: The First Phase, 1900–1913*. New Haven: Yale University Press, 1968.

Mau Mau

Aaronovitch, S. and K. *Crisis in Kenya*. London: Lawrence and Wishart, 1947.

Baldwin, William W. *Mau Mau Man-hunt*. New York: E. P. Dutton & Co., Inc., 1957.

Barnett, Donald L., and Njama, Karari. *Mau Mau from Within*. New York: Monthly Review Press, 1966.

Corfield, F. D. *Historical Survey of the Origins and Growth of Mau Mau*. London: Her Majesty's Stationery Office, 1960.

Corothers, J. C. *The Psychology of the Mau Mau*. Nairobi: Kenya Government Printer, 1955.

Delf, George. *Jomo Kenyatta*. London: Victor Gollancz, Ltd., 1961.

Henderson, Ian, and Goodhart, Philip C. *The Hunt for Kimathi*. London: Hamish Hamilton, Ltd., 1958.

Kenyatta, Jomo. *Facing Mount Kenya*. London: Martin Secker & Warburg, Ltd., 1938.

———. *Land of Conflict*. Manchester, England: Panaf Service Ltd., 1945.

Lambert, H. E. *Kikuyu Social and Political Institutions*. New York: Oxford Univ. Press, 1956.

Middleton, John. *The Kikuyu and Kamba of Kenya*. London: International Affairs Institute, 1953.

Montague, Slater. *The Trial of Jomo Kenyatta*. London: Martin Secker & Warburg, Ltd., 1935.

Worsley, Peter. *The Trumpet Shall Sound*. London: MacGibbon & Kee, Ltd., 1957.

The New Cuba

Beals, Carleton. *The Crime of Cuba*. Philadelphia: J. B. Lippincott Co., 1934.

Castro, Fidel. *History Will Absolve Me*. Havana: Liberal Press, 1961(?).

De Gámez, Tana. *The Yoke and the Star*. Indianapolis: The Bobbs-Merrill Co., Inc., 1966.

Dubois, Jules. *Fidel Castro*. Indianapolis: The Bobbs-Merrill Co., Inc., 1959.

Foner, Philip S. *A History of Cuba and Its Relations with The United States*. 2 vols. New York: International Publishers Co., Inc., 1962–1963.

Frank, Waldo. *Cuba: Prophetic Island*. New York: Marzani and Munsell, Inc., 1961.

Guevara, Che. *Guerrilla Warfare*. New York: Monthly Review Press, 1961.

Huberman, Leo, and Sweezy, Paul M. *Cuba: Anatomy of a Revolution*. New York: Monthly Review Press, 1960.

Jackson, D. Bruce. *Castro, The Kremlin, and Communism in Latin America*. Baltimore: The Johns Hopkins Press, 1969.

Mills, C. Wright. *Listen, Yankee: The Revolution in Cuba*. New York: McGraw-Hill Book Company, 1960.

Sartre, Jean-Paul. *Sartre on Cuba*. New York: Ballantine Books, Inc., 1961.

Szulc, Tad, and Meyer, Karl E. *The Cuban Invasion: The Chronicle of a Disaster*. New York: Frederick A. Praeger, Inc., 1962.

Taber, Robert. *M-26, Biography of a Revolution*. New York: Lyle Stuart, Inc., 1961.

Zeitlin, Maurice, and Scheer, Robert. *Cuba: Tragedy in Our Americas*. New York: Grove Press, Inc., 1963.

Revolution and the Power Structure

Cleaver, Eldridge. *Post Prison Writings and Sketches*. New York: Random House, Rampart Book, New York, 1969.

———. *Soul on Ice*. New York: Dell Publishing Co., Inc., 1968.

Cohn-Bendit, Daniel and Gabriel. *Obsolete Communism: The Left-Wing Alternative*. New York: McGraw-Hill Book Company, 1969.

Cruse, Harold. *The Crisis of the Negro Intellectual*. New York: William Morrow & Co., Inc., 1967.

Debray, Regis, and Deming, Barbara. *Revolution: Violent and Non-Violent*. New York: Liberation, 1968.

Djilas, Milovan. *The Unperfect Society*. New York: Harcourt, Brace & World, Inc., 1969.

George, Henry. *Progress and Poverty*. New York: Robert Schalkenbach Foundation, Inc., 1945.

Gregory, Dick. *The Shadow That Scares Me*. Garden City, N. Y.: Doubleday & Company, Inc., 1968.

Hoffman, Abbie. *Revolution for the Hell of It*. New York: The Dial Press, Inc., 1969.

Horowitz, David, ed. *Containment and Revolution*. Boston: Beacon Press, 1969.

Jordan, Winthrop D. *White over Black*. Chapel Hill, N. C.: University of North Carolina Press, 1968.

Knebel, Fletcher. *Vanished*. Garden City, N. Y.: Doubleday & Company, Inc., 1969.

Lasch, Christopher. *The Agony of the American Left*. New York: Alfred A. Knopf, Inc., 1969.

Lightfoot, Claude M. *Ghetto Rebellion to Black Revolution*. New York: International Publishing Co., Inc., 1968.

Marcuse, Herbert. *One Dimensional Man*. Boston: Beacon Press, 1964.

———. *Negations: Essays in Critical Theory*. Boston: Beacon Press, 1968.

———. *Soviet Marxism*. New York: Columbia University Press, 1958.

Mackinder, Halford John. *Democratic Ideals and Reality*. New York: Henry Holt and Company, Inc., 1919.

Mitford, Jessica. *The Trial of Dr. Spock*. New York: Alfred A. Knopf, Inc., 1969.

Salk, Erwin A., ed. *A Layman's Guide to Negro History*. New York: McGraw-Hill Book Company, 1968.

Schuchter, Arnold. *White Power/Black Freedom*. Boston: Beacon Press, 1969.

Spender, Stephen. *The Year of the Young Rebels*. New York: Random House, Inc., 1969.

Strachey, John. *The Coming Struggle for Power*. New York: Covici Friede, Inc., 1933.

INDEX